The Two Tocquevilles

The Two Tocquevilles
Father and Son

Hervé and Alexis de Tocqueville
On the Coming of
the French Revolution

EDITED AND TRANSLATED BY

R. R. Palmer

PRINCETON UNIVERSITY PRESS

Copyright © 1987 by Princeton University Press
Published by Princeton University Press, 41 William Street,
Princeton, New Jersey 08540
In the United Kingdom: Princeton University Press, Guildford, Surrey

All Rights Reserved

Library of Congress Cataloging in Publication Data will be found
on the last printed page of this book

ISBN 0-691-05495-9

Publication of this book has been aided by a grant from the
Paul Mellon Fund of Princeton University Press

Translations from Alexis de Tocqueville are published by
agreement with Editions Gallimard, publisher of the *Oeuvres
complètes d'Alexis de Tocqueville*, and with M. André Jardin, editor
of Tocqueville's unfinished work on the French Revolution in the
Oeuvres complètes. The present translator and publisher express
their thanks to both for their cooperation

This book has been composed in Linotron Bembo type

Clothbound editions of Princeton University Press books are
printed on acid-free paper, and binding materials are chosen for
strength and durability. Paperbacks, although satisfactory for personal
collections, are not usually suitable for library rebinding

Printed in the United States of America by Princeton
University Press, Princeton, New Jersey

For Esther

Contents

CONTENTS

Illustrations

viii

Introduction

by the Editor/Translator

The two Tocquevilles about 1827. Hervé, shown in full dress as a Peer of France, wears the medal of the Legion of Honor. Alexis is presented as his secretary, as if taking dictation.
Courtesy Beinecke Rare Book and Manuscript Library,
Yale University

The Two Tocquevilles

IT IS UNUSUAL for two men of distinguished social position, father and son, to publish books on the same subject only a few years apart—with the son's work becoming instantly famous, and the father's ignored and soon forgotten. Such is the story of the two Tocquevilles. As Frenchmen living in the first half of the nineteenth century, both sought to understand the Revolution of 1789 from which both had suffered. Both tried to explain its causes by examining the last years of the Old Regime. The difference between them is a matter of human interest, and it can also illustrate the larger question of difference between two kinds of history.

Alexis de Tocqueville published his *Old Regime and the Revolution* in 1856. It made an immediate sensation in France, and two English translations appeared in the very same year, one by Henry Reeve in England and the other by John Bonner in the United States. A German translation followed in 1857. Since the book in fact never reached the years of the Revolution, it was really an account of French thought and society in the two or three generations preceding 1789. The author intended to follow it with a sequel on the Revolution itself, on which he engaged in research, took many notes, and drafted a few chapters—all left incomplete at his premature death in 1859. Most nearly complete were seven chapters on the "pre-Revolution," involving the reforming efforts of the monarchy in 1787–1788 and the actual outbreak of revolution in 1789. A version of these seven chapters was published in French in 1865 and in English in 1873. It was not until 1953, however, that a French historian, André Jardin, published the whole mass of uncompleted work for Tocqueville's sequel—draft chapters, subheads, marginal corrections, reading notes, alternate versions, and memoranda and queries to himself—to be used in the course of a revision that he was never able to make. This heterogeneous and somewhat inconsistent material is translated in the present book.[1]

Everyone concerned with Alexis de Tocqueville has heard of his father, Count Hervé de Tocqueville, but few have ever heard of the count's publications, either in France or in the English-speaking

[1] See the Bibliographical Note at the end of this Introduction.

world, for which they were never translated. The father nevertheless published in 1847, at the age of seventy-five, and having never
written a book before, a *Philosophical History of the Reign of Louis
XV*, and in 1850, at the age of seventy-eight, a *Survey of the Reign of
Louis XVI*. Count Hervé died in 1856, only a few days before the
appearance of his son's *Old Regime* and only three years before the
death of Alexis.

It is enlightening to compare the work of father and son for what
they say on the immediate origins of the Revolution, for a period of
some three years before the fall of the Bastille. Hence the present
book offers for the first time a translation of over a third of Hervé
de Tocqueville's *Survey of the Reign of Louis XVI*. Most of what is
translated of Hervé's *Survey* concerns the same years and the same
events as Alexis's unfinished chapters. The similarities and differences may offer a curious exercise in comparative analysis for anyone interested in the French Revolution, in historiography generally, possibly even in family history, and in the intellectual outlook
of the eminent Alexis de Tocqueville.

The Clérel de Tocquevilles were an old noble family of Normandy, so ancient that one of that name had taken part in the Nor-
man conquest of England. Hervé, born in 1772, was married in
1794 to an almost equally high-born young woman, the grand-
daughter of Lamoignon de Malesherbes, who had been active in
government service since the 1750s. Known for his humane opinions, Malesherbes had favored a thorough reconstruction of the
French monarchy in the 1780s, but he then came forward to defend
Louis XVI at his trial before the National Convention in 1793, and
so died himself in the Terror a few months later. Hervé and his
young wife were imprisoned for several months, and might have
died if the Terror had lasted longer. Throughout the Revolution
Hervé remained inconspicuously in France—that is, he was not an
émigré—and he occupied no more than a minor village office during the years of Napoleon. His only public career was under the restored Bourbons. From 1814 to 1827 he served as prefect of several
French departments in turn, and enjoyed more purely honorific appointments as an officer of the Legion of Honor and gentleman of
the king's bedchamber. In 1827 Charles X made him a peer of
France, in which capacity he sat in the upper house of the Restora-

tion parliament and spoke on a variety of practical subjects, such as the postal service, the budget, and the development of the port of Le Havre. Eliminated from the Chamber of Peers by the revolution of 1830, and refusing to serve the Orleanist monarchy of Louis-Phi-lippe, he retired to private life. Why he waited until 1847 and 1850 to publish his two books is unknown, but from his prefaces and a few references in his books we know that they were written in the eighth decade of his life.

Alexis de Tocqueville, born in 1805, thus spent his childhood in a provincial aristocratic family withdrawn from affairs, nostalgic for former times, scarred by the Revolution, and detesting Napo-leon, and his adolescence in the same family under very different conditions, favored by the Bourbons, with his father busy as a pre-fect in matters of practical administration. Nevertheless, although coming from this milieu, and though most of his friends and cor-respondents throughout his life were members of the aristocracy, the young Alexis, aged twenty-five in 1830, accepted the conse-quences of the revolution of 1830. He took the oath to Louis-Phi-lippe, to the distress of his family and consternation of his friends. To remove himself temporarily from an embarrassing situation, and to study the "democracy" by which he was already fascinated and alarmed, but which he believed to be the wave of the future, he contrived to make an extended tour of the United States. Officially, he received a mission from the French government to study the American prison system, on which he and his traveling companion, Gustave de Beaumont, in fact submitted a report. Actually, his main purpose was to observe democratic institutions and ways of life, on which he published his two-volume classic, *Democracy in America*. This work won him admission to the Académie française in 1841 at the early age of thirty-six. He went into politics, was elected to the Chamber of Deputies, accepted the Second Republic in the revolution of 1848, and served on its constitutional commit-tee and as its foreign minister. He refused to accept the overthrow of the Republic by Louis-Napoleon Bonaparte in 1851 or the Sec-ond Empire and second Napoleon ("Napoleon III") in 1852. Be-coming a private gentleman like his father, he launched into the re-searches that produced his *Old Regime* in 1856 and the unfinished chapters on the Revolution itself. His consuming interest was to explain to himself, and if possible to others, how it could happen for a second time that France should succumb to a modern Caesar, why in France it seemed impossible to have a free and peaceable democracy such as he thought existed in the United States.

It may be unfair to compare the work of the two Tocquevilles as it is presented in the following pages. Hervé's *Survey of the Reign of Louis XVI* is a carefully composed and finished book, and it may benefit from my omission of passages that a modern reader might find trivial or digressive. On the other hand, no amount of editing of Alexis's unfinished drafts and notes can make them more than an inchoate jumble that he intended to rewrite. Hervé enjoyed good health until an advanced old age. Alexis began to cough blood at the age of forty-five, in 1850; he managed to finish his *Old Regime and the Revolution* in 1856 but was then soon afflicted by periods of declining health, as was his wife also. His letters to friends in 1857 and 1858, from which I have included excerpts at the end of this book, offer a pathetic revelation of the psychological and physical difficulties that he tried to overcome. His work was interrupted by the need of enforced rest, by travel to warmer climates under doctors' orders, by a trip to London to consult the collection on the French Revolution in the British Museum, and by the presence of house guests at the château in Normandy. The seven draft chapters of his sequel were hurriedly written between October and December 1857. He expected to rework them but was never able to do so. In short, the material in the present book does not represent Alexis de Tocqueville at his best.

Even so, and with all due reservations, Alexis's unpublished writings on the immediate causes of the French Revolution reveal something of his habit of mind. In Sainte-Beuve's canny phrase, Alexis was so bright that "he began to think before learning anything." To think before beginning research is both necessary and commendable, but it is a virtue that Alexis possessed to an extreme degree. He had expressed many of his main ideas on the Old Regime as early as 1836, and he developed them more at length in his finished book twenty years later. In the seven unfinished chapters of 1857 we see him putting down his main ideas as they came to his mind, to be later substantiated, verified, expanded, digested, and integrated from the mass of his notes and transcripts. These ideas

naturally echo those expressed in his book published the year before. It is anyone's guess what the sequel on the Revolution would
have been like, if ever completed.

Hervé de Tocqueville is remembered as an old-fashioned royalist, Alexis de Tocqueville as a nineteenth-century liberal. But
Hervé's royalism was open-minded and critical, whereas Alexis's
liberalism, with its warnings against centralization of government
and fears for democracy, was of a kind that is now considered conservative. He was certainly a deeper and more troubled thinker than
his father. He worried about the connections between liberty and
equality. He knew that under certain conditions each had the capacity to destroy the other. He tried to reconcile them, to determine to
what extent and on what terms they could coexist. He thus dealt
with a perennial problem that gives life to his work, while his father
wrote a more common-sense history of a kind that can be, and is,
superseded and replicated in every generation.

Two Kinds of History

It is strange that Alexis seems never to have mentioned his father's
books. That he did not do so in the *Old Regime and the Revolution* is
not surprising, for he made it a point, as he tells us, not to read his
predecessors' work lest his own judgment be swayed by the opinions of others. To keep a freshness of view, he said, he purposely
worked only with original sources—the pamphlets, periodicals, official orders, laws, and other printed materials of the period, and letters and government documents as he found them in local and national archives. But neither is there any mention of his father's
writings in his abundant personal correspondence, still in process of
publication in a modern critical edition in Paris. From the exchange
of letters over many years between Alexis and his intimate friends,
such as Gustave de Beaumont and Louis de Kergolay, as well as with
other acquaintances, it is evident that father and son were on good
terms with each other, often visited each other, and moved in the
same social circles. They were bound by ties of mutual respect and
affection. "I had for my father a warmth of attachment," he wrote
shortly after Hervé's death, "that only those who have habitually

7

seen us together can understand."[2] Or again: "There was nothing in the world that I was not in the habit of saying to him."[3] It is hard to believe that when Alexis began his historical researches on the Old Regime in 1853 he had not read his father's book on the reign of Louis XVI published only three years before. Yet we learn from André Jardin, the editor of Alexis's papers and his most recent and authoritative biographer, that Alexis had (to put it mildly) a re-served opinion on his father's books and even evaded his father's re-quest for assistance in getting them reviewed in the periodical press. It seems that Alexis even concealed from his father the fact that he was himself writing a book on the Old Regime.[4]

The explanation for Alexis's embarrassed silence must lie in the difference between the kinds of history in which the two Tocque-villes were interested—or of which they were capable. Alexis is known as a founder of analytical history, as distinguished from the older narrative history of which Hervé's work is an example. That Alexis was able to write a fast-moving narrative is clear from his published *Recollections*, in which he tells of his own experience in the revolution of 1848. Both of his more serious books, however, the *Democracy in America* and the *Old Regime and the Revolution*, are purely expository works with virtually no narrative content. Hervé's books are entirely narrative, though punctuated with ob-servations on why things happened as they did. It must be said also that Hervé's works were not very original. His *Survey of the Reign of Louis XVI* draws heavily, as may be seen in the occurrence of par-allel passages, on a larger work in two volumes published by Joseph Droz in 1839, whose very title defines the problem in which Hervé was interested: *History of the reign of Louis XVI during the years when the French Revolution might have been prevented or guided.*[5] If we look at other works of these years, we may conclude that Hervé's book

---

[2] To Mme de Circourt, July 5, 1856, in *Oeuvres complètes d'Alexis de Tocqueville* (henceforth OC in these notes), 18 vols. to date, Paris, 1951–, XVIII, p. 315.

[3] To Mme Swetchine, December 4, 1856, OC XV, 2, p. 300.

[4] Jardin, *Alexis de Tocqueville, 1805–1859*, Paris, 1984, p. 471.

[5] Joseph Droz, *Histoire du règne de Louis XVI pendant les années où l'on pouvait pré-venir ou diriger la Révolution française*, 2 vols., Paris, 1839, and new edition, 3 vols., Paris, 1858. Hervé drew also on the published memoirs of the period and on the first two volumes of the great compilation of P.J.B. Buchez and P. C. Roux, *Histoire par-lementaire de la Révolution française*, 40 vols., Paris, 1834–1838.

reflects only common knowledge. It is undoubtedly for this reason that Alexis thought it unimportant.

Yet a comparison of the two Tocquevilles can be important for us today. There is said now to be a revival of narrative history in reaction against the more analytic methods of the French *Annales* school and against other methods that present history as a social science. There may be an explanatory value in narration that a more general treatment, suppressing personalities, time, and contingency, does not attain. And if Hervé's book is taken to reflect common knowledge, or if its explanations of what happened in the 1780s were widely accepted in the 1840s, we can ask ourselves what Alexis contributed that was new. Certainly the intensity of Alexis's research in printed and archival sources, brief as it was by modern standards, was new at the time for historians of the French Revolution. It made possible his independence from his predecessors. It gave him concrete particulars with which to illustrate his argument. But it is legitimate to ask, in the case of Alexis de Tocqueville as of others less famous, whether a researcher in his enthusiasm for unexplored materials may not underestimate the importance of what is already known or believed. Newly found sources are not always the most significant.

As for any "influence" of Hervé's books on those of Alexis, there can hardly be said to have been any. Or it was negative, in that Alexis was determined to write something new, something different from what his father and other predecessors had said. He remarked in a letter to Beaumont in 1857, while at work on his unfinished chapters, that "to repeat the commonplaces we have heard since we were born is impossible for me."[6] He did share with his father one main idea throughout his career, that France suffered from an excessive centralization of government. As far back as 1832, while traveling in America, he had written to his father for information on centralization in France. His father had replied with a little essay on the subject. But here, too, the difference between father and son is apparent. For Alexis, the great disadvantage of centralization was the loss of local liberties. For Hervé, the disadvantage was pragmatic: the prefect of a department, appointed from Paris, found it

[6] See below, p. 239.

hard to determine the real needs of his locality or to find competent, informed, and representative local persons with whom to deal.[7]

Hervé called his first book a "Philosophical History," but what he meant by the term was the use of narrative to elucidate cause and effect. "The book which I offer to the public," he said of his work of 1847 on the reign of Louis XV, "is not a metaphysical work. The facts are narrated in detail, and I have tried to group them in such a way as to bring out their consequences."[8] He followed the same principle in his second book of 1850.

Alexis was far more the philosopher than his father. It is in the nature of philosophy to look for necessary, probable, hidden, or generally unrecognized connections between apparently unrelated matters. Applied to historical writing, such an attitude produces a history of broad scope and transcendent message, rising above or digging below the surface of passing events. It was this kind of history that Alexis wrote, while his father was more content to tell his reader simply what happened. Alexis, both in his draft chapters and in his notes, often remarked that he need not offer details on this or that topic because they had been set forth by predecessors whom he never names. He wrote for those who were already informed. As he once said, "I am discussing history, not narrating it." Or as he told his friend Beaumont, he intended to analyze ideas, "and yet not write a history properly speaking."[9]

In a "philosophical" history, in the sense now meant, we find attention to continuity and persistence or to changes that take place only over long periods, as distinguished from combinations of circumstances at a given time and place. The method is to present one aspect of a subject after another rather than to follow a chronological sequence. Particular events are subordinated or cited only to illustrate larger developments. The tone verges on the sociological

[7] Hervé's "Coup d'oeil sur l'administration française," written in 1832 but never published, is in the Tocqueville Papers at the Beinecke Library, Yale University, C III a, paquet 16. See also James T. Schleifer, *The Making of Tocqueville's Democracy in America*, Chapel Hill, 1980, pp. 128–129.

[8] *Histoire philosophique*, I, pp. ii–iii.

[9] OC II, 2, p. 48, and below, p. 160. Tocqueville's sense of his difficulties with the kind of history that he wished to write may be seen below in the excerpts from his correspondence, for example at pp. 232 and 239–240.

and avoids what has been scornfully called *histoire événementielle*. The preference for finding long trends and great social forces tends to diminish the importance of individual persons; kings, rulers, public spokesmen, and decision makers only express needs or movements greater than themselves. When such a history turns to "ideas," it prefers to explore widely shared states of mind rather than the thoughts of individual persons as they try to cope with specific problems. Or it takes the view that people are carried along by great developments of which they are unconscious, which their own statements do not reveal, and which produce other consequences than were intended or foreseen.

In such a history there is a tendency to suggest, if not affirm, that what happened could hardly have happened otherwise because of the magnitude of the forces involved. Everything is explained by such massive considerations that no alternative to what happened seems to be possible. The sphere of freedom of action open to policy makers is correspondingly minimized. There is less reason, when dealing with a particular problem faced by persons in the past, to revive the conflicting arguments or proposals of contending parties or to quote from them at length, since one already knows which arguments will prevail. What individuals say of their motives or purposes is incidental. Nor need the consequences of individual action be closely examined, since it may be supposed that the consequences would have been much the same anyway.

In any history there is likely to be an element of present-mindedness or some expectation of throwing light on the writer's own time. It is especially to be expected in a history dealing with events within living memory or barely beyond it. There is a kind of retrospective reflection in which the present is seen as the outcome of distant and irreversible causes still actively in operation. The corollary may be an attitude of resignation or helplessness. There is another kind of present-mindedness, especially for a historian dealing with recent times, and especially if he has known and talked with some of the surviving participants: he will try to explain and judge their actions, award praise and blame, think that some were wise and others foolish, or some self-regarding and others disinterested.

By no means, of course, are there only two kinds of history. But on the whole what I have called philosophical history applies to Alexis de Tocqueville, and what is suggested as the opposite applies to Hervé. In the following pages we see them both addressing the same question: How is it that France fell into a great revolution in 1789? They are trying to explain an "event." In Alexis's analysis, the Revolution came naturally out of the whole history of France, its effect was to continue rather than repudiate what had gone before, it had occurred in men's minds before they made it the work of their hands. Hervé concentrates on the combination of circumstances at the moment. His method is narrative and chronological. He is preoccupied with short-run causes, not with developments since the Middle Ages. He names individuals by name and discusses their conflicting proposals at some length; long quotations from them in their own words give his work some of the value of a source book. He thinks that some kind of revolution or sweeping change was inevitable, but not the Revolution of 1789 as it actually happened. He thinks that alternatives might have existed, or that firmer or wiser leadership might have made a difference. He thus peoples his stage with characters on whom he passes judgment. Born in 1772, a young adult at the height of the Revolution, he could talk with others a little older than himself who had been active in the 1790s and some of whom were still alive and well fifty years later. Like them, he had lived through the euphoria of 1789 and the horrors of 1793 and 1794, and could never forget them.

Father and son had both been hurt by the Revolution and its continuing repercussions. Not only had their inherited way of life been undermined, but Hervé's public career had been blasted in 1830, as Alexis's was in 1851. Both were personally involved with their subject. On the whole, Hervé seems the more calm observer, Alexis the more excitable and profoundly concerned. In Hervé's book of 1850 there is only the faintest reference to the Revolution of 1848. Alexis's book of 1856 and drafts for its sequel are full of dark references to the sinister despotism by which he thought Napoleon III was degrading France. Alexis's involvement was deeper than his father's because he believed more passionately that the whole future of his country, and indeed of civilization, was at stake.

Let us see how the two saw the outbreak of revolution in the short span of years ending in 1789.

"Reasonable Demands" or "Extraordinary Illness"

"On May 10, 1774, a new reign succeeded to one that had lasted for fifty-nine years. Will the men now inheriting power know how to measure the extent of the great movement of ideas in the preceding years? Will they be able to distinguish the reasonable demands of public opinion from the caprices produced from day to day by a rising taste for innovation?"[10]

It is thus that Hervé de Tocqueville began his *Survey of the Reign of Louis XVI*. He proceeds immediately to characterize Louis XVI, Marie-Antoinette, and others "inheriting power."

"During the ten or fifteen years preceding the French Revolution the human mind throughout Europe was gripped by strange, incoherent, and irregular movements, such as had not been seen for centuries, symptoms of a new and extraordinary illness by which contemporaries would have been frightened if they had been able to understand them."[11]

These are the words with which Alexis de Tocqueville opens his proposed book on the French Revolution. They are preceded by a chapter title in which the "human mind" suffers from a "violent and uncertain agitation." He illustrates his point by quoting from several minor German writers that he regards as typical of their time.

In his draft chapters, research notes, and letters written in 1857 and 1858, after publication of his *Old Regime* and while beginning work on its sequel, Alexis often referred to the state of thinking in France and in Europe before 1789 as a *maladie* or *malaise*, a sickness or illness, or an "agitation" variously described as strange (*bizarre*), violent, vague, uncertain, or feverish. He calls it also a "virus" and a "universal epidemic."[12] He was puzzled by it, and floundered for an answer. Hervé uses the phrase *maladie de l'esprit humain* only once in passing; he meant by it a chronic tendency of the French, which

---

[10] *Coup d'oeil*, p. 1, and below, p. 42.

[11] OC II, 2, p. 33, and below, p. 153. Readers wishing to compare Hervé and Alexis may also do so by consulting items in the index below, noting that references to pages 41–143 relate to the views of Hervé, while those referring to pages after 144 relate to those of Alexis.

[12] OC II, 2, pp. 33, 37n, 46, 48n, 49n, 67n, 135, and below, pp. 153, 155n, 157, 159, 161n, 163, 173n, 220, 233, 234, 242.

he thought lasted until his own time, to become overexcited for or against a politician without understanding his proposals.[13] It may be that Alexis's own poor health inclined him to use the metaphor of a malady. But to see the thinking of the 1780s as a malady has always appealed to those who view the French Revolution with disfavor, from Edmund Burke in 1790 to American neo-conservatives of more recent times. Others would more probably agree with the royalist count Hervé, who from his first page observes that much of the fermentation of the 1780s expressed "reasonable demands."

It was Alexis's belief that latent or potential elements of a democratic revolution existed throughout eighteenth-century Europe but that these became manifest and actual only in the French Revolution itself. He had expressed this idea at the beginning of his *Old Regime and the Revolution*, where he had briefly sketched the institutions of eighteenth-century Europe. Now, in beginning its sequel, he dwelt on diffuse feelings and general ideas. Expanding on what he meant by the agitation of the human mind, he drew his most specific examples from Germany, citing Jacobi, Basedow, and Georg Forster. He saw signs (but not causes) of the coming storm in Swedenborg, Cagliostro, and the *philosophe inconnu*, L. C. de Saint-Martin, and in the mysterious activities of Martinists, Freemasons, Rosicrucians, and Illuminati.[14] Through a third party he sought the opinion of Leopold von Ranke on the importance of the Illuminati in Germany, and was disappointed when Ranke replied that he considered them insignificant.[15] It was in this connection, after discussing the Mesmerists and Illuminati, that Alexis made his only reference to the American Revolution as part of the background to the French. "Do not look for particular causes in all these facts," he wrote; "they were all only different symptoms of the same social malady."[16]

Hervé also takes note of the Freemasons, Martinists, and Illuminati, in whose mystagogic activities he sees the "poverty [*misère*] of man's mind." For him, as for Alexis, they are signs of the times

---

[13] *Coup d'oeil*, p. 214, and below, p. 69.
[14] OC II, 2, pp. 41–44, and below, p. 157.
[15] OC XVIII, pp. 362, 376–377, 379, 385, and below, pp. 234–236.
[16] OC II, 2, pp. 44–45, and below, p. 159.

rather than causes. Quoting Louis Blanc (an altogether pro-Revolutionary historian), he credits Saint-Martin with the first use of the formula *Liberty, Equality, Fraternity*, and he asks his readers: "Do we not seem to hear in these words of Saint-Martin the language of communism seventy years later?"[17] But neither Hervé nor Alexis, after referring to these secret societies, makes much use of them again in his account of what happened.

For Hervé the influence of the American Revolution was entirely different from that of the secret societies and is never mentioned in the same connection. He even quotes the opening sentences of the Declaration of Independence at some length. He describes how French officers in Rochambeau's army, after the victory at Yorktown, went on peaceful journeys and visits throughout the United States and were impressed by the evidences of liberty and prosperity that they saw. He indeed thinks that in their enthusiasm they failed to perceive the great differences between France and America, but he sees them as the victims of a generous mistake rather than of a malady.

For both authors the acute crisis begins with the Assembly of Notables that met in February 1787. Alexis:

"I shall not relate how financial embarrassments brought Louis XVI to call to his side an assembly of members of the nobility, the clergy, and the high bourgeoisie, and to submit the state of his affairs to this Assembly of Notables. I am discussing history, not narrating it."[18]

Thus Alexis passes over the impending bankruptcy of the French government and is not surprised that the members of the Assembly belonged to the "privileged classes."

Hervé, after giving figures on receipts, expenditures, government borrowings, budget, and deficit, tells how Calonne, the controller general of finance, persuaded Louis XVI to convoke the Assembly of Notables.

"He wished to destroy the pecuniary privileges of the clergy and nobility, yet he called only privileged persons to the Assembly of Notables. The three orders were admitted, but almost all the rep-

---

[17] *Coup d'oeil*, p. 146, and below, p. 62.
[18] OC II, 2, p. 48, and below, p. 160.

resentatives of the Third Estate possessed municipal offices conferring nobility. . . ."[19]

Both, in a footnote, give figures on the number of princes of the
blood royal, *ducs et pairs*, archbishops and bishops, presidents of
sovereign courts, and municipal dignitaries in the Assembly. Alexis's note, however, was not published until 1953. He had not integrated the information into the draft of his chapter. Hence it was
missing from the text as published in French in 1865 and in English
in 1873. When the new American translation appeared in 1959 the
translator also omitted the note, although it had been published in
1953. One might suppose that Alexis thought the Third Estate ad-
equately represented in the Assembly of 1787. In that case, why
should there be any "agitation"? In fact, Alexis seems to have been
uncertain himself on the matter of tax privileges. At the close of his
Old Regime he had said that noble tax privileges were significant and
growing. A year or two later, commenting on the Assembly of
1787, he makes no objection to the claim of the nobility and clergy
that their "privileges on the matter of taxation were already reduced
to nothing."[20] In that case it would not so much matter who the
members of the Assembly were.

Both authors point out that the proposals of the government in
1787 anticipated the reorganization effected a few years later during
the Revolution. They agree that these proposals, if enacted, would
have overturned the existing legal order. Hervé observes that they
offered "various elements in the kingdom the degree of liberty that
the most advanced spirits at that time desired."[21] Alexis's view is
more cosmic: Calonne's program would "demolish the old political
system of Europe from top to bottom, replace all at once what was
left of feudalism by the democratic republic, aristocracy by democracy, royalty by the republic."[22] For Alexis, it is principles that are
in contention, more than persons. The principle by which Napoleon III seized power in 1851 with an overwhelming popular vote,
or "democracy," was already prefigured, as if genetically encoded,
in the royal program of 1787. Both authors stress the resistance of

[19] *Coup d'oeil*, p. 207, and below, p. 65.
[20] OC II, 2, p. 51. Cf. *Ancien régime*, OC II, 1, p. 244, and below, p. 162.
[21] *Coup d'oeil*, p. 219, and below, pp. 71–72.
[22] OC II, 2, p. 59, and below, p. 170.

the Notables to Calonne and the king. But where Hervé presents a debate between human beings, with quotations and counter quotations to show the arguments on both sides, Alexis offers a sweeping reflection on the long history of France. It is now the government that is "sick." It had submitted a vast program that it had no means of enforcing and which was unlikely to be accepted.

"The government had long suffered from an ailment, the ordinary and incurable malady of a power that has undertaken to command in everything, to foresee everything, and to do everything. It had become responsible for everything. However different their complaints, all now joined in blaming it, but what had hitherto been only a general inclination now became a universal and impetuous passion." The royal government, entangled in "ruined institutions," found itself the victim of "all the suppressed anger that had arisen from divided classes, disputed conditions, and ridiculous or oppressive inequalities."[23]

We hear in these words the echo of Alexis's great theme of everlasting monarchical centralization over the centuries, but also his belief that the Revolution arose from inequalities that would no longer be tolerated. There was an ambivalence here that troubled Tocqueville himself, but which was also his peculiar strength. It kept him out of the purely counter-revolutionary camp. It also offered something to those described in the United States a century later as conservative or liberal. Both those who wanted less central government and those who wanted more equality could always find something to quote in Alexis de Tocqueville.

The two authors agree on what followed: the Assembly of Notables in opposing the reforms enjoyed a wave of popular support; the government, having obtained no financial relief from the Notables and still facing a crisis, hoped to get an increase of taxes "registered," or approved, by the Parlement of Paris; the Parlement refused this registration; the government then silenced the Parlement, as well as the regional parlements, by transferring much of their jurisdiction to a new judicial system headed by a Plenary Court, which foreshadowed the reorganization later introduced in the Revolution; and the repressed parlements still enjoyed immense popu-

---

[23] Ibid., p. 52, and below, p. 163.

lar favor. As of these years 1787 and 1788, popular favor, or public opinion, meant what was expressed in hundreds of pamphlets written by nobles and bourgeois or by hired writers of no particular social class employed by their social betters.

For Alexis it seemed remarkable, or a sign of the general agitation, that the parlements were almost unanimously supported by public opinion in their opposition to the government, only to have public opinion turn abruptly against them toward the end of 1788. As he saw it, the French were at first eagerly committed to liberty, then suddenly shifted to demands for equality. In his view the love of liberty had barely reasserted itself in France when it was overwhelmed by another force, the "violent and inextinguishable hatred for inequality," which he thought had characterized the French since the Middle Ages.[24] It was a question of ideal types, of which one must prevail, since any blending of the two would be, if not impossible, at least very unstable.

Hervé was less inclined to see any mystery or paradox. He probably thought that a certain amount of liberty and a certain amount of equality could go together, or might even be normal. In his account of what happened it becomes understandable why the demand for equality became more insistent. It was, he thought, because of the obstinate and repeated demands of upper-class persons and corporate bodies for recognition of their own privileges, and more their political and honorific privileges than those concerning taxation. Rather than seeing a disturbance of the human mind, Hervé speaks with a nineteenth-century complacency that Alexis could not share: "It was evident that the progress of ideas would change all that. In 1788 it could not be doubted that the nation aspired to new institutions."[25]

There is really more of a puzzle for Alexis's readers than there should have been for him. For Alexis knew why the desire for more equality had arisen in France; his whole book of 1856 had gone to explain it, and in the drafts and notes for the unfinished book he explained it again. He observes that the judges in the parlements held their offices as a form of property, purchased by their ancestors and

---

[24] At the close of *Ancien régime et la Révolution*, OC II, 1, p. 247.
[25] *Coup d'oeil*, p. 318, and below, p. 108.

now mostly inherited; that a few rich families considered the administration of justice to be their particular privilege; and that they yielded to the impulse that "seemed to drive each particular body to become a little closed aristocracy, just as the ideas and habits of the nation made society incline more and more toward democracy." The idea of a judicial caste was repugnant to the new thinking. So the parlements that had thundered for liberty now "suddenly sank back and expired, unable to breathe even a sigh."[26] But he put these thoughts at the end of his discussion of the resistance of the parlements to the government's program, not at the beginning where they might have been more illuminating to the reader. What he offers is more his own reflections than an explanation.

The Estates General

Under pressure from the parlements and public opinion, Louis XVI promised an assembly of the Estates General, at first for 1792, then advanced to 1789. In such a gathering the three "estates" or "orders"—clergy, nobility, and "Third"—would be represented. Such an assembly, if not necessarily revolutionary, would signify a portentous change by the mere fact of assembling. Although nobles and clerics had always held high office as individuals, it had been many generations since the nobility and clergy as organized bodies had functioned as political institutions on a national level. The Estates General had last met in 1614. At that time the deputies of the three estates had convened in separate houses, each having one vote, so that the Third could be outvoted by the two other orders. In any case, the Estates General had exercised little power in their own right. But it was now expected that the Estates General would make weighty decisions of lasting consequence, take part in a general constitutional reorganization, limit the authority of the king's ministers, deal with the crisis in government finance and taxation, and in general address questions concerning liberty and equality for a long time into the future. In addition, the estates themselves were greatly changed since 1614. The nobility was more composite, internally

[26] OC II, 2, pp. 96, 103, and below, pp. 193, 201.

19

divided, and tied to the diverse interests of rural gentry, high finance, the law courts, and the court of Versailles, while the upper
level of the Third Estate, the bourgeoisie, was far more educated,
affluent, numerous, and vocal than in former times. A strong body
of opinion, shared by nobles and bourgeoisie, held that the Estates
General of 1789 should not follow the pattern of 1614. It seemed un-
reasonable to many that the organized clergy and nobility should
have two-thirds of the weight in public deliberations. From the
middle of 1788 the great question was thus the composition of the
coming assembly. Equality, in an immediate and practical sense,
now meant at the least an equality between the Third Estate and the
other two orders in the Estates General. Such an equality was
thought to require the "doubling" of the Third Estate—that is, that
the Third should have about 600 deputies while the clergy and nobility had only 300 each, and that the 1,200 deputies should meet in
a single body and vote as individuals, or "by head," with one man
having one vote, and not by "order" or "estate."

It is enlightening to see how the two Tocquevilles handled this
question. On the one hand, it is surprising to note what Alexis did
not say, that is, what he omitted. On the other, it is equally surprising to see Hervé, a septuagenarian writing in the 1840s, taking
much the line now followed by most historians in the twentieth century.[27]

For example, it is now common to see importance in the ruling
of the Parlement of Paris, on September 25, 1788, that the Estates
General should meet "in the forms of 1614," an order that precluded
the doubling of the Third and the vote by head. This action quite
abruptly turned opinion against the Parlement and more in favor of

[27] Cf. William Doyle, *Origins of the French Revolution*, Oxford, 1982, pp. 10–11,
36, 96–114, 138–148. Doyle gives both a summary of the historiography and his
own judgment of a new consensus in the light of recent research. Hervé's account
of the three years preceding July 1789 closely resembles the treatment by Georges
Lefebvre in his *Coming of the French Revolution* (Eng. trans., Princeton, 1947); Jean
Egret, *The French Pre-Revolution, 1787–1788* (Eng. trans., Chicago, 1977); F. Furet
and D. Richet, *French Revolution* (Eng. trans., New York, 1970); M. Vovelle, *The
Fall of the French Monarchy, 1787–1792* (Eng. trans., Cambridge, 1984). On the other
hand, some of Alexis's principal ideas have been greatly modified by recent research, such as his stress on the isolation of social classes from each other (especially
aristocracy from bourgeoisie) and on the great preponderance of Paris and the central government over the rest of France.

the king, from an attack on "despotism" to an attack on "aristocracy." Then came the recall of the Notables and the "second" Assembly of Notables of December 1788, composed mainly of the same persons who attended the first in 1787; it too, by a considerable majority (and hence overruling a not inconsiderable noble minority) opined that the Estates should assemble and transact their business as in 1614. At the close of this Assembly five of its members—five of the seven princes of the blood royal—published an address to the king objecting to innovations in favor of the Third Estate. In all this furor there was frequent mention of the American Revolution and the constitutions and declarations of rights that the several American states had adopted. There were also some prominent people who urged Louis XVI to take a clear stand in favor of the Third Estate by resisting noble opposition; among them were the nobleman Malesherbes and the bourgeois P. V. Malouet, who had occupied important office under the royal government. Running through everything, and hard to trace, were the machinations of Louis XVI's distant cousin, the duke of Orleans, who subsidized pamphleteers and worked to build a party of his own, with the thought that if Louis should be forced off the throne he himself might become king.

All these items are mentioned by Hervé, none by Alexis—with one exception soon to be considered. Of the Parlementary ruling of September 1788, calling for the Estates in the form of 1614, Hervé observes: "The fanatical support of the Parlement in its opposition to the government immediately disappeared; its opposition was now seen as selfish egotism, and its popularity vanished like smoke in the wind."[28] Of the second Assembly of Notables he says that its meeting to debate a matter already admitted by a great majority of the French (that is, concessions to the Third Estate) "could only rearouse opinion and broaden the agitation indefinitely. It was bound to result in augmenting the irritation that already existed between the Third and the other two orders. And this is what happened."[29] On the letter of the princes of the blood: "It inspired a hatred of these princes that soon obliged them to emigrate." And he adds, in

[28] *Coup d'oeil*, p. 312, and below, p. 104.
[29] Ibid., p. 315, and below, p. 106.

a rare reference to later times, that "it transmitted a bitter memory from father to son, so that the reign of Charles X [whom Hervé had served in the 1820s] was received with cold distrust, because that prince was believed to be still the protector of privilege and the inequality of ranks."[30] As for the impact of American constitutional ideas, Hervé notes it several times throughout his book. Disliking as he did the Orleanist monarchy of Louis-Philippe, he could more freely speculate on the intrigues of Louis-Philippe's father, the duke of Orleans, who played with revolutionary politics and, though called Philippe-Egalité, perished in the Terror.

Hervé devotes several pages to the role played by his wife's grandfather, Malesherbes. "The royal council should have been vividly impressed by the general movement of opinion, yet only one of the ministers, Malesherbes, appreciated the gravity of the position in which the crown now found itself." Malesherbes therefore urged the king strongly, in July 1788, to take a firm initiative on the coming meeting of the Estates General. The king should not let matters drift, to be settled later and perhaps forcibly by others, but plainly and positively raise a standard to which all men of good will could rally. He should declare that periodic assemblies would meet in the future and be so composed that "each member should be elected by all citizens having the right to vote in the electoral district." That is, there should be no house of nobles chosen only by nobles, of clergy chosen only by clergy, or a third house chosen only by persons not belonging to the other two. Thus, as Hervé interpreted Malesherbes, a preponderance of popular interests would be assured, "and this great change would emanate from the crown, which would get the credit for the satisfaction of public opinion."[31]

With one exception, these points made by Hervé are absent from Alexis's explanation of the crisis of 1788. Neither the second Assembly of Notables nor the letter of the royal princes is mentioned. There is no reference to the American Revolution, probably because Alexis did not believe that there had been any real revolution in America; for him, equality had existed in America from the first settlement, "since the first Puritan who landed on its shores."[32] His

[30] Ibid., pp. 322–323, and below, p. 109.
[31] Ibid., pp. 288–295, and below, pp. 94–96.
[32] *La démocratie en Amérique*, OC I, 2, p. 292; or early in chapter 9 of volume I in

silence on the duke of Orleans's intrigues may have arisen from a certain embarrassment, since Alexis had accepted Louis-Philippe, but it is more likely that he considered the Orleanist machinations relatively unimportant, a conclusion on which many later historians would agree with him. It is more curious to find him saying nothing of his own great-grandfather, Malesherbes, whom we know Alexis greatly admired, and who had advised the king to come out strongly in favor of the Third Estate. Possibly this was because Alexis was not much concerned to consider alternatives in 1788, or speculate on might-have-beens, or note that some of Louis XVI's advisers were perceptive and intelligent men. His argument was that the monarchy was bound to fail.

The exception concerns the ruling of September 25, 1788, by which the Parlement of Paris announced that the Estates General should meet as in 1614. This ruling is not mentioned in Alexis's chapter, but it does figure in one of the research notes found after his death. In this note he observes that the ruling provoked a storm of attacks by pamphleteers on the Parlement and that these pamphlets revealed "the true mother passion of the Revolution, the passion of class which the Parlement did not represent. . . ."[33] He thus saw an emerging class conflict, in which, however, he considered the Parlement to be uninvolved. There is no way of knowing whether he made this note before or after writing the chapter. If before, he must have thought the ruling of little importance for an explanation of what happened. If after, he might have incorporated the ruling into his chapter if he had been able to revise it. In that event, the agitation might have seemed less incomprehensible or less of a malady.

In any case, as usual, Alexis saw in these arguments over representation of the Third Estate a principle loaded with significance for the future. "At first they talked only of a better balance of powers,

any translation. But Alexis briefly notes the importance for France of the American Revolution in his book of 1856, OC II, 1, p. 199; see the *Old Regime*, Book III, chapter I in some translations, Book II, chapter 13 in others.

[33] This note went unpublished until the Jardin edition of 1953, OC II, 2, p. 100, and below, p. 198. It was not used by Beaumont in 1865 in his presentation of Alexis's unfinished materials, and so did not appear in the Reeve translation of 1873. Nor was it used by Lukacs in his reconstruction of Tocqueville's unfinished book in 1959.

a better adjustment between classes; soon they walked, they ran, they threw themselves on the idea of pure democracy. . . . The notion of government was simplified. Numbers alone became the basis of law and right. Politics was reduced to a question of arithmetic. The root of everything to follow was planted in these ideas."[34] We can accept this more as an oversimplification of a basic truth than as an explanation of why people in 1788 thought as they did or what they thought they were doing.

Both Hervé and Alexis accuse the king—or rather, his chief ministers in turn, Calonne, Brienne, and Necker—of raising class hostility in France, either intentionally or by clumsiness and ineptitude, and especially of setting the bourgeoisie against the aristocracy. Alexis, of a younger generation than his father, uses more modern language. The terms "class struggle" and "class war"—*lutte de classe* and *guerre de classe*—occur in his draft chapters and his notes. Hervé is more likely to speak only of "the division of various classes of society."[35] There are nuances of difference on who should be blamed for this igniting of class conflict. Hervé is more inclined to blame the aristocracy, and especially the high aristocracy of the parlements and the royal court, and in general the irresponsible and fashionable persons at Versailles who surrounded Louis XVI. Alexis is more inclined to blame not so much Louis XVI personally as the "royal power."

For example, Alexis takes note of a pamphlet of 1788 which charged that the nobility and parlements "continue to humiliate the Third Estate whom the king alone defends and raises up." He thinks that this tract may have been paid for from government funds. It revealed a "premature attempt," he says, "at that union of democracy and absolute power to destroy privileges and aristocracy for the benefit of despotism. An attempt so often and so successfully renewed since."[36] (By the two Napoleons, of course.) The trouble was that the aristocracy did not know how to defend itself. They, too, believed in the virtues of equality; they agreed with the bourgeoisie that the differences among men should depend on merit, not on birth and fortune. "None of them had ever thought about what had

[34] OC II, 2, pp. 106–107, and below, p. 204.
[35] Ibid., pp. 69, 71, 106, 115, and below, pp. 175, 176, 198, 203, 209n, 210–212, 222; *Coup d'oeil*, p. 296, and below, p. 97.
[36] OC II, 2, p. 85, and below, p. 185.

to be said to justify their privileges in the eyes of the people." It should have been shown that "only an aristocracy can preserve the people from the oppression of tyranny and the misery of revolutions. . . ."[37] The thought here reflects one of Alexis's principal themes, which he had expressed in many other connections and notably in his *Democracy in America*: the need for an aristocracy or some functional equivalent thereof, some grouping of persons who stood above the multitude, who derived their strength and influence from some other source than the government, and who could therefore, if necessary, boldly oppose it. Some measure of institutional inequality was necessary for the preservation of liberty.

Hervé, who probably would have agreed with this maxim in principle, was less inclined to invoke it, or rather the ignorance of it, as a cause of the French Revolution. For him, it was the ambition of incompetent ministers, not the king or the royal power, that set one class against another in 1788 and 1789. It was the privileged persons in the parlements and the second Assembly of Notables who exploited the common people, who pandered to the populace to strengthen themselves against the king, and who even proposed packing the Estates General with simple country priests, humble peasants, and ordinary workers in the belief that "democracy" would redound to the benefit of the aristocracy, the traditional superiors to whom lesser people looked for guidance. "The system adopted by the Notables, if we may suppose that they had a system, appears to have been to keep the Third Estate weak by refusing it the advantage of numbers [that is, no doubling of the Third], and in the Estates General to compose the Third of men accustomed by habit or interest to follow the way traced for them by the upper classes."[38]

When the two are set side by side, Hervé stands as more of the monarchist, with some sympathy for the bourgeoisie, and Alexis as more of an aristocrat than his father, the count, and more inclined to see the bourgeoisie as agitated by confused ideas. They agreed on much, and the differences are differences of emphasis. Both explicitly declare that the upper classes started the Revolution. Both see a class conflict between aristocracy and bourgeoisie. Both found fault

---

[37] Ibid., pp. 108–109, and below, p. 206.
[38] *Coup d'oeil*, p. 319, and below, p. 108.

with the French aristocracy for its actions in 1788 and 1789, but Alexis blamed it for its ignorance of political principles, Hervé for its stubborn defense of its own privileges until concessions that came too late. Alexis seems to have thought that what France needed in 1788 was a better aristocracy, able and willing to lead the people; Hervé, that France needed a better monarchy, a stronger government, willing and able to resist the clamors of special interests: "The French thought that they were oppressed without feeling that they were governed."[39] For Alexis, the French nobility had become decadent, more a caste than a true aristocracy, corrupted by the Bourbon monarchy that had taken away its old feudal powers and granted privileges in exchange, leaving the aristocracy with no powers of government, no experience in political affairs, and no ability to combine with and lead the unprivileged common people. The monarchy, for Alexis, in seeking power for itself, had divided the classes of French society against each other; it had initiated the process leading to a fatal class struggle between aristocracy and bourgeoisie, and resulting in the despotism first of one Napoleon and then another. For Hervé, it was the weakness of the monarchy, its failure to check the overambitious but hardly decadent prelates and nobles, that had brought on a perfectly understandable resentment on the part of the unprivileged elements in the population.

A Concluding Assessment

Alexis de Tocqueville is thought of today even more as a precursor to political science and sociology than as a historian in a strict or academic sense of the word. He himself sometimes said that only the contemporary scene fundamentally interested him.[40] It was Hervé whose interest was more purely historical. Both Tocquevilles had the present in mind as they wrote, and they punctuated their work with advice to contemporaries on what they took to be the lessons of history. But where Hervé offers practical tips to statesmen on how to conduct their business, Alexis tells his readers in general that they must understand the science of politics and be aware of deeper historical forces.

[39] Ibid., p. 244, and below, p. 82.
[40] See below, p. 227.

With Alexis we have an interpretation more than an explanation of what happened in 1787–1789; with Hervé, more explanation and less of a probing interpretation. Alexis, in contemplating the past, seems always to be asking himself, "What is the meaning of it all?" Hervé seems to be asking, "Why did these people act as they did?"

Alexis found it difficult to keep his attention fixed on any given person or historical moment; in treating a particular matter it was his habit to relapse into retrospective background or get ahead of himself by noting portents of what was then the future. He did not easily think in chronological terms or see human affairs as a succession of events or phases. His way of understanding a matter was not to refer to what had immediately preceded it but to show how it fitted into a general pattern or long-continuing process. Hervé, with his narrative method, was well aware that the crisis of 1787–1789 came from changes evident in the reign of Louis XV, to which his book on the reign of Louis XVI was a sequel. But the latter book was conceived along the lines of a drama, not of a treatise. It begins with the accession of a young and good-hearted king and queen in 1774, proceeds through the difficulties of their reign with the erosion of their power and prestige, and comes to a definite end, a climax and dénouement, on June 23, 1789, the day on which sovereignty passed from the Bourbon dynasty to the new National Assembly. Hervé's narrative was thus far more than anecdotal, since the transfer of sovereignty was precisely the issue that signified the passage from the Old Regime to the Revolution and to a more modern world.

Alexis, though perhaps a political scientist or proto-sociologist, remains more significant as a historian than his father because he could not be satisfied with the easy or obvious explanation of events in terms of what merely preceded them. Trying to dig deeper, seeking what was less obvious, he took the risk of bold generalizations, statements of fact not confirmed by later researchers, and declarations of belief arising more from ethical attitudes than from empirical observation. But he also gave more to think about. In his metahistory or metaphysics he is clearly an idealist, repeatedly distinguishing between what he calls "ideas and feelings" and what he calls the "facts." Assiduous in closely reading his sources, he is always looking for more than they actually say. Events, speeches, laws, and institutions, he insists, are underlain by something more fundamental and pervasive which he sometimes calls *moeurs*, the habitual, recurrent, and almost unconscious system of values and behavior of a whole people. Or sometimes this underlying current appears as national character, whether of the Americans in *Democracy in America* or of the French in both his finished and his unfinished work on the *Old Regime and the Revolution*. Despite all his fears and disapproval of what had happened in France for the past two hundred years, he concludes the seven chapters of his unfinished book with a soaring paean to the character of his country that would make the purest patriot blush.

What, then, did Alexis de Tocqueville add to what his father and others had already said? On the whole, it was a sharper, more vivid, and more memorable presentation of not wholly unfamiliar ideas, made possible and more durable by his superior literary gifts. Sainte-Beuve and others, reviewing his *Old Regime and the Revolution*, while admiring it, observed that its main ideas were less new than the author supposed. Probably no work that is altogether original can become a "classic." If Alexis's *Old Regime* became a classic, it was because he presented ideas understandable to his readers with a new clarity and emphasis, with a whole aura of collateral implications, and in his own distinctive voice.

The main themes of his *Old Regime* published in 1856 reappear in his unfinished book, though in a more confused way, since his strength was ebbing and his health failing in 1857, and his view of the current political situation was more disillusioned and pessimistic. The main theme was the growth of both centralized government and of equality or democracy since long before the Revolution. The idea was not new. As long ago as the 1730s the Marquis d'Argenson had written of "that fortunate progress of democracy which we admire in the reigns free from civil war."[41] The idea had been obscured or forgotten in the clash of the Revolution. Tocqueville revived it, very clearly in his youth in an essay written in 1836,[42] and with more mixed feelings in his writings of the 1850s.

---

[41] D'Argenson, *Considérations sur le gouvernement ancien et présent de la France*, Amsterdam, 1765, p. 151. Written about 1735 but not then published.

[42] "L'état social et politique de la France avant et depuis 1789," written in 1836 at the request of John Stuart Mill for the *Westminster Review*. Mill translated and pub-

In the 1850s it was those who accepted Napoleon III, such as Sainte-Beuve, who thought that monarchy and strong government had promoted equality and who found that Tocqueville gave insufficient credit to the pre-Revolutionary monarchy for this desirable development.[43]

Alexis's treatment of centralized government and democracy, especially in the seven unfinished chapters, was indeed somewhat equivocal. He was made more fearful of both, and more strictly liberal, by the despotism of Napoleon III and the violence of popular revolution in the June Days of 1848. On centralized government before 1789, he dwelt mostly on the negative aspects, not on how it promoted equality but on how it destroyed liberty, a kind of liberty that he saw in an idealized Middle Ages. He scarcely perceived what has interested many more recent historians: the growth of a more professional, competent, reformist, and in some ways more equitable administrative monarchy of the Old Regime. With regard to democracy, he used the word in varying contexts and senses. Sometimes it seemed to mean only the absence of a recognized aristocracy, a society without institutionalized legal orders. Sometimes, and very often in the unfinished chapters, it meant the influence of untutored masses to be exploited by dictators and despots. Sometimes it meant a kind of fraternization or mutual acceptance between persons of different social rank. One of his insights in the book of 1856 had been to observe that Frenchmen before the Revolution, noble and bourgeois, were becoming more alike, and in a sense more equal, though still separated by privilege and legal distinctions. Not much of this idea appears in Alexis's seven chapters on the crisis of 1787–1789. We find something of it in Hervé. Developing this thought, more recent historians have identified a whole category of "notables," composed of both nobles and bourgeois, who cooperated in bringing on the Revolution of 1789 and were its principal beneficiaries in the following century.

The growth of centralized power and of "democracy," however defined, was the basis of two more of Alexis's principal ideas: the

---

lished it in English, but it was not known in French until after Tocqueville's death. It is included in OC II, 1, pp. 33–66.

[43] Richard Herr, in *Tocqueville and the Old Regime*, Princeton, 1962, pp. 107–119, quotes reviewers and others on Tocqueville's book; for Sainte-Beuve, see p. 117.

inevitability of the Revolution, and the continuity from before it, through it, and after it. The idea of inevitability of the Revolution was not new. Guizot, Michelet, and Louis Blanc had thought it inevitable that the French should reject the main features of the Old Regime. They saw a sharp break, a decisive new moment in history. Hervé de Tocqueville, stressing the revolt against obstinate privileged classes, was within this general school of thought. Alexis's innovation was to combine the ideas of inevitability and continuity. The Revolution, as he saw it, prolonged or developed further what had existed before it. It was the Old Regime itself, not the repudiation of it, that produced the Revolution. As the title of the last chapter of his book of 1856 expressed it, the Revolution simply "came out of" the Old Regime—"sortie d'elle-même de ce qui précède." Or, as he wrote in a note on his readings, probably in 1857 while working on the unfinished book, "How after reading all these papers . . . can one not see that the Revolution was inevitable, or rather, that it was made in advance?"[44]

To some degree also, Alexis made a new contribution in his perception of social classes and of their different interests as causes of the French Revolution. That the Third Estate had rebelled against the privileged classes was of course a commonplace in everything written on the Revolution since the year 1789 itself. Alexis analyzed and developed what had been said before. Within the Third Estate, he gave a picture of the French peasantry that was new to his readers, stressing that many peasants had been owners of land before the Revolution. Here again the idea was not new; a Physiocrat, the Abbé Baudeau, had asked his readers in 1766 to remember that "our peasants are *citoyens et propriétaires*."[45] It was another idea that had been forgotten in the turmoil of the Revolution. Except for Alexis de Tocqueville, it might have waited longer to be recovered. His idea of the working classes in the towns was hardly more than a sense of their ominous presence, a potential menace that became a "monster" when enraged. He was aware of their importance, however, as indeed was Hervé also, though both were mainly concerned with the activities of middle- and upper-class persons. An attentive

[44] OC II, 2, p. 117, and below, p. 212.

[45] A series of articles, "De l'Education nationale," in *Ephémérides du Citoyen, ou chronique de l'esprit national*, Paris, 1765–1766, vol. III, pp. 17–32.

reader may notice also that Hervé shows a more positive attitude than Alexis toward the activities of women in political matters.[46]

Both Tocquevilles see the Revolution of 1789 as a victory of the bourgeoisie over the aristocracy and thus belong within what the late Albert Soboul liked to call the classical historiography of the French Revolution. Yet, although for both of them the bourgeoisie is an important collective protagonist, neither analyzes it into any component parts. Alexis, during his political career under the July monarchy, had come to think of the French bourgeoisie somewhat like Karl Marx—as selfish, grasping, shortsighted, and lacking in the larger views necessary in a governing class. Hervé, in passing phrases, shows more sympathy for the feelings of the bourgeoisie and more respect for its spokesmen than does Alexis. Alexis is more positive and explicit than Hervé in seeing an actual class war and in his belief, again as with Marx, that a class conflict between aristocracy and bourgeoisie would be followed by one between bourgeoisie and common people. His sense of inevitability, however, had nothing to do with Marx's dialectical materialism. Neither Alexis nor Hervé would define the bourgeoisie in economic terms as the possessor of capital and the means of production. They were well aware that nobles possessed such things also. Their bourgeoisie was more simply a class that possessed advantages but without the legal privileges of nobles and clergy.

It has been said that Alexis was the first writer to see that the Revolution was started by the aristocracy or nobility, that he invented, so to speak, the idea of an Aristocratic Revolution in 1787 and 1788 preceding the French Revolution of 1789.[47] But Hervé said much the same, almost as emphatically as Alexis and more plainly than his own predecessor, Joseph Droz, on whom Hervé drew so heavily in writing his book.[48] A later French historian, Georges Lefebvre, who since his death in 1959 has become a kind of classic, also gave a prominent place to this pre-Revolutionary Aristocratic Revolution. As a natural result, more recent historians, hoping to modify the

[46] See below, pp. 44, 49, 54, 74, 123, 141, 156, 169, 196, 211. And see the index under Marie Antoinette.

[47] Jardin's view, in *Alexis de Tocqueville, 1805–1859*, Paris, 1984, p. 490, shared by Jacques Godechot in *Un jury pour la Révolution*, Paris, 1974, p. 116.

[48] See below, pp. 86, 91–92.

views of their predecessors, have in effect doubted whether any such Aristocratic Revolution ever took place.[49] They generally wish also to lessen the use of class conflict in treating the Revolution, often from a dislike of its Marxist associations. They argue that the Parlement of Paris in 1787 and 1788 had no desire to increase the powers of the nobility as a whole, that it was concerned not so much to advance its own position as to uphold constitutional and individual liberties, and that in any case those who launched the Revolution were not so much a social class as a group of notables, both noble and bourgeois, who desired a new regime to be based on civil equality, but also on liberty, property, education, and participation in government.

All this, however, seems hardly enough to refute the idea of an Aristocratic Revolution. The same people can be both constitutional liberals and aristocrats. The parlements could both uphold the public liberties and be concerned with strengthening themselves as important and largely hereditary bodies within the state. In any case, the true locus of an Aristocratic Revolution, if there was one, was the insistence of the nobility on obtaining special representation in the coming new representative government, that is, of persisting as a separate order in the Estates General and in the future organization of French government and society. This much can be seen in Hervé's account of what happened at the Estates General from May 5 to June 23, 1789. Alexis seems to have been blocked on the subject or to have postponed confronting it, for in what he actually wrote— that is, his seven chapters as distinguished from notes and fragments—he never got beyond May 5, 1789.

To conclude, Alexis carried on a tradition of aristocratic liberalism in the manner of Montesquieu; Hervé, the outlook of the professionalized, bureaucratic, and reforming monarchy in the tradi-

[49] For Lefebvre, see his *Coming of the French Revolution* (Eng. trans., Princeton, 1947), pp. 7–37. For recent critiques, William Doyle, *Origins of the French Revolution*, New York, 1982, pp. 7–40; Joseph Shulim, "The Continuing Controversy over the Etiology and Nature of the French Revolution," *Canadian Journal of History*, 16 (1981), pp. 357–378; Vivian R. Gruder, "A Mutation in Elite Political Culture: The French Notables and the Defense of Property and Participation, 1787," *Journal of Modern History*, 56 (1984), pp. 598–634; Lynn Hunt, *Politics, Culture and Class in the French Revolution*, Berkeley, 1984; and Bailey Stone, *The French Parlements and the Crisis of the Old Regime*, Chapel Hill, 1986.

tion of Turgot. All four of these men had sprung from a long background in the nobility of France. Turgot and Hervé de Tocqueville had spent years as working government servants, accustomed to dealing with people of all classes in the day-to-day business of administration. Although Montesquieu had sat in the parlement of Bordeaux and Alexis de Tocqueville had held elective office for a dozen years after 1839, they were both more fundamentally students of society and political commentators who preferred to see events in a long and large perspective. We can go to Alexis for the background and to Hervé for the foreground of the event that concerned them, to Alexis for the necessary causes without which the Revolution could not have occurred and to Hervé for the efficient causes that produced it at the time as we know it, to Alexis for the long-accumulating pile of combustibles and to Hervé for the spark that set off the explosion.

The Two Texts

The two texts raise entirely different problems of presentation. With Hervé's book it is purely a matter of selection and omission. More than half is omitted; but since the purpose is to compare Hervé and Alexis, and since Alexis begins essentially with the year 1786, the latter part of Hervé's book is presented almost in its entirety. Omitted, therefore, is his treatment of the important ministry of Turgot, the first ministry of Necker except for a few sentences, and miscellaneous details and digressions, such as court intrigues, the deaths of Voltaire, Rousseau, and Frederick the Great, and the explorations of La Pérouse in the Pacific Ocean. What is presented here from the first half of Hervé's book is mainly the opening pages and the impact in France of the American War of Independence, included partly for its interest to English-speaking readers and also because of the importance that Hervé attached to it, as may be seen in the fact that it is one of the few items other than the names of ministers to be found in his chapter titles.

All seven draft chapters by Alexis are presented without omission, as reconstructed by André Jardin for the critical edition of Alexis's *Oeuvres complètes*. Omitted, though presented by Jardin, are a few of the notes pertaining to these seven chapters (those seeming quite trivial); all the heterogeneous short fragments concerning the Revolution after the meeting of the Estates General; and two finished chapters on the condition of France on the eve of Bonaparte's coup d'état of 1799, written in 1852 for another purpose. Anyone wishing to make a more thorough study of Tocqueville's work on his unfinished sequel must go to the critical edition published in French by Jardin. I have added, however, excerpts from Tocqueville's correspondence relating to his work on the unfinished book. These excerpts contain about everything that can be found on the unfinished book in his correspondence as published until now in the *Oeuvres complètes*.

In Hervé's book and in the excerpts from Alexis's correspondence, the use of three dots (. . .) signifies omissions made by me in the translations. In Alexis's draft chapters, however, the three dots are in Alexis's original text as edited by Jardin. All dashes, parentheses, italics, and small capitals are in the originals, as is the paragraphing, whether the long paragraphs of Hervé or the short ones characteristic of Alexis. Square brackets, mostly in footnotes but occasionally in the text, indicate matter inserted by me, except for a few cases where Jardin's notes are translated, with credit given to him.

Footnotes are of various kinds. They are by the original author unless in square brackets. Those in Hervé's book require no explanation; they are ordinary afterthoughts, supplements, or references. Those accompanying Alexis's draft chapters are more diverse. They do not appear as footnotes in Alexis's manuscript, though some are presented as footnotes by Jardin. Some are words or phrases written by Alexis in the margins of the draft chapters or on the covers of containers in which the manuscript was enclosed. Others, written on separate sheets, were judged by Jardin to relate to a particular subject and presented by him as a footnote. What appear here as Alexis's own footnotes are mainly variants or alternative wordings, additional matter, or comments and queries on his work as he read it over with a view to revision.

Other, longer notes appear at the end of Alexis's chapters. Unlike the footnotes, most of these seem to have been written before the chapters were drafted. They consist of memoranda of thoughts or data not to be forgotten, summaries and paraphrases of his readings in the course of his researches, and versions written but later rejected when the chapters were composed. I have omitted many notes of this kind. In the notes of both kinds—those accumulated before the act of writing and those jotted down after the writing with a view to alteration or improvement—we can catch a glimpse of a historian actually at work.

There is in fact no great difference between Alexis's chapters and his notes. The chapters are full of phrases like "analyze rapidly," "put here," "verify," "here strengthen with facts," or "insert quotations." The frequency of the first-person singular ("I think," or "it seems to me"), the exclamation points, the short and unintegrated paragraphs, and the incomplete sentences all show a manuscript halfway between a mass of notes and a finished composition. There are blanks where a word has yet to be filled in. There is sometimes no transition from one paragraph to the next; such places, and others, are often signified by dashes. There are two or three cases of repetition of the same phrases. There are a few downright errors, and some obvious overstatements. There are places where a reader will feel a circularity and repetition of the argument, or inconsistencies yet to be ironed out. The diversity in the length of the chapters, though characteristic of Tocqueville's two famous books, is so extreme (with Chapter III over three times as long as IV, VI, or VII) as to suggest a manuscript on which much work had yet to be done. But in all this material the care and scrutiny that Alexis put into his writing are apparent.

Bibliographical Note

For particulars on the publication and translation of Alexis de Tocqueville's *L'ancien régime et la Révolution*, see the excerpts from his correspondence, pp. 229–230 below. The materials accumulated for its sequel were published shortly after Tocqueville's death by his friend and first editor, Gustave de Beaumont, working with Mme de Tocqueville, in *Mélanges, fragments historiques et notes sur l'ancien régime, la révolution, l'empire . . .* , Paris, 1865, pp. 55–148. This book is volume VIII of the *Oeuvres complètes d'Alexis de Tocqueville*, 9 vols., Paris, 1864–1866. Beaumont, expressing some reluctance, wove together Tocqueville's materials on the "pre-Revolution," consisting of seven draft chapters, fragments, and notes, into a smooth and connected account such as he thought Tocqueville might have had in mind. This reconstruction of Tocqueville's work by Beaumont was translated and added by Henry Reeve as a "Book III" to the third edition of his translation of the *Ancien regime*, called in English *The State of Society in France before the Revolution of 1789 and the Causes which Led to That Event*, London, 1873, and subsequent editions. After the Second World War a new and critical edition of the *Oeuvres complètes d'Alexis de Tocqueville* (OC in the notes here), was launched under the direction of J. P. Mayer, with assistance from the Rockefeller Foundation and the Centre national de recherche scientifique. In this edition, still incomplete (1986), Tome I (in two volumes) contains *La démocratie en Amérique* and Tome II, also in two volumes, contains *L'ancien régime et la Révolution*. Tome II, volume 1, contains Tocqueville's *Ancien régime* with an important introduction by Georges Lefebvre. Tome II, volume 2, edited by André Jardin and published by Gallimard, Paris, 1953, presents the draft chapters, fragments, and notes for a sequel left by Tocqueville at his death. In 1959 John Lukacs, drawing on Jardin, edited and translated a work called *Alexis de Tocqueville: The "European Revolution" and the Correspondence with Gobineau*, New York, Doubleday Anchor Books, 1959, of which pages 33–87 are a translation and reworking of the chapters and notes on the pre-Revolution as presented by Jardin. Lukacs in 1959, however, like Beaumont in 1865, attempted to combine the notes, fragments, and chapters so as to produce a piece of connected historical exposition such as he thought Tocqueville might have written.

Jardin's edition of 1953 maintains the distinction between the chapters as Tocqueville actually drafted them and the alternative versions, variant wordings, disconnected sketches, comments, notes, transcripts, summaries of his readings, etc., in the mass of handwritten and sometimes illegible material that is the only source of all these editions. I have followed Jardin exactly, except that I have omitted some of his annotations and some of Tocqueville's notes when they seem of minor importance, such as paraphrases or summaries that Tocqueville made of what he was reading.

On the seven chapters here in question, see Jardin's "note critique" in OC II, 2, pp. 7–26; François Furet, "Tocqueville and the

Problem of the French Revolution," in *Interpreting the French Revolution* (Eng. trans., Cambridge, 1981), pp. 160–163; Richard Herr, *Tocqueville and the Old Regime*, Princeton, 1962, pp. 100–106; and André Jardin's new biography, *Alexis de Tocqueville, 1805–1859*, Paris, 1984, pp. 485–492.

Hervé de Tocqueville's two books are *Histoire philosophique du règne de Louis XV par le comte de Tocqueville*, 2 vols., Paris, 1847, with a second edition in the same year; and *Coup d'oeil sur le règne de Louis XVI depuis son avènement à la couronne jusqu'à la séance royale du 23 juin 1789, pour faire suite à l'Histoire philosophique du règne de Louis XV, par le comte de Tocqueville*, 403 pp., Paris, 1850. Hervé's first book, the one of 1847 on the reign of Louis XV, was favorably known in the United States. See Charles Kendall Adams, *A Manual of Historical Literature, Comprising Brief Descriptions of the Most Important Histories in English, French and German . . .* , New York, 1882, third ed., 1888, p. 349. But Adams seems to have had no knowledge of Hervé's book of 1850. Nor is it mentioned by others writing on Alexis or on the historiography of the French Revolution.

Hervé de Tocqueville

Excerpts from *Survey
of the Reign of Louis XVI*
Paris, 1850

Count Hervé de Tocqueville in middle life.
Courtesy Beinecke Library, Yale University

Preface

THE MAIN AIM of my previous book, *A Philosophical History of the Reign of Louis XV*, was to recognize and emphasize the successive causes of the great changes that took place at the end of the eighteenth century. Accumulating through faults committed during that reign, these causes still produced no apparent results so long as Louix XV lived. The volcano gathered strength ominously in the depths of society. Louis XVI succeeded to the throne, but passions were not assuaged by his good intentions. His irresolution undermined his will and compromised the dignity of his government. So the workings of sixty years erupted in revolution. The crater spread its lava over France, and little by little over all Europe.

The considerations set forth in our first book required as a sequel a narrative of the reign of Louis XVI from his accession to the crown until the day when the Constituent Assembly, spurning his authority, declared itself the supreme power. Such a narrative is necessary for a full appreciation of the events produced by the movement of public opinion in the preceding period.

We have made an effort to remain within the limits of strict impartiality. We have adopted neither the language nor the spirit of the parties. All of them made mistakes; all committed faults; we have felt obliged to point these out, but have denounced nothing but crime. We earnestly wish the reader to use his judgment as we have done, and at the conclusion of this work grant it the same favorable reception as to its predecessor.

Introduction

ON MAY 10, 1774, a new reign succeeded to one that had lasted fifty-nine years. Will the men now inheriting power know how to measure the extent of the great movement of ideas in the preceding years? Will they be able to distinguish the reasonable demands of public opinion from the caprices produced from day to day by a rising taste for innovation?

Calm reigned in material things, but there was moral restlessness everywhere. The fall of the duc de Choiseul had raised opposition among the higher nobility, who began to grumble against the royal authority. The lower classes were dreaming of liberty. Political passions quivered behind the mask of tranquility. Religious restraint no longer existed since the victory of philosophism was complete. Why attack beliefs already destroyed? Victorious over religion, writers were turning to an examination of political systems. The revolutionary storm that had shown its first signs during the reign of Louis XV would continue to spread under his successor unless he possessed enough intelligence, strength, and energy to prevent its outbreak and preserve the social order entrusted to him.

Louis XVI ascended the throne at the age of twenty. He had been taught to be more afraid of himself than to know men. His education had been such as to make him incurably timid and distrustful of his own judgment. The late king had never allowed him to be initiated into affairs, to which he therefore remained a stranger. He had a good mind. He saw a difficulty and its remedy; but since he lacked breadth of knowledge and force of character, he would prove unable to remain firm in measures suggested to him by his wisest advisers and which his own reason had accepted. Instability in the march of government would mean that moments of gratitude were followed by murmurs of discontent, and confidence in authority by the frustration of disappointed hopes. Yet no king would seem more worthy of the love of his people, for no king had loved them more. Louis XVI's passion was for the public good. "Under the predecessors of Louis XVI the French had made a cult of their monarch; under Louis XVI the monarch made a cult of the French."[1] The king was religious and his morals were above reproach, so that an example of all the virtues descended from the throne. Yet there was a general air of uncertainty, because by the vacillation of his own will he commanded no respect. He was more moral than his time, and his contemporaries, with his court at their head, enlarged on his faults, ridiculed his virtues, and shook off the restraint that they seemed to impose. In person the king was rather heavyset and massive, and the elegant world laughed at him. His good nature sometimes took the form of bluntness, and he was said to be lacking in grace. He liked hunting and found relaxation from the labors of his cabinet in manual hobbies; he was accused of laziness and of tastes unsuited to the dignity of a king. He reigned over France, but without governing its opinions, modifying its morals, or guiding its thinking; an easygoing king who in another age might have passed for one of the best monarchs remembered in history. But at a time when the difficulties surpassed his abilities, he would be continually blown about by the winds and finally carried off in the storm.

At his side on the throne was a young princess of nineteen years, brought from Vienna by the duc de Choiseul to seal the union of the houses of France and Austria. She seemed surrounded by love, admiration, and prosperity. Marie Antoinette, without being a regular beauty, possessed a great personal dignity; her complexion was fresh and bright, her figure well formed, and her bearing full of nobility. People noticed her pointed remarks and her touching traits of humanity and kindness. At her accession to the throne she was idolized by the French.

But she had the misfortune to arrive in a court divided by hostile coteries, one favoring the duc de Choiseul and known as the Austrian party, and the other led by the duc d'Aiguillon, behind whom those opposed to the Franco-Austrian alliance were rallied. The latter party was the more numerous. It was composed of those who remained faithful to the policy created by Cardinal Richelieu and pursued until the ministry of the duc de Choiseul; its adherents were

[1] *Mémoires historiques*, by Soulavie.

annoyed by the marriage of the dauphin to an Austrian princess, and their prejudices were increased by their fear that she would obtain Choiseul's recall to favor. They soon showered on the queen the hatreds they felt for the Austrian coterie. Everything she did was interpreted in the most unfavorable manner, and the accusations formulated on various pretexts in the loftiest circles ended up by spreading down to the people.

The young queen liked some liveliness in her surroundings. In the etiquette established at the French court and strictly observed by Marie Leczinska she found a profound boredom. At Vienna, such etiquette was reserved for gala occasions and days of great ceremony. The ordinary life of Austrian princes was simple and without ostentation. The queen, from both personal taste and the impressions received in childhood, rejected the constraints imposed by our customs. It is dangerous to disdain the habitual forms that some believe necessary to the majesty of the crown. All the older ladies of the court were indignant. Several of them made comments that the queen responded to with irony, and the d'Aiguillon party took up and exploited this new kind of discontent. . . .

Princes, those august slaves, are obliged to remain enclosed in their dignity. They cannot yield to gentler sentiments without arousing violent jealousies and murmurs. Friendship is forbidden to them, for it is soon seen as odious favoritism. Marie Antoinette misunderstood this unfortunate necessity. . . .

While royalty struggled under these disadvantages an unknown enemy, working with imperturbable persistence, was to attack it unceasingly and undermine the existing social order. This enemy was the spirit of association acting clandestinely through the medium of secret societies. This formidable power worked in France at first under the name of Freemasonry, then of Illuminism.

"Freemasonry, composed of men of all countries and ranks bound to one another by symbolic conventions, subjected to tests, and committed by oath to keep the secret of their internal affairs, was divided into three classes, the apprentices, the journeymen, and the masters."[2]

---

[2] See the *Histoire de la Revolution* by Louis Blanc, vol. II. [Paris, 1847, p. 103.]

The ordinary members knew nothing of the secret of Freemasonry except its general confraternity and the meetings that it held for pleasure or sociability. They were left to enjoy in peace the natural satisfaction felt on leaving their daily rounds and entering into the unknown. It was not so with the higher grades. To them, after a series of tests, were confided the plans for political change; they then took the name of masters and engaged themselves to direct the action of the society toward the agreed-upon ends when the proper time came.

Princes and men of the great world sought the favor of admission to the society. Frederick II wished to be one of the brothers, but the secret of the masters was never communicated to him. One prince, however, the duc de Chartres,[3] was fully initiated. In 1772 the Freemasons chose him as their grand master, either supposing his absolute adherence or hoping to bind him by promises to lend him aid in his own ambitions. It may indeed be assumed that the society assisted in the plots in which he later involved himself against the government of Louis XVI. . . .

These innovators knew the weaknesses of the human heart and its taste for the marvelous. After philosophy had dissipated the marvels associated with Christian belief, the empire of the charlatans took over. Cagliostro, Mesmer, and various others recruited numerous adepts, and this poverty of man's mind would henceforth play its part in the work of destruction.

At the same time, a new passion, a passion for popularity, came to dominate the depositories of public power and even the organs of justice. It was no longer enough simply to work for one's country. In discharge of duty it was not enough to gain the esteem of the enlightened or the witness of one's conscience, but one must have the approval of the multitude for a reward. From that time, the king descended from the throne and public opinion took his place; and this power also soon had its courtiers and its flatterers.

3 [Later the duc d'Orléans, the Philippe-Egalité guillotined in 1793.]

Ministry of M. de Maurepas
and M. Turgot

[MOST OF THIS chapter is devoted to the program of reform initiated by Turgot, assisted by Malesherbes, which the author believes was favored by Louis XVI but which unfortunately failed because the king could not stand up against the opposition of the threatened vested interests. He relates how the Assembly of the Clergy in 1775 complained against the trend toward toleration of Protestantism in France, and thinks that the effect was to discredit the Church itself.]

While the clergy compromised the future of religion, civil society was deeply shaken by events on the other side of the Atlantic. North America called for liberty in defense against the violent despotism of the home country. Since 1769 [*sic*: the author's information was a little uncertain] the American colonies had conducted an armed struggle against the demands of England. Always fighting, sometimes defeated, never submitting, they proclaimed to the world the sovereignty of peoples and the rights of nations. This republican program re-echoed in Europe across the depths of the ocean, and nowhere more so than in France. For fifty years philosophers and magistrates had repeated the word *liberty*, and the imagination roamed in confusion among various systems that publicists recommended. The American Revolution clarified this chaos and threw a strong light on questions that had hitherto been obscure.

In 1774 the Congress adopted a declaration of rights. "This declaration," said Lacretelle, "had a character of abstraction and philosophical boldness that would spread its principles very far." On July 4, 1776, the Congress proclaimed the definitive separation of the American colonies from the mother country and the independence of the United States. In this proclamation we find the following sentences:[4]

---

[4] [The following paragraph is obviously not retranslated from Hervé's French.]

"We hold these truths to be self-evident, that all men are created equal, that they are endowed by their Creator with certain unalienable rights, that among these are life, liberty and the pursuit of happiness, that to secure these rights governments are instituted among men, deriving their just powers from the consent of the governed, that whenever any form of government becomes destructive to these ends, it is the right of the people to alter or abolish it, and to institute new government, laying its foundations on such principles, and organizing its powers in such form, as to them shall seem most likely to effect their safety and happiness. . . . [Dots in the original.] When a long train of abuses and usurpations, pursuing invariably the same object, evinces a design to reduce them under absolute despotism, it is their right, it is their duty to throw off such government, and to provide new guards for their future security."

Even before the Americans declared their independence, public opinion approved their efforts. In Europe as in the New World there was much irritation at the haughty superiority affected by England. The king of Prussia and the czarina praised the courage of the insurgents, and these sovereigns seemed not to appreciate the importance of the principles of the insurrection, principles that would one day overturn thrones. But nowhere did the exaltation for the American cause develop so excitedly as in France.[5] The French were delighted at the humbling of the pride of Great Britain. Many applauded a revolt in the name of liberty. They admired the combination of steadfastness and moderation in the American people, of genius and firmness in Franklin, of prudence and courage in Washington. Everywhere the demand rose for the government to come to the support of America and efface the shame of the Seven Years War. The ministry was interested, but undecided. Louis XVI, who was too upright to favor hostilities that the British crown had done nothing to justify, desired to preserve an exact neutrality. Maurepas inclined to a war that he might be praised for launching. Vergennes and Turgot opposed. "The English power," they said, "will be more weakened by a long war with its colonies that it would be by losing them." Turgot also thought that the active cooperation of

[5] "The American insurrection became fashionable everywhere. The complex English game of whist was suddenly replaced in the salons by a less serious game, called boston" (*Souvenirs de Ségur*).

France would bring new embarrassments to the finances and increase the difficulty of reforms that he meant to introduce.

Pushed by widespread pressures on the one hand, and held back on the other by moral and political considerations, the government chose the least worthy course. It continued to assure the cabinet at London of its peaceful intentions but at the same time put no obstacle in the way of help for the Americans through commercial channels.[6] Such an abnormal situation could not last. Not much time passed before it was replaced by open hostilities.

[6] It was through the commercial intermediation of Beaumarchais that the American envoys obtained the aid that they sought. The author of *Figaro* showed great zeal and granted M. Deane a long term for repayment. Deane, fearing that Beaumarchais might not be reliable, went to consult Vergennes, who completely reassured him.

Ministry of Maurepas, Clugny, and Necker. American War (1776)

M. DE MAUREPAS replaced M. de Malesherbes with M. Amelot, whose only merit was to be the son of an old friend. "No one can accuse me of choosing him for his intelligence," said Maurepas. The office of controller general of finance was given to M. de Clugny, the intendant of Bordeaux. He arrived with an eagerness to satisfy the court and comply with any requirements it expressed, so that extravagance was almost immediately introduced into the state finances and was well known to all except the king, who was deceived.

At the same time, the new administration set to work to undo everything that Turgot had attempted. The gild masterships were restored, and the edict suppressing the *corvée* was indefinitely suspended. When the country people found themselves condemned to bear again the burden from which they thought themselves delivered, their irritation was great and gave rise to troubles. Enlightened observers were dismayed at the instability of the royal will, and superficial and malicious people made the monarch and royalty itself into a laughingstock.

Is it not strange, in fact, to see the king suddenly renouncing measures that he had so recently supported against the opposition of the Parlement and used his own authority to get adopted? Such vacillation diminished the respect necessary for the preservation of power. . . .

[The author goes on to tell how the Swiss-born Paris banker Jacques Necker became controller general of finance and then touches on the international situation, involving the visit of the Emperor Joseph II to Paris to consult on the affairs of eastern Europe.]

In Paris the enthusiasm for the American insurgents grew more fervid. The women, who were very influential during the reign of Louis XVI, became passionately committed to the Americans and made it a point of honor to demand aid for them. The simplicity of the American envoys, with their unpowdered hair and bourgeois attire, was a delectable novelty. Everyone who came near Franklin was charmed by his sagacity; he was venerated as the founder of a great people's liberty, and this very liberty was the cause of the excitement. But the situation of these two peoples was so different that it should have been evident how differently liberty was understood. The American colonists, who had come to their new land seeking a security that religious persecution in Europe had denied them, shared in the same feelings and the same goal: to assure subsistence for themselves and their families by opening up the virgin country that was their refuge. These citizens of the wilderness marched toward liberty with equal rights and without the embarrassment of complex social distinctions as on the old continent.

Among us, the scale of ranks was subdivided into a multitude of gradations, from the serf still attached to the soil in some provinces up to the man who wore the crown. Hence the instinct for liberty aroused by the American example was not accompanied by the warm fellow-feeling that a complete establishment of the reign of law might imply. With us, those aspiring to liberty hoped to raise themselves to the level of a higher class, never to descend to the class below. This inherent vice in the yearning for liberty gave rise to deep divisions, which were harmful from the beginning and of which traces still exist. Courtiers indeed affected to wear bourgeois clothing, because it was more comfortable and because it was the fashion. But the new uniformity of costume produced no taste for social equality. Some of these patrons of liberty merely followed along in an exaltation felt by all classes; others hoped to arrive, through liberal institutions, at a sharing in the sovereign power.

Among them a young man of nineteen, the marquis de La Fayette, seemed wholly devoted to this cult of liberty which so many others talked about without understanding it. Of firm and serious mind, he remained immovable in his ideas and inflexible in resolve; the passing of the next fifty years brought no change; throughout a long life he worked tirelessly to import American institutions into France. With such fixed ideas, he made no allowance for the fundamental differences between the French and American societies. His first efforts would lead to anarchy in France and the despotism of the Committee of Public Safety, and his last efforts to setting up a government which has since disappeared in the revolutionary tempest.

La Fayette, in 1777, resolved to devote himself and his fortune to the American cause. He solicited authorization from the French government, which refused it so as to avoid a premature act of hostility against England. La Fayette then fitted out a vessel of his own in a Spanish port, found a few experienced officers to go with him, and departed in secret from Paris. He was stopped on the way but managed to escape, gain his ship, and set sail. On disembarking, he applied to Washington and offered to serve as a volunteer under Washington's orders. The general appreciated his zeal, admired his disinterestedness, and accorded him his friendship, which did honor to both of them as long as they lived. La Fayette was soon made a major general by the Congress, and at the Battle of Brandywine, won by the insurgents against Lord Howe, he received a ball in his leg.

While the fighting was going on in America, and several officers brought glory to the French name, the envoys of Congress sought the help of Louis XVI's government. An unexpected advantage won by American arms gave decisive weight to their efforts after the surrender at Saratoga, where the British general Burgoyne laid down his arms before a body of insurgents commanded by General Gates. Strengthened by this success, the ambassadors of the United States renewed their solicitation and were favorably listened to by MM. de Maurepas and de Vergennes. The king still hesitated. They took advantage of his inexperience by persuading him that no more was involved than a commercial treaty by which neutrality would not be broken. But treaties are not made with a people whose independence is not recognized, and to recognize the liberation of its colonies was in itself a hostile act toward Great Britain. The treaty was signed on February 6, 1778. When the news reached London, George III recalled his ambassador, the French ambassador returned to Paris, and both sides gave orders to open hostilities.

So began this war undertaken by a monarchy to found a republic. We shall see how ideas of liberty developed in part of the nation and in the army, and how the British hatred for France was carried to an extreme, provoking them later to terrible reprisals. "The government," as one writer has put it, "taught the French to side with the rebels; a taste spread for maxims of independence and republicanism, and the word 'insurrection,' little used until then, replaced the word 'revolt' without having its unfavorable sense."

[About thirty pages follow on operations of the French and British navies during the War of American Independence; the triumphal return of Voltaire to Paris and his death; and the formation of the Armed Neutrality of the North against Great Britain.]

La Fayette, returning to France, as we have seen, to take part in plans for an invasion of England, worked to obtain more effective and decisive assistance to the Americans. His efforts were successful, and it was decided at the beginning of 1780 that 6,000 men should be sent under M. de Rochambeau as auxiliaries to the United States. The war was on the point of becoming more active in the four quarters of the globe and would require great sacrifices by the royal treasury. Necker was in charge of the finances of the state, and his administration and his own character were of such great influence on later events that one must attempt to define them.

Necker combined an immense vanity with the talents of a businessman rather than the genius of a statesman. He had arrived at a system based on unchangeable ideas. Later on, at the time of his second ministry, it would be recognized that his mental resources were insufficient when his ideas ran against triumphant facts. At the time we are now discussing, he thought himself destined to govern France, and even regenerate it. He was a partisan of the absolute royal power of which he expected to be the chief agent, and he accepted a principle contrary to the ancient French law which held that taxes must be consented to by the nation that pays them. According to Necker, it was the power of ordering taxes that constituted sovereign greatness. He meant to relieve the crown of the resistance of the parlements and to overcome the antagonism of the privileged elements in society. He would do so by appealing to popular interests.[7] Hence his ideas resembled those of Turgot, whom he

---

[7] We see this idea dominating the whole reign of Louis XVI, repeatedly under a succession of ministers. They were tired of the resistance to the royal authority by the privileged bodies and gladly adopted measures to reduce their power. The most effective method seemed to be to increase gradually the influence of the bourgeoisie, which was doubtless expected to be amenable to the royal wishes. They forgot that

had earlier opposed more from a desire to promote himself than from conviction.

To achieve his own ambitions he had to show himself the adversary of abuses. But the destruction of abuses makes numerous enemies, whose combined efforts lead the reformer to disgrace. He called on that new and rising power that was stronger than magistrates, stronger than the privileged elements: the power of public opinion, of which he became the flatterer so that it would become his supporter. He charmed it first by an exceptional disinterestedness in refusing the emoluments of his office, then by the marvels of an administration that was not understood. He would provide for the expense of a costly war without raising new taxes. In brief, the basis of his system was to establish provincial assemblies, suppress all useless expenses, improve the public credit by a reputation for strict economy, and meet the expenses of state and of war by successive borrowings every year. . . .

[Necker's difficulties as a foreigner and a Protestant; his atempted reforms, his experiment with new provincial assemblies, and his resort to new loans and financial expedients.]

But credit is used up when too often called upon. Frequent resort to it causes concern. At the end of 1780 the minister foresaw embarrassment in paying for the campaign of 1781. He took the unheard-of step of letting the French know the condition of the State's finances, intending to present it in a favorable light, as he did in his *compte-rendu*, or accounting to the king.

The resulting publicity was almost a revolution in itself. The condition of the finances has a great effect on all operations of government. The public, if invited to examine the finances, will also examine all acts of authority and then discuss, praise, judge, and make objections. . . .

[War of pamphlets attacking and defending Necker; actual reforms, improvement of hospitals, abolition of vestiges of serfdom on the royal domain. Necker's resignation compromises the royal authority, which is again accused of weakness.]

---

a nation awakened after a long sleep is like a raging torrent that carries off everything opposed to its course.

CHAPTER III

Continuation and End of the
American War

[AFTER A FEW paragraphs on naval operations and the siege of Gibraltar the author returns to the affairs of the newly proclaimed United States.]

While all this was happening, the affairs of the insurgents in North America were rapidly deteriorating. Discouragement, penury, and above all the disunity among the thirteen states joined only in a loose federation brought a series of new disasters. The disunity was evident in the relation between Congress and the states, the former not daring to issue orders and the latter obeying only at the dictates of their own interests or caprices. Armies were hard to form; and, once formed, the militiamen of whom they were composed, disheartened by their distress, deserted and went home.

This troubled situation was made worse by the treason of one of their generals, one most outstanding for his military talents and courage. General Arnold sold himself to the English and then acted with as much zeal against his country as he had formerly shown in its defense. The other leaders, with Washington at their head, were far from despairing of the triumphs of liberty, but they could not prevent other partial reverses. The British General Clinton occupied New York, from which he threatened the northern part of the confederation. Cornwallis, after gaining control of Georgia and taking Charleston, laid waste to the two Carolinas. While the men lost courage, the women were unshaken. They pressed their husbands and sons to take arms and sometimes joined in the fighting themselves. Their names were at the head of all subscriptions; they made and delivered linen to the soldiers; if pursued and obliged to hide, or even if taken prisoner by the English, they went on writing letters to arouse energy and provoke revenge. Their heroic intervention renewed the patriotic spirit. Their men were ashamed to be less firm than the weaker sex. Recruitment began again with less difficulty, the militias refilled their ranks, and the generals who had been so recently left almost alone found themselves surrounded by imposing forces, so that new misfortunes could be prevented.

At the same time, the Americans received an aid that their own pride had forbidden them to ask for but which La Fayette brought about during his return visit to France. Louis XVI opened his treasury and made a loan of 16 million. He sent as his ambassador a man well qualified to figure in American counsels, the chevalier de La Luzerne. A fleet of seven ships of the line escorted 6,000 soldiers commanded by the comte de Rochambeau to the United States. To avoid division and from a sense of delicacy that did honor to France, it was ruled that Rochambeau should be under Washington's orders.

The French general disembarked in Rhode Island on July 7, 1780, and, while awaiting the opportunity for conferring with Washington on a plan of operation and for joining up with the American army, fortified himself in Rhode Island so as to make impossible any British move against him; but he was soon blockaded by the British fleet, which our squadron could not attack before receiving reinforcements. . . .

[Death of Maria Theresa; Gordon riots in London; British obliged to keep troops at home against possibility of French invasion of England or Ireland.]

Rochambeau received reinforcements of 3,000 men brought by a French squadron under Barras, who took command of all French naval vessels in the area. Rochambeau's freedom of action was restored. In talks with Washington they agreed on a plan of campaign. The comte de Grasse at this time directed a fleet of twenty-one ships toward the West Indies. His move obliged the British squadrons to separate. One of them under Admiral Hood, leaving the coast of the United States, attacked de Grasse and was repelled with losses. Soon Bouillé and Blanchelandes occupied the island of Tobago.

We have seen how at the end of 1780 the American position was precarious. Gates and Greene had been beaten by Cornwallis, but the arrival of Rochambeau restored confidence and made Clinton so afraid of an assault on New York that his movements were paralyzed.

As Cornwallis continued to make progress, the Congress sent La Fayette and 3,000 militia against him. It was common enough in this war for small bodies of men to conquer or defend immense territories, since the population of the United States, still sparse and scattered, was unable to form large masses of troops. La Fayette, only twenty-five, showed the skill of an old general in his defense of Virginia. He outwitted the enemy by ingenious marches, stopped him before strongly held positions, harassed him unceasingly, destroyed his detachments, and finally forced him to retreat.

Washington and Rochambeau joined forces. They decided to attack Cornwallis and force him to shut himself up at Yorktown, where he could be besieged. But the success of this plan depended on threatening New York so that Clinton would not dare to send troops to the aid of Cornwallis. He must also be prevented from retreat by sea. At the request of the two allied generals the comte de Grasse directed his fleet to Chesapeake Bay, on whose shore Yorktown is situated. He also brought to Rochambeau 3,000 men commanded by the marquis de Saint-Simon. Arriving without difficulty at the bay, he drove off Admiral Hood, sent to oppose him.

With some French and American units, Washington made a few feints against New York in order to hold Clinton there. Then, leaving one division three leagues from that place to keep up the threat to the enemy, he moved rapidly toward the south. He passed with his army through Philadelphia to the acclamation of the citizens of that great city. The British outposts were quickly pushed back toward Yorktown. All avenues of retreat were now closed to them, and Cornwallis was obliged to concentrate his troops there where they could be surrounded. The allies opened their trenches on the night of October 6–7. The American force numbered about 9,000, the French about 7,000.

In this memorable siege French and Americans rivaled each other in daring. Two defensive redouts were carried by assault. Neither wounds nor sickness could stop the officers, some of whom, unable to walk, were carried at the head of their columns. Cornwallis, attacked in force and blockaded by the French fleet on the side toward the sea, capitulated on October 19. He and the 8,000 men under his command became prisoners of war. The victors captured 214 cannon and 22 flags.

The British troops, with drums beating, defiled between the two allied armies and laid down their arms. O'Hara, commanding the British in the absence of Cornwallis, who was ill, began by offering his sword to the comte de Rochambeau, who, however, said, pointing to Washington, "I am only an auxiliary," so that the leader of the rebels saw the sword that had been intended to subjugate him fall at his feet. This action in itself was an anticipated recognition of American liberty and the sovereignty of the United States. All the provinces resounded with cries of joy. Congress voted its thanks to Generals Washington and Rochambeau and Admiral de Grasse, and ordered the erection at Yorktown of a column with emblems of the alliance and inscriptions in honor of the victors. A religious holiday was also established, to give thanks to Providence every year. The French government rewarded its warriors; La Fayette received the rank of *maréchal de camp* at the age of twenty-five. Everyone felt the enthusiasm, including the queen.

In effect, the surrender of Cornwallis marked the end of hostilities on the American continent. The British, soon obliged to evacuate the Carolinas and Georgia, concentrated their forces in New York, Savannah, and Charleston and made no further efforts. The Americans made no attempt to force them out, awaiting the final liberation by a peace treaty that could not be long in coming. They thus saved precious blood that would have been spilled by more hasty action.

The French officers took advantage of this tacit truce to make visits in many places. They were everywhere eagerly received; France was eulogized; wherever they stopped they heard blessings on the names of Louis XVI and Marie Antoinette; there was no dinner where toasts were not offered to the good king whose timely intervention had assured the deliverance of their country. This republic of a few days had the qualities of youth in being profoundly grateful to those who had served and helped it. It showed also the energy of youth. Land was cleared everywhere. On sites of wild and majestic nature there now arose clean and well-maintained habitations. The towns were alive with a hard-working population. There had of course been divisions and opposed parties, but liberty restored a cordiality between citizens who now had to bear only the equal yoke of the law.

It is therefore not surprising that the French officers conceived such an enthusiasm for liberty, which seemed to them the surest guarantee of union of the people and prosperity for the state. On their return to France their admiration for free institutions could hardly not have a notable influence on public opinion. In the inexperience of that time, no difference was seen between our old continent with its vices and this virgin land still innocent of political dissensions. It was not foreseen how this liberty, so bright when crossing the ocean, would succumb among us, along with its own best friends, to the storms raised by repressed old hatreds and triumphant jealousies.

[Birth of the dauphin; continuing naval operations in the West and East Indies; Franco-Spanish siege of Gibraltar and threat of invasion of the British Isles; terms of the peace treaty.]

Ministry of Vergennes and Calonne.
First Assembly of Notables

THE GLORIOUS peace of 1783 seemed to strengthen the monarchical principle. The national pride was satisfied. Louis XVI loved his people, and his people were content with their king.

Maurepas died on November 21, 1781. The king declared that he would now govern himself and never again have a first minister. The government, freed from the restraints that the self-serving Maurepas had put upon it, would now surely go forward at a firm and more steady pace.

Yet hardly had the calm arrived that follows on the troubles of warfare when the existing social system became weaker and weaker. Day by day, royalty lost its prestige; its decline became visible year by year.

Several causes had long been preparing this surprising outcome. One of the first was the character of the chief of state. We have already had occasion to observe how the inconstancy of his decisions had painful consequences for his subjects. He did harm by his excessive fear of doing so. Weakness in a monarchy leads to revolutions, with everyone supposing himself authorized to discuss public questions; hence a confusion of ideas, and then anarchy.

We should also recognize a more distant and still active cause. There had been a time lasting for several centuries when the nation had been consulted on its gravest interests; it now endured the suppression of this right with impatience. The writings of philosophers and works of several well-known publicists had increased this dissatisfaction. Popular desires were formulated under the banner of a love of liberty; this liberty shone brightly in the New World and was reflected in the minds of many in France.

There was then at the top levels of the nation a society whose ideas, not very deep, followed the empire of fashion and had no faculty for penetrating the future. In our previous book we saw how the vogue established itself of admiring everything that was done in England and on the other side of the ocean. It required one to seem above all prejudice of religion or caste. Pride changed its face, as if a country tired of being so long the first among monarchies now wished to be the first in freedom. This empire of new ideas, this apparent abnegation of self for the benefit of liberty, overwhelmed even the high magistracy of the parlements. From the lofty height of their bench, these bodies, which had styled themselves little estates general, gave up this fine prerogative and began to demand, in all their remonstrances, the convocation of the real Estates General, the ancient national assemblies.

This initiative, these appeals for intervention by the country itself, could not fail to have a prompt and decisive impact on a wealthy and enlightened bourgeoisie. These people desired a freer system that would inevitably give them a more important position; but the love of liberty was joined with another passion: the love of equality. Social relations between the nobility and the bourgeoisie under Louis XVI were what they had become during the last years of his predecessor. Wealth, science, and literature were admitted in the salons. But under the appearance of perfect politeness could still be seen the protective forms that maintained a social distance. In addition, the middle class was hurt by seeing all the highest places, even in the Church, reserved for the nobility. Discontent was made worse by an ordinance published in 1781 that required any young man aspiring to become an army officer to prove four degrees of nobility. There were no waivers, except for soldiers promoted from the ranks for merit, who were called *officiers de fortune*. What the French will support least of all is humiliation, and this mistake contributed to the depopularizing of the king.

Quite apart from these unsettling tendencies, the spirit of investigation continued to grow. Dogmas, government, arts, and sciences were all analyzed. The search for new knowledge moved on boldly into the unknown, scorning the experience of the past. It was in vain that past ages showed how an absolute logic was often not applicable to human affairs. Reason, whether enlightened or muddled, laid claim to an unlimited empire, whose seductions would lead to destruction instead of to reform and progress.

This taste for analysis, this inflexible logic that dominated these years, was unfavorable to works of the imagination. Literature became dull; while it discussed and philosophized, it lacked warmth of feeling. Sometimes praised by party spirit, it left nothing for posterity.[8] But this tendency toward abstract ideas that chilled the imagination was more favorable to the exact sciences, so that the reign of Louis XVI is particularly notable for progress in these subjects. Mathematics developed, and astronomy made great advances in the vast region of the stars. The king gave his encouragement. He conceived the project for a voyage around the world, of which he put the unfortunate La Pérouse in charge. He himself drafted the instructions given to that famous navigator. Chemistry penetrated to the elements of matter, discovered principles of the creation of new beings, and examined the basic means used by the Eternal in the formation of complex bodies. Bold spirits ascended into the highest regions of the atmosphere, and people applauded the genius that seemed to soar above human destinies and steal the secrets of the heavens.[9]

But the movement of ideas did not stop with the exact sciences. It soon claimed to introduce itself into the sciences of government and explore the mysteries of the social order. Thinkers were impressed by the abuses, which they angrily pointed out, but they lacked experience and were unable to propose remedies. Everyone had his own ideas, and the resulting chaos could hardly be sorted out even by revolutions.

At the beginning of this book we mentioned the secret societies and their influence. They were joined by a new sect called Martinist, after a certain Saint-Martin who formulated its doctrines in a work all the more admired by its adepts because, as they thought, its obscurity concealed great profundity.

"Grafted on Freemasonry, the new doctrine set up a rite in ten grades or degrees of instruction through which those who adopted it passed.

[8] From Voltaire and Rousseau to the Revolution, in imaginative works, nothing worth remembering remains except the poetry of Delille.

[9] It was in 1783 that Montgolfier found a way to lift himself in a balloon filled with rarefied air, lighter than atmospheric air. His discovery was soon improved on by other students of physics.

"Saint-Martin, in the name of a pious spirituality, objected to all human religions; he humbled himself before sovereigns while undermining their thrones; as for religions, their diversity condemned them. As for governments, their instability, variety, and mutual conflicts were enough to show the falsity of their basis. Civil law, entangled in debates over the illegitimate distribution of the common domain, wandered aimlessly in search of justice without ever finding it.

"According to Saint-Martin, there was no salvation for societies until they accepted what he called the *active and intelligent principle*, and the motto for this enigma was *Liberty, Equality, Fraternity*, a formula which in his symbolic style he called the holy triad, and which he spoke of in a tone of fervent solemnity."[10]

Do we not seem to hear in these words of Saint-Martin the language of communism seventy years later?

From all the preceding it was obvious that the social order was profoundly shaken. A lever of moderate strength was enough to overturn it. This lever was supplied by the bad administration of finances and the deficit.

[Further financial troubles after the resignation of Necker. Resistance in Brittany and Franche-Comté against new taxes.]

Credit was exhausted, the royal treasury was empty, and the government services were on the point of collapse. The need was for a capable man to prevent the financial disaster that seemed imminent. Vergennes understood the necessity and tried to persuade the king. There was one man who had made himself talked about by declaring repeatedly that he knew how to direct the finances and restore credit, and so seemed suitable for the post of controller general. This man was Calonne, the intendant of Metz. Louis XVI felt an aversion to him, seeing him as a frivolous and immoral character. He was said to be lost in debt; he had moreover won a regrettable celebrity in the trial of La Chalotais, so that his promotion would make the parlementary magistrates unhappy.

Calonne overcame these obstacles with the aid of court intrigue. He had a brilliant mind and was gracious and amiable. He was known to disapprove of Necker's severe and pedantic economies.

---

[10] *Histoire de la Révolution*, by Louis Blanc. [Paris, 1847, vol. II, p. 103.]

He won the favor of the count of Artois and the intimates of the queen. Vergennes, to influence the king, had a letter written to himself by a court banker, d'Harvelay, praising Calonne as the only person who would revive the confidence of the capitalists.[11] Shown to the king at an opportune moment, this letter overcame his repugnance, and he yielded.

Calonne was a man of strange contrasts. His inventive mind quickly found a solution to a problem. He never seemed upset or embarrassed, and his self-assurance aroused the confidence of others. The administration of the finances, so complicated for his predecessors, seemed only an amusement for him. His good spirits were inalterable, as was his taste for pleasure. He knew how to banish boredom in his conferences with the king. But in this brilliant man, with his lively imagination and quick understanding, there was a superficiality that prevented him from seeing the distant consequences of his system and of the plans that he claimed to be executing. He proved to be more ingenious than circumspect; his audacity was not tempered by prudence. So in four years he brought the public fortune to ruin and left the way wide open for changes that came later.

He began by wishing to seem generous and even prodigal. Since money would be profusely distributed, it would seem that the State had unknown resources. "A man who wants to borrow," said Calonne, "must give the appearance of being rich, and to seem rich he must dazzle the world by his expenditures. Let us act this way in public administration. Parsimony is doubly bad; it makes the capitalists fear lending to an overburdened treasury, and it depresses the arts and trades that are stimulated by liberal expenditure." For a while the controller general obtained the success that he hoped for, but his eagerness to please and the extreme facility of his character would not let him stop on the dangerous slope he had entered; and we shall soon hear the frightful word *deficit* resound in the ears of the French and mark the hour of revolutions.

[The author now devotes about fifty pages to examples of Calonne's extravagance, his renewed borrowings, the Diamond

---

[11] [At this time *capitalistes* meant financiers who organized loans to the government or took part in its tax-collecting activities.]

Necklace affair by which Marie Antoinette's reputation was damaged, and the furor over Beaumarchais's *Mariage de Figaro*, in which aristocracy and social rank were ridiculed on the stage. He then states that in the budget for 1786 the expected revenues were at least 60 million francs short of expected expenditures.]

This deplorable situation inspired some very serious reflections in the mind of the controller general. How could he admit to a deficit when he had repeatedly lulled the public into hopes for an early liberation from debt? In any case the king, on the assurance of his minister, believed his finances to be sound.

In ten years the government borrowings had risen to 1,338 million, and of this enormous sum 487 million had been incurred during the administration of M. de Calonne in time of peace. Yet payments on the debt were about to stop!

The controller general called on all the resources of his imagination. Some great service to the nation might induce it to forgive his earlier prodigalities, and he would retain the confidence of the king if he could show that his proposals would bring relief to the people. Abuses were numerous. Calonne would try, like Turgot and Necker before him, to re-establish the finances by a reform of abuses.

In this plan there was a great difficulty, since it would require the registration of royal edicts by the sovereign law courts, which were the faithful guardians of privileges. But they could not possibly refuse, or their resistance could be easily overcome, if the edicts reached them for registration on a broad wave of national support. The Estates General had not been assembled for 172 years, and the progress of ideas, especially the American war, had developed an instinct for liberty in France. But a new danger would be created if members of the Estates General, chosen by elections, should arrive with mandates from their constituents. Calonne remembered that assemblies whose members were appointed by the king had been convoked several times by Louis XVI's predecessors, under the name of Assemblies of Notables. As emanations of the royal power they had not dared to go in their deliberations beyond the limits that the king set for them. So Calonne proposed that the king call together an assembly of this kind, strengthening his argument with the precedent of Henry IV.

He obtained the royal consent both for the assembly and for the projects that he would present to it. He was encouraged when he overcame a greater difficulty by winning over the minister who most fully enjoyed the king's confidence, the count de Vergennes. It was agreed that until the convocation was publicly announced it would remain a secret known only to the king, Vergennes, the keeper of the seals, and Calonne. Even the queen was not told.

The controller general, nonchalant as always, was lacking, as we have already remarked, in the foresight that might have assured the success of his plans. He was fascinated by the abundance of his own ideas and had no doubt of their success.

He wished to destroy the pecuniary privileges of the clergy and nobility, yet he called only privileged persons to the Assembly of Notables. The three orders were admitted, but almost all the representatives of the Third Estate held municipal offices conferring nobility. With mistaken confidence, he designated as representatives of the clergy the prelates who had shown the most talent in the provincial estates, including Loménie de Brienne, of whose ambitions to be minister he was well aware, and who would soon pose as his adversary.[12] Yet he also wished to replace the provincial estates with provincial assemblies created on a uniform model. He was deluded enough to expect no resistance and to think that his proposals would be accepted by acclamation.

The meeting of the Notables was set for January 29, 1787, and they all assembled in Paris before that date. But Calonne, always inclined to mix his own pleasures with the business of state, was unable to have his program ready by that time. The opening of the assembly was postponed until February 7, then to the fourteenth, and

[12] The Assembly of Notables was made up as follows:

Princes of the royal family and princes of the blood	7
Archbishops and bishops	14
Dukes-and-peers, marshals of France, gentlemen	36
Councillors of state and masters of requests	12
First presidents and attorneys-general of the sovereign courts, and other magistrates	38
Deputies from the *pays d'états*, of whom four were of the clergy, six of the nobility, and two of the Third Estate	12
Municipal officers	25
	144

finally to the twenty-second. The delay built up a strong prejudice against both the minister and the proposals he intended to make. The Notables had arrived with ideas of conciliation in mind. The enemies of the controller general used their leisure to turn feelings against him and managed to arouse an incurable distrust. Rumors of a large deficit were already spreading. Calonne's opponents, with some success, pointed to a work published by Necker in 1784 entitled *De l'administration des finances de France*; it was a time when charlatanism carried more weight than truth.[13]

A misfortune now made the controller general's position more difficult. Vergennes, who had favored his projects, died on February 13, 1787. He had agreed to the convocation of the Notables as a necessity. But he had foreseen the discontent that a revelation of the deficit would arouse and the shock that the ensuing discussions would give to public opinion. He thought also that when foreigners learned of the bad state of our finances the British would attempt measures harmful to France. To avoid this danger, he decided to flatter the commercial interests that were so influential in British policy, and he signed on September 26, 1786, the commercial treaty that had been promised when the peace treaty was signed. The new treaty was based on free trade. Soon the products of British manufactures poured into France at a price that many could afford. Since Anglomania was all the rage, it became stylish to dress in British fabrics. Our own manufactures were adversely affected, but the damage was only transient, for the competition stimulated our manufacturers to imitate their rivals by offering better made, cheaper, and quickly available products to the public.

As February 22 approached, some rejoiced, but others were concerned at this convocation of a new assembly at a time when everyone's thoughts were turning to innovations. Would the assembly remain within the limits assigned to it by the royal authority? Though not emanating from the people, it was summoned to discuss the people's interests. Named by the king, it represented nei-

[13] Necker's aim was to exalt himself and indirectly belittle his successor. He had already declared, in his *compte-rendu*, that at the time of his resignation the receipts exceeded expenditures by 10 million; this fabulous allegation was blindly believed in, and it was asked how so favorable a situation could have changed to distress in only six years.

ther royalty nor the nation. Would the nation be satisfied with interpreters who were not of its choosing? Would this experiment not inspire the wish for a more direct and hence more logical deputation? Public attention had been sharply provoked. The government's measures, the faults it had committed, the projects that it announced, and the debates that would follow, all became the staple of everyone's conversation. The French would claim the right to penetrate the secrets of state and would soon develop that public opinion which is stronger than government and more powerful than a king.

Such were the anticipations by which many were disturbed. If they reached the ears of Louis XVI, they did not trouble his confidence. The day after he announced the convocation of the Assembly of Notables he had written to Calonne, "I was awake last night, but it was from pleasure." The king judged others by the sentiments of his own heart, devoted as he was to the prosperity of the country and the improvement of his subjects' lot.

Finally the day came that was to open the era of deliberative assemblies in France. This one, ordained by the king himself, was opened by him with pomp. He announced his intention in a simple and succinct speech: "On the one hand," he said, "to improve the revenues of the state and make them more flexible by a more equal distribution of taxes, and on the other to liberate trade from the barriers that block its circulation, and so to relieve the poorest of my subjects so far as circumstances allow me to, such, Messieurs, are the views that I have come to entertain and on which I have settled after mature examination."

After a few insignificant improvised words by the keeper of the seals, Calonne rose to speak and tried to win over the Notables by an eloquent exposition of the needs of the treasury and the means of providing for them. According to him, the deficit went back to the time of John Law and the Regency. Since then, it had never been possible to restore a balance between revenues and expenditures; neither the thrifty administration of Cardinal Fleury nor the financial devices of Abbé Terray had made the differences between the expenses of the state and its income disappear. "The deficit was over 74 million when Abbé Terray was called to the administration of the finances, and it was still 40 million when he left it.

"In 1776 the deficit was estimated at 37 million by the very man [Necker] who shortly thereafter became the director of finances. Between that date and May 1781 the rebuilding of the navy and the needs of war required the borrowing of 440 million. It is evident that the revenue produced by all the reforms and improvements made in the interval, however high we may put it, was far from compensating for the increased expenses made necessary by the interest on these loans, which must always be reckoned at nine to ten percent, whether we consider the payments on life annuities or other repayments, and that this burden of interest has risen to more than 40 million a year. The deficit has thus increased, and the actual accounts prove it."

Accused on all sides of wastefulness, Calonne hoped to excuse himself by the definition he gave to the word *economy* in the administration of a great state.

"In general, economy for a minister of finance may exist in two ways, so different that one may call them two kinds of economy.

"There is one that is easily obvious by its appearance of severity, which shows itself in spectacular and harshly worded refusals, which affects rigor in small things so as to discourage the crowd of those seeking favors. It seems impressive while proving nothing in reality, but it has an impact on public opinion. It has the double advantage of discouraging importunate demands and of quieting the worries of the uninformed.

"The other kind, arising more from the minister's sense of duty than from his personality, can accomplish more by showing less. Strict and careful for everything important, it makes no affectation of austerity in minor matters. It lets people talk about what it grants, but is silent on what it saves. Since it is seen as accessible to requests, people are unaware that most requests are rejected. Since it tries to soften the bitterness of refusal, it is thought to be incapable of refusing. Since it has no useful and convenient reputation for inflexibility, it receives no credit for its wise restraint. While by assiduous attention to all details it protects the finances from the worst abuses and most ruinous incompetence, it seems open to the charge of a superficial facility, which is then exaggerated by those who wish to discredit it."

Those who listened saw that he wished to draw in his own way the portraits of Necker and himself. In addition, he demolished Necker's *compte-rendu* by affirming, against the contrary assertion of the former director general of finance, that the deficit existed when Necker left office. The fanatical supporters of Necker were infuriated, and there were many of them. Since the ministry of the Genevese banker, many of the French had acquired the habit of becoming very excited in favor either of particular men or of systems all the more admired the less they were understood; and this malady of the human mind has lasted until our own times.

Indignation grew when it was learned that Necker had asked the king's permission to come and defend the facts in his *compte-rendu* in the presence of the king and Notables, and that the only reply he received was to be forbidden to return to the capital. A verification of the budgets during his administration has since proved that his assertions were lacking in truth. But that was of slight importance at the time. He enjoyed the sympathy always aroused for a man who is respected but believed to be persecuted unjustly.

Calonne, after exhibiting the sad state of the finances, went on to indicate remedies.

"What, then, remains that can supply what is lacking and procure all that is needed to restore the finances?

"The abuses.

"Yes, Messieurs, it is in the abuses themselves that the wealth can be found which the State has a right to reclaim and which can serve to restore order. It is in the elimination of abuses that we have the only means of meeting our needs. It is in the very depths of disorder that we shall find the source to fertilize all parts of the monarchy.

"The greatest of all abuses would be to attack only those of least importance, those that concern only the weak and would thus arouse only a feeble opposition to their reform, and which in any case could not produce an adequate result.

"The abuses that must be eliminated today for the public good are the most considerable and the most protected ones, those with the deepest roots and the widest ramifications."

In thus allying the public good with the reform of abuses, Calonne should have foreseen that those profiting from them would think the remedy worse than the disease. In his relations with the Notables he would have to struggle against the irritated and numerous partisans of Necker, against the implacable suspicions of all those who feared the reforms, and against public opinion itself, aroused by his unpardonable levity and inexcusable prodigality. He did indeed enjoy the support of Louis XVI and the king's promise to defend him against his enemies. But the king was weak, and it was known that his excessive fear of being deceived took away all perseverance from his resolutions. The minister had managed to win over the comte d'Artois, but Monsieur was not favorable.[14]

The Notables subdivided themselves into seven "bureaus," each presided over by a member of the royal family.[15] They deliberated by bureau, but the votes were counted by head.

The deficit was announced as amounting to 115 million. Many believed that Calonne exaggerated the figure so as to arouse the fears of the assembly on the state of the finances and more easily gain approval for the measures he proposed.

These measures were the following:

The differences would disappear between *pays d'états, pays d'élections, pays d'administration provinciale*, and *d'administration mixte*. They would all be replaced by a uniform system of provincial administration for all parts of the kingdom. Each province would contain municipal and parish assemblies composed in each case of municipal officers; notables of areas comprising from twenty-five to thirty rural parishes or towns would form districts, with each district assembly composed of deputies named by the parish and municipal assemblies; and finally a provincial assembly, the highest echelon in this hierarchy, would consist of deputies named by the secondary assemblies.

These three kinds of assemblies, corresponding with one another and subordinated according to their several levels, were intended to apportion the public charges, draw up proposals for roads, canals, and charitable works and workshops, and to make known the local and general needs of the province. They would meet only once a

[14] [The king's two brothers. "Monsieur," *tout court*, was the common way of referring to Louis XVI's next oldest brother, who became Louis XVIII in 1814. The youngest of the three brothers, who became Charles X in 1824, was known simply as the comte d'Artois.]

[15] These princes were Monsieur, M. le comte d'Artois, the duc d'Orléans, the prince de Condé, the duc de Bourbon, the prince de Conti, and the duc de Penthièvre. [For the "bureaus," see the Glossary.]

year, but the provincial and district assemblies would have permanent offices at work between their meetings. All these bodies were meant to become a means of communication between the government and the population. They would have the power to make formal requests and present views on which the government reserved the right of judgment; none of their operations could be implemented, even provisionally, without authorization by the intendant of the province; and finally, all jurisdiction and all executive authority were explicitly denied to them.

The levy of the twentieth-tax, or *vingtième*, was to be replaced by a "territorial subvention," a land tax falling without distinction or exception on all lands belonging to the royal domain, the clergy, the nobility, and all others.

The taxes known as the *taille* and the *capitation* were preserved, with significant reductions.

Agriculture would be freed in perpetuity from the *corvée* in kind, which would be converted into a monetary payment equivalent to a sixth of the *taille* and of the *capitation taillable*.

All barriers to trade between the provinces were pushed back to the frontiers of the kingdom. Taxes on trade would be replaced by payments on a uniform scale, in which political needs and the interests of manufactures would be allowed for.

The abuses and vexations in guild masterships were to be ended for the whole of France.

The strict obligations of the salt tax were moderated in regions subject to the general farm, and the price of salt in these regions would be reduced.

Taxes on the regulation of documents were converted into a single stamp tax, at a higher rate, applicable to all persons and extended to items hitherto exempt.

The sale of subinfeudated leases of the crown domain was to be used as a means of reducing the public debt.

Finally, by proposed economies in all government departments and in the king's household, an annual savings of 20 million would be obtained.

The purposes behind these innovations won public approval. The establishment of provincial assemblies would give various elements in the kingdom the degree of liberty that the most advanced spirits

71

at that time desired. But so great was the distrust inspired by Calonne's administration that everyone thought that the proposals
were good and should be adopted, but only if their execution could
be confided to someone else.

The Notables received favorably the proposal for provincial assemblies. They asked only that rights of precedence and the presi-
dency should be granted to the two highest orders. They agreed
that the Third Estate should have a number of deputies equal to
those of the clergy and nobility combined and that deliberation
should be in common. Two bureaus even asked that the two highest
orders should have only a third of the total number of deputies.

The assembly approved the liberty of the grain trade and the
suppression of the *corvée*. It voted against alienation of the crown
domain as apparently contrary to the constitutional law of the State.

So far, all went well. But when the question of the land tax was
taken up, all the affected interests began to revolt. They formed little groups. Each class of Notables that saw one of its privileges
threatened met during the evening at the house of one of its members to plan resistance. The bishops, who would have to defend the
immunities of the clergy and its right not only to tax itself but also
to apportion these taxes, met at the residence of Dillon, the archbishop of Narbonne. The prelates, more politicians than Chris-
tians, experienced in affairs by their habit of sitting in provincial estates, were to be the most formidable adversaries of the controller
general. The archbishop of Toulouse, who said little in his bureau,
so as not to incur the king's displeasure by any public expression,
sowed discord in the private gatherings and used his talents to make
conciliation impossible.

The first presidents and attorneys general of the parlements combined in an opposition which they made to seem moderate, expect-
ing to make it more vehement when the edicts should come to their
courts for registration. Even so, M. de Castillon, attorney general
at the Parlement of Aix, challenged the king's right to levy taxes
and the right of the Assembly of Notables to consent to them.
When the comte d'Artois, presiding over the bureau of which Castillon was a member, tried to bring him back to the subject under
discussion, Castillon replied, "Your Royal Highness will allow me
to say that no authority exists that can accept a land tax as now pro-

posed, neither this assembly, august as it may be, nor the parlements, nor even the king; only the Estates General would have such a power." M. d'Alligre, first president of the Parlement of Paris, also gave signs of bitterness toward the controller general in several of his speeches.

It did not seem that the nobility had reached any collective opinion. But within the assembly several members, the marquis de La Fayette more than any other, took the opportunity to advance ideas of liberty and put royalty on the downward slope leading to the need for representative government.

One provision in the proposal for a land tax was the object of justified criticism. Calonne had specified that the tax should be collected in kind. Such a procedure would require complicated and almost impossible methods of enforcement. It would mean the establishment of storage depots with numerous employees for the receipt, preservation, and redistribution of agricultural products. The expense would have absorbed most of the value received. Calonne was too intelligent to have overlooked this inconvenience, but in the levity of his character he was tempted by the chance to create a great many jobs and so satisfy his supporters and win new partisans for his plan.

The bureaus pronounced unanimously against collection of the land tax in kind. Calonne seemed willing to concede on this point. Then the Notables raised another difficulty. They were unable, they said, to approve a new tax unless the need for it was made clear; they must therefore be informed of the causes and extent of the deficit, and they asked that the accounts showing revenues and expenses should be communicated to them. The initiative in this matter came from the first bureau, presided over by Monsieur, who was known to find Calonne not congenial.

Calonne at first passed off the demand of the Notables with a jest. "These gentlemen are very curious," he said; but a more official reply was needed. The minister objected that the king had not summoned the Notables for any such investigation as they now contemplated. The situation of the treasury had been examined and determined in the royal council; there had been no intention of asking their advice on the administration of the finances but only of consulting them on the best means of levying and collecting a tax.

The Notables were thus reduced to the simple task of drafting an edict. But even admitting such narrow limits, could they not argue that some notion of the finances was necessary before they could determine the mode of taxation most productive of revenue and least onerous for the taxpayers? How could Calonne have persuaded himself that men brought together to rescue the State would agree to new taxes without knowing why they were necessary? Moreover, grave changes in established practices had to be envisaged. The Notables were not only princes, nobles, and prelates; they were also privileged Frenchmen, and they felt a double responsibility to France and to their order.[16]

When the minister's reply was known, all the bureaus resounded with a unanimous protest. The archbishop of Arles, the archbishop of Narbonne, and the marquis de La Fayette joined in demanding the early convocation of the Estates General.

The dissatisfaction of the Notables soon spread to the general public in the capital. Then began the war of witticisms, pamphlets, and cartoons that assailed the controller general without respite during the rest of his ministry. The women attacked him excitedly. For them it was not enough to drive him from office; he must be brought to judgment. Carried away by the reigning fashion to disparage him, even the courtiers who owed the most to his favors came out against him. All the influences outside the assembly were hostile, and in the salons the evenings passed in urging the Notables on to resistance.

The opposition most feared by Calonne was that of the prelates who were members of the Assembly, for they enjoyed great credibility. In the attempt to win their favor he arranged a conference with the archbishops of Narbonne, Toulouse, Aix, Bordeaux, and Reims. During the conversation he said to Loménie de Brienne, "Support my plan and then you will take my place." He had read the archbishop's mind, but Brienne turned the remark off with a

[16] During this discussion of serious matters the French trait of lighthearted malice remained alive. A print circulated a caricature showing a farmer surrounded by his chickens, cocks, turkeys, and ducks. The words at the bottom read:

FARMER: My good friends, I have called you together to know in what sauce you wish to be eaten.

A COCK, *raising his head*: But we don't wish to be eaten.

FARMER: You are avoiding the question.

pleasantry. The archbishop of Narbonne terminated the meeting with more candor: "You want war? Well, you shall have it, and we will fight you frankly and openly. At least you present yourself to our blows with good grace." "Monseigneur," replied Calonne, looking at the archbishop of Toulouse, "I am so tired of blows from behind that I have decided to provoke them in front."

The clergy did not dispute the justice of a proportional distribution of public taxes. Their hostility arose, as we have seen, from their fear that their immunities would be jeopardized. They were afraid to open the way to the destruction of their other privileges.

At the request of the controller general, a committee of six members from each bureau met at the home of Monsieur. For four hours Calonne developed his ideas and replied with urbanity and talent to the objections, but no one felt any confidence in him. Neither his courteous and witty manner nor the light that he threw on these arid discussions could win him any partisans. He went so far as to say that the king could impose his will, as he thought no one in the assembly would doubt. "I doubt it," said the archbishop of Narbonne, "and I shall not be the only one. A tax, whether in its amount or in its duration, should have the same limit as the public need that requires it and which alone justifies it." The archbishop of Arles, as impressive for his character as for his learning, expressed strong doubt that any assembly except the Estates General could take the responsibility for adding to the taxes already borne by the nation. The minister ended the meeting by announcing, in the king's name, that the Notables had the power to deliberate not only on the form but also on the substance of the proposed measures.

After this concession it became clearly necessary to submit the accounts of revenue and expense to the bureaus of the Notables. It was decided to provide them only after removal of those records of expenses deemed improper for the Notables to see. The material submitted gave rise to innumerable objections. There was no understanding, and no wish for an understanding.

To put an end to these difficulties, Louis XVI held a solemn "royal session." Calonne was the main speaker. Hoping to gain approval by taking it for granted, he thanked the Notables for all that they had agreed to. As he put it, the differences of opinion between them and the government turned only on matters of form. But the assembly accepted no such agreement, and on the next day all the bureaus protested.

This new attack made worse the bad feeling already existing. The public became more incensed. In calling the pecuniary privileges into question, Calonne's projects were favorable to the people. The Assembly of Notables made itself a defender of the abuses. It did not matter. The Notables were popular because they opposed a minister who was generally detested. They were thanked for rejecting a benefit that came from him.

Yet in all this agitation there were some signs of hope for conciliation. The ducs de Nivernais and du Châtelet proposed that the provincial assemblies should be organized without delay and then be consulted on the least burdensome means of filling the void in the public finances. Pending the decision of these assemblies, the government would receive temporary help to carry on its functions. This expedient was favorably received. Monsieur the king's brother supported the idea and worked personally to win over many others.

It was at this moment, when Calonne's position seemed strengthened, that he committed the fault that achieved his ruin. He had endured the most vehement opposition and lively attacks without seeming moved, but he had reached the farthest limits of his patience. He had had enough, his courage gave way and his mind became helpless against the forces unleashed in the war against him. He now imagined that he could make the public the judge between the assembly and himself. He printed the papers submitted to him and wrote a long preface to their publication, in which he characterized the Notables in the harshest terms, implying that they were sacrificing the interests of the people in order to keep their own privileges. This tract was widely diffused; every curé received a copy.

The Notables, who had left Versailles on Saturday in a mood of accommodation, returned on Monday filled with indignation and demanding vengeance. Every bureau complained to the king. The archbishop of Toulouse, who since the convocation of the Notables had been sending notes to Louis XVI informing him of their proceedings, now used them to make accusations against the controller general. It was becoming obviously necessary to choose between the dissolution of the assembly and the retirement of Calonne. Ver-

gennes's successor, Montmorin, together with the baron de Breteuil, obtained the queen's interest in Calonne's dismissal, pointing
out that a minister who had aroused such resentment could not restore health to the country's affairs and that the very success of his
projects, supposing them desirable, required his disappearance
from the scene. The last blow came with the revelation to the king
that Calonne, without consulting him, had had the use of 12 million
to support the market in public securities and that this sum had been
wasted.

The king liked Calonne; he appreciated his wit and lucidity in the
treatment of public business. Convinced of the need of parting with
him, he gave him the satisfaction of seeing the removal also of the
keeper of the seals, regarded as his enemy and accused of encour-
aging in advance the opposition of magistrates in the Assembly of
Notables. M. de Miroménil was discharged and replaced as keeper
of the seals by Lamoignon, a presiding judge in the Parlement of
Paris. On the next day, April 8, 1787, the king asked the controller
general for his resignation.

What an unheard-of thing in the absolute monarchy of the kings
of France! A minister succumbed before the opposition of a deliberative body. The will of the monarch was thwarted by the will of
an assembly. This victory was the precursor to immense changes
that were to come in our institutions. The royal authority would
show itself for a while, but in the end would be destroyed by a
power stronger than itself.

Ministry of Loménie de Brienne. End of the Assembly of Notables

[THROUGH INFLUENCE at court and by special arrangement, Loménie de Brienne, the archbishop of Toulouse, became a member of the royal council, although Louis XVI disliked him for his religious skepticism and loose morals. But as archbishop of Toulouse, Brienne had been an important figure in the provincial estates of Languedoc, and he was thought to be an effective administrator.]

It was thus that Loménie de Brienne was admitted to the king's council. He soon came to dominate it, supported as he was by the queen and by Lamoignon, the keeper of the seals. The duc de Nivernais and M. de Malesherbes joined the council at this same time, though without portfolio.

The elevation of the archbishop of Toulouse won general assent. But it soon became evident that his skill in handling the affairs of a province disappeared entirely when it was a question of dealing with the great interests of the State. He touched on everything but on nothing thoroughly, all the while believing that he had resolved the problem. He lacked foresight, candor, and energy of character. Quick-witted but without depth, he was presumptuous and disconnected in his thinking, clever but without real ability, bold but without courage. He made important decisions and followed them with acts of authority, only to recoil before obstacles and abandon what he had begun. He would stir up discontent, then give his adversaries the advantage of a triumph over the royal authority.

His first error was the prompt dissolution of the Assembly of Notables. "People at Versailles are tired of all these discussions," he said. Yet since the removal of Calonne, the greatest calm had prevailed in the assembly, which had ceased to oppose the stamp tax and the land tax, being content simply with a few modifications. At a royal session held on April 27, the best of feeling seemed to exist between the assembly and the government. The king promised considerable reform in the households of himself, the queen, and the princes. The Notables voted in favor of a loan, which the Parlement did not dare to refuse.

The Assembly of Notables did honor to its last labors by requesting the restoration of civil status to Protestants. It expressed the wish for revisions in the civil and commercial law and in ordinances pertaining to waterways and forests. The closing of the assembly took place on May 25, 1787. Its final session, presided over by the king, passed in mutual congratulations. Yet some words pronounced by the first president of the Parlement of Paris seemed to foreshadow future opposition. When all the magistrates who were members of the assembly had risen, the first president spoke as follows:

"The Notables have viewed the depth of our troubles with alarm. . . . A prudent and moderate administration today should reassure the nation on the unfortunate consequences which your Parlement has more than once foreseen. . . . The various plans proposed to Your Majesty deserve the most careful consideration. . . . It would be indiscreet for us, at this time, to be so bold as to suggest which should merit your preference. . . . Our role at the moment is a most respectful silence."

This speech was evidently meant to reserve the right of the sovereign courts to discuss the government's projects in the future and to withold their sanction.

The speeches of the keeper of the seals and the archbishop of Toulouse sent up characteristic signals that are particularly worth repeating. The keeper of the seals told the Notables: "You have been your king's council; you have prepared and facilitated a most desirable revolution with no other authority than confidence, which is the greatest of all powers in the government of states."

After him, the first minister spoke these even more remarkable words: "Since only one and the same interest should animate the three orders, it might be believed that each should have the same number of representatives. But the two first orders have agreed to be counted together, and thereby the Third Estate, assured of having as many voices as the clergy and nobility combined, will have no fear that a special interest will distort the vote. It is only right that this portion of His Majesty's subjects, so deserving of his interest and protection, should receive, at least in the number of votes, some compensation for the influence that naturally follows from superior dignity, wealth, and birth."

We see that from this early date the minister had the idea of overcoming the resistance of the privileged classes by increasing the influence of the Third Estate.

So Loménie appropriated much of Calonne's system, to which in any case he knew the king had given his approval. It was expected that the edicts concerning measures approved by the Assembly of Notables would be registered at a *lit de justice* immediately after the closing of the assembly. The Parlement then would not dare to protest against the desires formulated by the elite of the nation. The keeper of the seals insisted on prompt action on a matter for which opinion was well prepared. But the archbishop judged that there was no need to hurry. He considered a *lit de justice* a more extreme action than the existing state of affairs required and preferred to send separate edicts to the Parlement in succession. This was a serious mistake. When the edicts arrived for registration, the memory of the Notables had lost its influence.

The edicts on the provincial assemblies, the grain trade, and the abolition of the *corvée* were the first to be registered, on June 17, 22, and 27. The Parlement reserved its judgment on laws that would have more impact on public opinion, on which it was counting for support of its own authority. It did not foresee that its resistance, if carried too far, would strengthen those causes which, since the beginning of the century, were gradually disposing the nation to great changes in which royalty and the magistracy itself would disappear.

Dominated only by the interests and emotions of the moment, the magistrates failed to understand that all foundations of the existing social order had been weakened: religion, by the philosophy and unbelief on which the elite of French society now prided itself; royalty, by the degradation to which Louis XV had brought it; the nobility, since suppression of its great fiefs and privileges, by the abuse of new ennoblements and the antagonism of a class that was more enlightened and more wealthy; the clergy, by its claims to preserve its immunities and by the low morals of some of its pontiffs; monarchical institutions, to sum up, by Anglomania and republican ideas imported from America. . . .

THREE EDICTS remained for the Parlement to register: those on the stamp tax, the land tax, and the civil status of Protestants. The hostile attitude of the Parlement was well known. It was important, therefore, to face it with the alternative of either offending public opinion by refusing a measure favorable to the people or else of adopting the projects of the government. The land tax, by falling on the privileged, would diminish the tax burden on the Third Estate, so that the Parlement could rightly fear that its refusal would be attributed to its own personal interest; but with a blindness hard to explain, Loménie provided the magistrates with arms for their attack by first submitting the stamp tax to them for registration, a new tax that fell on all transactions relating to property and so affecting all classes. By this false step, he opened the conflict that he should have attempted to avoid.

One mistake followed another. It had been the custom of his predecessors to submit proposed legislation first of all to the first president of the Parlement, who then communicated it to the other presidents and members that he thought he should consult. Thus the consent of influential magistrates was gained in advance. Loménie neglected this precaution, which he should have taken under the circumstances even if it had not been observed before.

Parlement began its deliberations on July 6, 13, and 15, with the peers present and taking part. In the *chambre des enquêtes* there were a good many younger councillors imbued with the new ideas, eager for popularity, and making it a point of honor to pose as eloquent organs of resistance to power.[17] In their opposition they had strong support in many quarters, even among the courtiers who were injured by the reforms introduced in the households of the king,

[17] The two principal leaders were d'Eprémesnil and Duport. With a lively intelligence and engaging eloquence but little judgment, d'Eprésmesnil was fanatically attached to his "company," the Parlement, which he thought could never have too much consideration or too much authority. He was cruelly disabused in his reliance on popular favor. Attacked a few years later on the Feuillant terrace as he was leaving the Constituent Assembly, of which he was a member, he escaped death only to perish in 1794 under the blade of the Revolutionary Tribunal.

Duport was entirely different. With cold intelligence and imperturbable character, he was strongly imbued with philosophical principles and American ideas, which he carried to the point of exaggeration, applying them without the slightest deviation from his inflexible logic.

queen, and princes. The stamp tax furnished matter for many objections and declarations on the misery of the people. Nothing was clear; nothing seemed to justify the government's program. What was the true figure on the deficit? Some doubted its very existence.[18] What revenue would the new taxes produce, and how long would they last? The Parlement, for its information, asked for the accounts of the royal treasury. These were refused, and the refusal increased the general effervescences among a huge crowd gathered outside the hall where the magistrates deliberated. The sessions of the Parlement were secret and the members had taken an oath of silence on what passed within, but the oath was forgotten. Some, on coming out of the assembly, were willing to answer the crowd's questions. Several passed out handwritten bulletins. Even the peers were questioned, and the archbishop of Paris was insulted because he mentioned his oath on refusing to reply. By such publicity, the agitation in the capital spread throughout France.

The Parlement presented its remonstrances to the king on July 16. The great word was now pronounced. The Parlement proclaimed the principle that only the Estates General had the power to consent to a *perpetual tax*.

This declaration, resounding everywhere, was hailed with universal acclamation. A desire for a representative body no doubt follows on ideas of liberty. But we have seen how much these ideas owed to the weariness caused by the uncertain and varying actions of the royal power. Absolute government may be supported when it is firm enough to guarantee order. But authority was in this case vacillating, weak, and irresolute. The French thought that they were oppressed without feeling that they were governed.

Such was the frivolity of the national character at this time that no

---

[18] In 1787 the revenues of the State were 474 million; expenses for the current year were 660 million, so that there was a deficit of 126 million, of which 52 million represented redemptions of the public debt for that year. These were called redemptions on fixed term and would continue for several years in varying amounts. The life annuities owed by the State, amounting to 96 million, would be naturally extinguished year by year. It was thus hoped that expenditures could be reduced by 50 or 60 million. The real deficit then was not very large, and could have been easily met by the new stamp tax and land tax proposed by M. de Calonne to the Notables. The provincial administrations that were to be established would provide a convenient and exact means for apportioning the tax.

one foresaw the consequences of what was happening. But an evil genius peering into the future saw a coming revolution, the fall of a dynasty, and a chance for usurpation. It inhabited the Palais-Royal. It took for its agents the confidants of the prince who lived in this palace. The corrupt soul of the duc d'Orléans welcomed every intrigue that was proposed to him. He was not without hope of the moment arriving when he might replace Louis XVI on the throne. From this moment, his agents encouraged the Parlement in its opposition and the people in their discontents. Henceforth he was a stranger to none of the attacks on the existing royal authority.

On August 6, in a *lit de justice* held at Versailles, the king forced the registration of the edicts on the stamp tax and the land tax. The latter had not been sent to the Parlement until the opposition to the stamp tax reached its height. Hence the magistrates had instantly referred it to the Estates General.[19]

On the next day, August 7, the Parlement assembled and moved boldly against the royal power. Rather than limiting itself to the customary protests against a *lit de justice*, it declared null and void the *transcriptions ordered to be made on its registers*.

Hearing this, the first minister decided to send it into exile. The necessary sealed letters were about to go out when Malesherbes obtained a delay until the next deliberation of the Parlement, on August 13. In the interval the Parlement ordered an inquiry into the *dilapidations, abuses of authority, and all other abuses* attributed to the ex-controller general Calonne. The effect was to turn public animadversion against the courtiers who had benefited, it was said, from Calonne's "dilapidations." Pamphlets multiplied. Some of them attacked the queen, so that the baron de Breteuil felt obliged to advise her not to go to Paris. Calonne took refuge in England.

Finally, on August 13, came the deliberation that would either alleviate or aggravate the offenses of the Parlement against the royalty. Instead of the hoped-for calm, the opinions were more heated

---

[19] Later, a disillusioned public opinion would not excuse the magistracy for their obstinate rejection of the land tax. Retrospective rancor was the cause of the indifference felt when these great courts of justice were suppressed by the Constituent Assembly. It would be an error to suppose that culpable actions arising from personal interest do not sooner or later find their punishment. Society in the end always avenges itself for the harm done to it or the good denied to it.

than ever. The stamp tax was called as disastrous as the salt tax, or *gabelle*, so disastrous that even calling it a *gabelle* was not enough. The Parlement declared the edicts incapable of denying the nation its rights or of authorizing the levy of taxes.

The crisis had come. On August 14, 1787, all members of the Parlement received orders to leave Paris within twenty-four hours and to proceed to Troyes within four days.

[Other law courts resist, the people of Paris become unruly, and France suffers setbacks in foreign policy, being unable to support Turkey against Russia or the Dutch Patriots against intervention in the Netherlands by Prussia and Great Britain.]

At Troyes the Parlement met every day, but its sessions were empty. There were neither attorneys to initiate cases nor advocates to plead them. As a diversion in their idleness, the magistrates had the pleasure of receiving promises of support from all the courts within their jurisdiction. The provincial parlements also continued in opposition. All demanded recall of the Parlement of Paris and convocation of the Estates General. Several objected to the establishment of provincial assemblies; and the Parlement of Bordeaux, for forbidding the meeting of the provincial assembly of Limousin, was exiled to Libourne.

We have seen how it was characteristic of the archbishop of Toulouse to begin with violent measures and then back down before obstacles. He showed an inclination to withdraw the edicts concerning the stamp and land taxes, but on certain conditions made necessary by the financial situation, which was extremely precarious, with the treasury empty and further credit impossible.

Abandoning his main objective, Loménie counted on the boredom of exile to make the magistrates more amenable to his secondary aims. He proposed to annul the edicts if in return the Parlement would authorize a new verification of the twentieth-taxes, declare the clergy liable to these taxes, and extend by two years the second twentieth that was due to expire in 1790.

But the Parlement wanted a complete victory. It preferred to have the edicts on the stamp and land taxes suppressed unconditionally. It agreed, however, to an extension of the second twentieth, thus violating the principle that it had itself proclaimed, that only the Estates General had the right to consent to taxes.

The new edict was soon registered, and the Parlement was re-called to Paris at the end of September 1787. It now entered on a pe-riod of vacation, during which a vacation chamber sat as was cus-tomary.

The return of the Parlement was greeted by enthusiastic disor-ders. For several nights the law clerks and the populace demanded the lighting of houses in the neighborhood of the Palace of Justice and broke the windows of anyone not promptly obeying their or-ders. An effigy of Calonne was tried and burned in the Place Dau-phine. The minutes of his "trial," when they became known the next day, declared that the former controller general was con-demned "for making the king lose the love and confidence of the French people." Other effigies, representing the baron de Breteuil and the duchesse de Polignac, were paraded through the streets amid shouts of derision. The vacation chamber tolerated these ex-cesses and put an end to them only upon repeated complaints from the lieutenant of police.

We may be astonished at this coalition of all the judicial bodies against the perfectly justified demands of the royal authority. The wheels in the machine of government can do nothing if the main en-gine has no power. It is not superfluous to dwell on the causes of such a singular anomaly. We find them mainly in the passion of van-ity, which in France often misleads the most enlightened minds. The royal authority being feeble and vacillating, the parlements meant to take advantage of its weakness to elevate themselves to the point of direct intervention in the affairs of state. They claimed that nothing could be done without them, that everything should be de-cided by them. The convocation of the Notables had deeply of-fended them, because they thought its purpose was to reduce the in-fluence that they arrogated to themselves. If their demands were opposed, their vanity found another object; they would put them-selves at the head of an aroused public opinion. There is an appear-ance of greatness in giving up the power over taxes to a nation rep-resented by the Estates General; but in truth, they expected that the Estates General, when not in session, would delegate all its powers to them. In that case the government of France would be greatly changed: the highest authority would be in the Estates General; the second in the parlements; and in third place, the royal power would be subordinated to the other two.

Magistrates whose duty was to restrain public opinion within reasonable bounds now gave it an irresistible impulsion. Under their banners were arranged all the innovators trained by the lessons of philosophy and the example of America, and the whole crowd of people who delighted in resisting whatever was above them. The mistakes of the government fanaticized the partisans of the sovereign courts. It was these courts that implanted in France the revolution that would soon drag the magistrates from their bench and shortly thereafter cut off their heads.

[Further disputes over government borrowings; measures for the legalization of Protestant marriages.]

While these serious discussions went on concerning the civil status of Protestants, the ministers were busy with plans for overcoming the persistent opposition of the parlements to the crown. . . . They adopted the idea of creating a new body, a Plenary Court, to be charged with the registration of edicts. The ministry was not deterred by the thought of changing the constitution of the State as established by customary usage. . . .

The ministry prepared the new edict in the utmost secrecy, taking care that the men who printed it should be confined to their shops and forbidden to leave under any pretext. Nevertheless, the Parlement found out what was happening; it is said that d'Eprésmenil, by suborning one of the workers, obtained a copy of the edict on the Plenary Court. He communicated the news to his colleagues without delay. The emotion was extreme. All the chambers met together in a general assembly and invited the peers to join them. They drew up the following manifesto, which defined the rights of the king by restricting them and the prerogatives of the Parlement by expanding them.

"The court, justly alarmed by the calamitous events whose too constant notoriety seems to threaten the magistracy and the constitution of the State; considering that the unshakable opposition of the magistrates to two disastrous taxes and their repeated calls for the Estates General, etc., etc., are now the grounds on which ministers wish to crush the magistrates and subvert the laws;

"Considering also that the system of a single will, clearly expressed in various replies obtained by surprise from our lord the king, reveals on the part of ministers the ruinous project of destroying the principles of the monarchy and leaves the nation no recourse except in a precise definition by this court of the doctrines that it is charged with upholding and of the sentiments that it will continue to profess;

"Declares that France is a monarchy governed by the king, according to the laws;

"That among these are fundamental laws embracing and consecrating:

"The right of the reigning house to the throne, from male to male, by order of primogeniture and excluding daughters and their descendants;

"The right of the nation to consent freely to taxes, through the organ of the Estates General, regularly convoked and composed;

"The customs and capitulations of the provinces;

"The irremovability of magistrates, the right of the courts to verify the wishes of the king in each province and to order registration only so far as these wishes conform to the constitutional laws of the province and fundamental laws of the State;

"The right of every citizen never to be brought for any matter before other than his natural judges, who are those designated by the law;

"And the right, without which the others are useless, of not being arrested by any order whatsoever, except to be brought without delay before competent judges.

"The said court protests against any violation of the principles expressed above;

"And unanimously declares that it will in no case deviate therefrom; that these principles, being equally certain, are binding on all members of the court and are comprehended in their oath; that consequently no member of the court should authorize, or let himself be thought to authorize, the slightest innovation in this matter, nor accept a place in any company that is not this very court itself, composed of the same persons and vested with the same rights;

"And in the event that force, by dispersing this court, should render it powerless to maintain the principles contained in the present order, the said court declares that it places the inviolate safekeeping of these principles in the hands of the king, his august family, the peers of the realm, the Estates General, and each of the orders, united or separate, which form the nation."

Loménie and the keeper of the seals, exasperated by the disappointment that they felt, resolved to avenge themselves on the magistracy that had defied them; but their rage troubled their judgment and impelled them to measures that were unduly irritating and ill considered.

The declaration of the Parlement was annulled (May 5), and an order went out for the arrest of d'Eprémesnil. By the same order, Goilart de Montsabert was also to be arrested; he had recently led the resistance of the Parlement to verification of the twentieth-taxes. Someone in the royal council gave them a secret warning, so that they hastened to the Palace of Justice, believing that its great hall would be an inviolable place of refuge.

All members of the court, promptly alerted, met together in a general assembly. The peers were invited to sit, and came immediately. The court, thus constituted . . . , ordered that its first president should lead a deputation to the king. It announced that it would remain in session until their return. . . .

That evening the members of the deputation presented themselves at the door of the king's apartments but were refused entrance on a pretext: they had omitted the indispensable formality of sending an officer to receive His Majesty's orders on the hour at which he wished to admit them.

Then, in the middle of the night was heard the sound of marching soldiers. The regiment of Gardes françaises surrounded the Palace of Justice. Sentinels were stationed at all the doors, with orders to let no one leave until d'Eprémesnil and Goilart were taken away. D'Agoult, an officer of the Garde, entered the hall where the court was sitting and read a message signed by the king, ordering MM. d'Eprémesnil and Montsabert to be seized "in the *grand' chambre* or anywhere else."

Consternation was extreme, and indignation showed on every face. The sanctuary of the laws was profaned, and in the eyes of most Frenchman the king's justice was transformed into an act of violence. The feelings of the magistrates were shared by the peers of France. All seemed to join in a single exclamation: "We are all d'Eprémesnil and Montsabert!" Disconcerted, d'Agoult withdrew, saying he would seek orders from his superiors.

At eleven in the morning he returned and again asked to be admitted. In the name of the king, he called on the two magistrates to make themselves known. Profound silence was the only reply. D'Agoult brought in a lesser functionary of the court and ordered him to point out the two men whom he sought. This person declared that he did not see them in the hall.

An impulse of generosity now swept over d'Eprémesnil, who resolved to surrender himself so as to end this painful scene. Still seated and wearing his judicial cap, he said to d'Agoult: "I am the magistrate you are looking for in this sanctuary of justice. I call upon you to declare whether, if I do not follow you willingly, you are under orders to remove me from this place." D'Agoult replied affirmatively and seemed on the point of ordering in the troops. "Enough," said the magistrate; "lest this sanctuary of the laws be further profaned, I yield to force." Then rising and removing his cap, he made a formal protest to the assembly against the violence to which he was subjected. Montsabert also gave himself up after a similar protest. He was taken to Pierre-Encise and d'Eprémesnil to the Iles Sainte-Marguerite.

May 8, 1788, was the date set for registration of the measures adopted by the ministry. But violence makes a bad prelude for innovations, since it arouses suspicion or even revolt, or leads to an inertia against which authority is powerless. A *lit de justice* was convoked at Versailles. The king presided and spoke as follows:

"There are no lengths to which the Parlement of Paris in the past year has not allowed itself to go, and it has been imitated by the parlements of the provinces. . . . I owe it to my peoples, to myself, and to my successors to repress such aberrations.

"I wish not to destroy my parlements but to bring them back to their duty and to their purpose as institutions. I intend to turn this moment of crisis into a salutary time for my subjects; to begin a reform of our judicial system by a reform of the law courts; to render justice more prompt and less costly for those who are subject to it; to renew for the nation the exercise of its just rights while reconciling them with the rights of the sovereign. A great state needs thorough cohesion and complete unity of views. There must be one king, one law, and one procedure for registration; one single court as depository of laws common to the whole kingdom; and, finally, estates general assembled not only on one occasion but whenever required by the needs of the state. Such is the restoration that my love for my subjects has prepared and dedicated today for their happiness."

After a few observations by the keeper of the seals, the king ordered the registration of several edicts.

One curtailed the overextended jurisdiction of the parlements by creating *grands bailliages* with appellate powers in all cases involving less than 20,000 francs. Since the establishment of such *bailliages* would reduce the number of cases brought before the Parlement, it seemed natural to reduce also the number of magistrates attached to that court. There would thus be relief from the crowd of younger councillors always disposed to oppose the wishes of the government. An edict ordered the parlement to be henceforth composed of only sixty-seven members.

The great improvements that Malesherbes had worked on were introduced into the criminal code. Torture was definitively abolished. The criminal courts, which had prefaced their condemnations with the formula, "condemned to such-and-such penalty for causes made known at the trial," would now have to specify in detail the reasons on which their judgments were based.

After these wise measures came the famous edict of which advance knowledge had stirred up such agitation. The king deprived the courts of justice of the power of registration, to be confided henceforth to a single body under the name of a Plenary Court. This court would be composed in the following manner: the keeper of the seals, the grand almoner, the grand master of the royal household, the grand chamberlain, the grand equerry, two archbishops, two bishops, two marshals of France, two governors of provinces, two lieutenants general, four other persons of quality in the kingdom, princes of the blood, peers, the *grand' chambre* of the Parlement of Paris, ten councillors of state or masters of requests, one member from each provincial parlement, two from the *cour des comptes*, and two from the *cour des aides*.

Appointment of members of the court would be by the king. They were to be irremovable. The king would preside, or in his absence the chancellor or keeper of the seals. To this court would be granted the privilege of verifying and publishing edicts applying to the whole of France. Those of local interest would continue to be registered by the parlements. The Plenary Court would register taxes provisionally, pending the next meeting of the Estates General. The king reserved to himself the power of contracting for loans.

The new court would have the right of remonstrance, but in exercising this right, four of its members would appear before the royal council to discuss the reasons for remonstrance; the king as sovereign would then decide.

The *lit de justice* ended with registration of an order forbidding the Parlement to assemble until the new judicial system was in place. The governors were instructed to have the edicts registered in their respective provinces, by act of authority, and to keep the doors of the palaces of justice closed.

Let us suspend the narration of facts to take account of the effect produced by the edict on the Plenary Court.

The edicts by which it was preceded were all dictated by an enlightened philanthropy. They made civil justice more accessible and relieved criminal justice of its most odious rigors. The unity of government to be established in such a large kingdom as France was a good thing. Yet the paternal views of Louix XVI won no adherence and inspired no gratitude. The violent, clumsy, and thoughtless acts of the ministry had alienated everyone. The talk was only of the abuses of an arbitrary regime and of its abolition at any price.

The parlements had the support of public opinion because they raised the banner of liberty.[20] Everything coming from absolute power seemed suspect. The provisions of the edict on the Plenary Court were scrutinized for hidden meanings favorable to despotism. Even ridicule had its day, for the edict had been awkwardly entitled "Reorganization of the Plenary Court," as if there had ever been any such thing in France in the past.

And where was the strongest opposition to be found? In the peerage, in the nobility, in the magistracy, even in the clergy, and in the

---

[20] The same men who were fanatical partisans of the Parlement applauded a year later when the Constituent Assembly destroyed the magistracy and established administrative unity.

most enlightened part of the middle class. The rest of this class and the ordinary people remained calm and almost indifferent. But Loménie did not end his disastrous ministry without finding a way to excite the passions of this hitherto inert mass.

The Revolution was beginning, and, as always, it was the upper classes that gave the signal for it, without foreseeing that they would soon become the victims of the fire they had lit. The army was already beginning to think about the conditions of obedience; its officers were imbued with the spirit of opposition and acted with regret when ordered to repress insurrection against the will of the government.

The ministers tried to persuade the king that they would obtain the adherence that was refused to him. The Châtelet protested, as did the other law courts, until the truths reached even to the throne. Louis XVI was deeply hurt on seeing his intentions misunderstood by his people. He could find no remedy, fell into discouragement, and sought relief from his sorrows by going hunting every day.

[Nobles in Brittany and Dauphiny led insurrectionary movements in defense of provincial liberties against the government's program. In Dauphiny the nobles invite the aid of the higher clergy and town council of Grenoble to join in an unauthorized revival of the provincial estates of Dauphiny at the neighboring château of Vizille.]

Seeing that the nobility was against him everywhere in France, since all the provinces showed the same opposition, Loménie conceived a new plan that he hoped would fortify his power. In past times the crown had won the confidence of the people by defending them against the feudal lords. The times had indeed changed, and the authority of the lords was no longer feared, having been destroyed by royalty. That was of no importance to Loménie de Brienne. Let us create antagonism between the nobility and the Third Estate (such was his reasoning); the Third, not feeling strong enough to prevail alone, will throw itself into the arms of the royal power and join it in common cause; and this power is now mine. But his experiment would give the people the idea of demanding a preponderance for itself, and this idea, even after Loménie's fall, would greatly influence the decisions of government.

The municipal officers of Grenoble were summoned to Versailles. The minister concluded his instructions to them by observing: "Your ancient local estates are about to be restored to you. Surely you do not want them with all those feudal vices and Gothic arrangements in which the people counted for so little."

But in Dauphiny the clergy, nobility, and Third Estate got along with one another very well. The seeds of division that the minister tried to plant did not germinate there. When the estates met at Vizille, the deputies of the Third, by consent of the other two, were equal in number to those of the clergy and nobility; they deliberated in common and took the vote of head. Yet their example was not without success for Loménie's system, because less benevolent parties used it to demand its application, willingly or by force, to an assembly representing the whole country.

The good understanding at Vizille continued. The estates, guided by Mounier, adopted a series of resolutions with unanimity in almost all cases. They declared themselves ready to make sacrifices and claimed only the rights of Frenchmen. They severely condemned all who would accept appointment under the new edicts. By common accord, they decided that the tax replacing the *corvée* should be paid by all three orders and that the Third Estate should have the double representation already obtaining in the new provincial assemblies. Finally, remonstrances were sent to the king requesting withdrawal of the edicts, the abolition of *lettres de cachet*, and the convocation of Estates General for the whole kingdom as well as provincial estates for Dauphiny.

Soon there was another, even more striking proof of the astonishing progress of public opinion. Loménie saw his plans becoming impossible to execute and the resources of the State diminishing day by day, with the nobility and the bourgeoisie both against him. Supposing that he would find solid support in the order to which he belonged, he called together an extraordinary assembly of the clergy of France and asked it to grant the government a free gift of 1,800,000 livres for the year 1788 and another of the same amount for the year 1789. The prelates refused the free gift and criticized all the activities of the principal minister; they appointed fifteen commissioners, namely three archbishops, four bishops, and eight members of the subordinate clergy, who were instructed to wait upon the king and present remonstrances containing the following language:

"When the first order of the State finds itself the only one that can raise its voice, when the public urges it to bring the wishes of all others to the foot of the throne, and when the general interest and its zeal for your service command it, there is no glory in speaking but it is shameful to remain silent; our silence would be a crime from which neither the nation nor posterity would ever wish to absolve us."

On the Plenary Court, the prelates declared: "Even if it had once been the highest court of our kings, it cannot now be such a numerous gathering of prelates, barons, and feudal vassals. The nation sees in it only a tribunal created by and submissive to royal officials, and one whose activities and intrigues would be dangerous in times of regency or minority of the king." And the clergy added: "The glory of Your Majesty is no longer in being the king of France but in being king of the French, and the heart of your subjects is the fairest of your domains." Finally, oblivious to the danger for the clergy of a national assembly in which philosophic doctrines were widely spread, the prelates ended by insisting on the prompt convocation of the Estates General.

So, on the one hand, we see confusion in the acts of the men in power, and, on the other, complete uniformity in the movement of public opinion.

The royal council should have been vividly impressed by the general movement of opinion, yet only one of the ministers, Malesherbes, appreciated the gravity of the position in which the crown now found itself.

[The author quotes at length from the memorandum drafted by his wife's grandfather, Malesherbes, and submitted to Louis XVI in July 1788, urging the king to recognize the legitimate grievances being expressed by an aroused public opinion.]

Malesherbes would have preferred that the new provincial assemblies should gradually habituate the nation to the use of deliberative bodies and an understanding of public affairs, with the Estates General to follow at a somewhat later date; but since the government had committed itself to a meeting of the Estates in the near future, he now felt that the king should not abandon the initiative for changes demanded by public opinion and which the public would require its representatives to bring about. "The king," he said, "must make a declaration in terms that can leave no doubt of his intentions for the good of the nation. He must open his heart in the presence of the nation, as he has done several times in the presence of his ministers."

Malesherbes was insistent because of the distrust aroused, in the highest degree, by government measures for which the edict on the Plenary Court was the pretext.

"All the acts of authority for whose enforcement a *lit de justice* has been thought necessary have had the consequence that every citizen trembles in his own home and sees the cause of the magistracy as his own personal cause." Hence Malesherbes urged a declaration *that could leave no doubt.*

In summary, he asked that either in the edict of convocation or in the opening address to the Estates General the king should announce his wish that the Estates consider the following:

1. The periodic return of the Estates.
2. Their composition to be such that each deputy should be elected by all citizens called upon to vote in a given electoral district.
3. The need of a vote by the assembly for any kind of tax.
4. The formation in every province of an assembly charged with allocation of the tax and discussion of local affairs.
5. A law on the liberty of citizens that would destroy the arbitrary character of *lettres de cachet* and legalize their use.

This last proposal could not fail to be agreeable to Louis XVI, "since," Malesherbes added, "during my first ministry not a single *lettre de cachet* was issued by will of the king."

With the desired changes submitted to the Estates General by the crown itself, all uncertainty as to the royal wishes would disappear and gratitude would take the place of doubt. There would be no more fear of that distressing vacillation that we have been obliged to observe in the decisions of the chief of state. Bound by his own words, the king would henceforth go forward with his people, and his people with him. Such was the hope of this man of good will.

But a great difficulty presented itself. The rules on composition of the Estates General would have to form part of the new constitution, to be drawn up by the Estates General with the approval of the king. But how would the Estates General themselves be composed before a new constitution was in being? In the Estates of 1614, the last to have met, the clergy, nobility, and Third Estate had rendered their opinions by order and the deputies of the bourgeoisie had been equal in number to those of only one of the other two. Could this method be preserved at a time of effervescence, when all rights and principles were under discussion? The people form the mass of the nation; could they be granted only a third of the representation? Or could the minority that made up the two other orders be given the advantage of numbers and the power of personal opposition? Interests were divided and sometimes conflicting in other ways also. Was an antagonism going to be authorized between the two higher orders and the Third that would be harmful to the public interest and perhaps dangerous to the higher two?

Malesherbes wished to take as a model the newly created provincial assemblies, in which the delegates of the people were equal in number to those of the two privileged orders combined, and the vote was taken by head. In the Estates General, as Malesherbes proposed, the two privileged orders would count only as half, and their deputies would be chosen, like those of the Third, by the universality of all voters in the electoral district. By this combination a preponderance of popular interests would be assured, and this great change would emanate from the crown, which would get the credit for the satisfaction of public opinion.

In revolutionary times, when the progress of ideas makes people conscious of their rights and their strength, sovereigns and privileged bodies can sustain themselves only by making all the concessions compatible with the preservation of order. But such concessions must be timely and appear to be freely made; if extorted by circumstances, they lose their value and lead only to further demands. In France, the royalty, clergy, and nobility did make great concessions; but coming too late, these won no acknowledgment and were useless in preventing the ruin of royalty, clergy, and nobility.

Loménie had too little judgment to appreciate, like Malesherbes, the danger by which his imprudence and the progressive march of public opinion threatened the monarchy. We have seen how his plans were lightly conceived and violently carried out, to be followed by discouragement and then by repudiation. On August 8 he obtained an order in council suspending establishment of the Plenary Court and setting the date for convocation of the Estates General for May 1, 1789.

He had already (on July 5) published another order in council which, "in view of the approaching meeting of the Estates General" (whose date he had not yet announced), invited municipalities, provincial assemblies, and all judicial jurisdictions to search in their archives and transmit to the government any documents they found concerning the composition of the Estates General. The same order exhorted "all men of learning and educated persons of the kingdom to send in information or commentaries on the method to be followed in making the assembly of the Estates General as national as it ought to be."

This call, which seemed to be made out of respect for public opinion, was really only an expression of the ruthless ambition of the principal minister, who wished to maintain his own position by causing division among the various classes of society. The political error thus committed was of no use for clarification of the question. The crown was later obliged to settle a difficulty that it could have resolved in the first place with advantage to itself, without provoking the investigations of writers.

When the aim is to establish liberty solidly among a people long shaped by absolute power, it is important to make the enjoyment of freedom come gradually by successive stages. The people are surprised and troubled by too much haste; not knowing how to use their new rights, they abuse them, and from one excess to another fall back into the lassitude of despotism.[21]

Freedom of the press, at the time we are talking about, by abruptly replacing a strict censorship, heightened the agitation that was already too far advanced. France was inundated with pamphlets scrutinizing the origin of privileges and violently attacking their existence. The king, fearing to provoke discontent among the clergy

---

[21] The history of our first revolution shows this truth.

and nobility by his personal decision, had ineptly put the bourgeoisie in a state of hostility against the two other orders.

Yet we must consider the king's very difficult position. He was importuned and resisted by the higher classes that exclusively surrounded him. It would have taken a more than ordinary strength of character to keep up resistance to such pressures; and this strength is what Louis XVI lacked.

When great changes are about to be made, and when parties are forming and the nation is dividing, the chief of state must rally to his side, frankly and clearly, the party that he believes to be in the right and useful to his interests; if he tries to keep a kind of balance between the parties, then those that he does not agree with will regard him as an enemy and the others as an impotent friend, so that he benefits from neither.

Loménie had triumphed, and the privileged bodies saw the futility of their opposition, which had served only to raise up a rival power stronger than they were. But the triumph was short-lived. The principal minister soon succumbed under the difficulties produced by his own incompetence, resulting from the deplorable state of the finances. On the one hand, the receipt of indirect taxes went badly because of doubts about the future. On the other hand, the resistance of the Parlement to the edict on loans made it impossible to deal successfully with the capitalists.[22] The royal treasury was empty, public services might be suspended, and the moment was even approaching when the army would go unpaid. Yet an increase of expense was becoming inevitable. The harvest was unsatisfactory, and on July 12 a region extending over sixty leagues had been devastated by an extraordinary hailstorm. A shortage making necessary a considerable importation of grain from abroad could be foreseen.

The first minister found resources by inexcusable means. There were some savings in the fund for retired soldiers, and he took them. A lottery had been opened to provide relief for victims of the hailstorm, and he appropriated the proceeds. Finally, he proclaimed the bankruptcy of the State by publishing an order in council to the

[22] [On "capitalists" see p. 63 above.]

effect that, until December 31, 1789, payments would be made partly in coin and partly in treasury bills bearing interest.

This news caused general alarm. It was feared that creation of paper money was a disguise for bankruptcy; imagination ran wild; it was rumored that the government would seize the funds of the Discount Bank, and holders of the bank's paper rushed to turn it into coin. The minister was obliged to order the bank to refuse to exchange its paper for specie until the following January 1, and to order the acceptance of bank paper in payment for letters of exchange and other such instruments.

The financial crisis reached its climax, as did popular discontent.

Nevertheless, Loménie could not bring himself to surrender the power that it had been his life's ambition to attain. He now had a new idea, to delegate the administration of finances to M. Necker while keeping the direction of other affairs of state to himself. Proposals were sent to the former director general, and the queen was urged to give her consent. Necker replied that "a year ago he might have been ready to share in the labors of M. the archbishop, but at the present moment he neither could nor would share in his discredit."

This refusal decided Loménie's fate. The comte d'Artois made it clear to the king that, with the fermentation in Paris, the dismissal of the principal minister was absolutely necessary. Marie Antoinette, now convinced, ceased to use her influence in his favor. At a conference in the queen's apartment Loménie broke into tears that proved touching to his masters. The poor man had exchanged the archbishopric of Toulouse for that of Sens, which was much richer, with a revenue of 678,000 livres a year. In his farewell audiences with the king and queen he won their consent to nominating him for a cardinal's hat, the co-adjutorship of his archdiocese and a rich abbey for his nephew, and a place as lady of the palace for his niece. On these conditions he agreed to submit his resignation (August 25, 1788). He left hardly 400,000 livres in the treasury. On the day of his retirement he sent for the 20,000 livres due him as his salary for the month of August.

Thus ended this bungling administration that precipitated the monarchy into the abyss of revolution. Loménie was an intelligent man, but intelligence is not enough to govern if it is not accompanied by the judgment that can evaluate difficulties or by the principles that can resolve them while following the rules of good faith and public morals. A prelate without religion, Loménie could not subject himself to the rules that religion prescribes. In him, the light of intelligence was obscured by deviousness of character. He prepared the storms that we shall see rising with frightful speed.

CHAPTER VI

Second Ministry of Necker. Meeting
of the Estates General

THE RETURN of Necker as director general of finances soon restored the confidence of the capitalists, so that the embarrassments that had overwhelmed the State slowly subsided. The task was difficult: on the one hand, there was a complete void in the treasury; on the other, the disaster of the great hailstorm and the poor harvest led to unexpected expenses. The heavens seemed prophetic, as if their extraordinary rigors presaged the upheavals to come. The winter of 1788–1789 was the most severe seen in France for a long time, and suffering was extreme. Necker poured two million livres of his own fortune into the State's coffers to help fill the gap; he found resources in the confidence he inspired; some capitalists made advances; the notaries provided 6 million. By his reputation and talents the director general met many needs without imposing new burdens on the nation.

Necker at this time showed himself to be a capable financier, but his knowledge of political science hardly matched his administrative skill. Loménie had brought about an anarchy in ideas that his successor could not prevent from passing into actions. Circumstances required a minister with common sense and a broad and firm grasp of the issues. Necker was a financial expert, with only the corresponding qualities.

No one then had a sound judgment of the situation in France.

Since the beginning of the reign of Louis XVI a series of ministers had come to power with the thought of reducing the importance of the nobility and judicial bodies, which had often engaged in annoying opposition to the crown. They hoped to achieve this end by increasing the preponderance of the bourgeoisie. The first consequence of this system was the creation of provincial assemblies in which members of the Third Estate equaled those of the two privileged orders. We have already noted how several parlements, disliking such equality, had opposed the meeting of provincial assemblies. The king had shared the view of his ministers; he had been deeply hurt by the provocations of the law courts and by the strong opposition of the nobility of Brittany and several other *pays d'états*, but had been held back at the same time by the fear of offending the higher strata in the class that surrounded him. Too weak to rise above this secondary consideration, instead of ordering himself the changes that his heart favored and his judgment approved, he allowed Loménie to appeal to that formidable power of public opinion that overthrows everything blocking its passage. Never did the effects of a decision follow so fast. Hardly had the edict calling for the investigations of writers appeared when the clubs began to discourse on politics, and other gatherings of the same kind were formed that were even more outspoken. Pamphlets poured forth disparaging the royal authority. We see the dogma of the sovereignty of the people sprouting up, to replace the idea of respect for the king's authority accepted until now.

The nobles misunderstood the kind of sacrifices that the middle class wished to impose on them. In general, they showed a willingness to give up pecuniary privileges, a reform that would be useful to the people. But the people still took no part in the dispute; the lion was still sleeping on his bed of straw. The dispute was with the bourgeoisie alone, for whose pride the abolition of honorific privileges was more important than that of pecuniary ones.

The parlements harassed the government to give themselves more importance, whatever might happen.

Philosophism hated the clergy and hoped to use the curés to destroy the bishops, until all could be encompassed in a common ruin.

Beside these various groups were men whose imaginations had been exalted by the American war and who professed to believe that republican government was best suited to the human race.

Such were the outlines of society as left by Loménie to the direction of Necker.

Possibly the agitation could have been calmed by publication of royal resolutions sanctioning the just desires of the most numerous part of the nation. But the director general of finance wished to support his own ambitions with something other than the royal authority that had let him down once before. He expected to find a more solid backing in the popularity to which he owed his return to power. Thus strengthened, he would brave all intrigues, and the king would be obliged to retain him after he became not merely the royal minister but the minister of the nation.

His first acts were to obtain the dismissal of the keeper of the seals, Lamoignon, and authorization for the parlements to meet.

In Paris, the assembling of the Parlement gave a pretext for serious disorders. Led by law clerks and law students, the people burned two mannequins representing Loménie and Lamoignon. Numerous groups took over the Place Dauphine and the Pont-Neuf, where they forced passers-by to stop and salute the statue of Henry IV and shout "Long live Henry IV, to the devil with Brienne and Lamoignon!" Persons riding in carriages were obliged to descend and offer the same salute, and coachmen who were not quick enough in obeying the order to stop were dragged from their seats and mistreated. In the evening, the glass was broken in windows that the occupants failed to illuminate; women were injured and men were forced to give money to contribute, it was said, to the cost of the illumination.

The disorder spread to other parts of the city. Then began the signs of a vast conspiracy throughout France, of which the secret threads remain unknown but which were believed to be sustained by the wealth of the duc d'Orléans.[23] Vagabonds from the provinces streamed into Paris, and from this time secret agents departed from the capital to spread agitation in the provinces.

It suited the leaders to push the people into such excesses as would bring on a bloody repression. Sedition would thus doubtless be quieted, but it would leave a feeling of hatred and a desire for vengeance that could be used later.

A municipal force called the foot watch and the mounted watch was charged with suppressing disorders in the streets. It was put to flight by the populace setting fire to its guardhouses. A crowd went to the hôtel de Brienne to pillage and burn it, from which it was prevented only by armed force. The same crowd then rushed with the same intention to the house of Sieur Dubois, the commandant of

---

[23] While most people avoided crossing the Pont-Neuf, the duc d'Orléans had himself driven there to show his popularity and enjoy the applause of the multitude (*Histoire de Louis XVI*, par M. Droz).

the watch. The riot was stopped and the rioters dispersed by musket fire; a few men were killed. The Parlement opened an inquiry, but its way of conducting the proceedings did more to encourage the anarchy than to check it. It ordered to appear before it, to examine their conduct, both Commandant Dubois and the lieutenant of police, who were insulted with impunity as they entered the Palace of Justice. The Parlement sought to inform itself only on so-called excesses committed by the military. Of all the persons arrested in the disturbances, only one was condemned to a few days in prison; the rest were all acquitted.

As for the government, it showed its weakness by transferring Dubois from Paris to a post in the provinces.

At its first session on September 24 [1788] the Parlement received the royal letters-patent recalling it to its functions and an edict annulling what had been done in the most recent *lit de justice*. It refused to register the letters-patent, on the ground that no law was necessary to restore it to what it called its imprescriptible right to assemble. So the highest court in the kingdom declared itself independent of royalty. This pernicious example would soon find numerous imitators.

The abolition of the Plenary Court met easily with public approval. There was less satisfaction with abolition of the *grands bailliages* that were so suited to the convenience of litigants. But the worst damage was the humiliation of an authority forced to repudiate what it had already done.

We shall see that punishment of the Parlement was not long in coming. The government sent to it for registration the edict of convocation of the Estates General for the following May 1, 1789. The Parlement registered it, but added a clause providing that the Estates should meet in the form of 1614. The fanatical support for the Parlement in its opposition to the government immediately disappeared; its opposition was now seen as selfish egotism, and its popularity vanished like smoke in the wind. A profusion of writings against the Parlement and the Estates of 1614 was spread everywhere. It was in vain that the Parlement tried later to modify its ruling. It had prepared its own destruction.

The claims of the bourgeoisie became increasingly vociferous. Petitions demanding the doubling of the Third came in from all the provinces. The clubs, various other associations, and even the provincial assemblies addressed similar messages to the government. The same plan had been agreed to by the king, Necker, and most of the ministry. Why not, then, settle the difficulty by an act of the still potent royal will? It was because Necker was afraid of drawing the hatred of the nobility on himself. He hoped to persuade the nobles to sacrifice willingly and with good grace the advantages they enjoyed by ancient custom. This minister was so self-confident that he could not see the difficulties in the way of his projects. Like all men infatuated with their own merit, he saw only one aspect of affairs without penetrating to their depth.

Necker had no thought of destroying the monarchy, and to arm the people against the nobility was always far from his mind. But he wished to give a new form to the government and to provide the nobles with different prerogatives from those they possessed. His plan was to create new institutions in France like those established in England, with the Third Estate forming a house of commons and with an upper house composed of the elite of nobles and bishops. He expected that laws voted by the two houses would take effect only after royal approval.

Since the revolution of 1688, England had enjoyed prosperity at home and glory abroad because of its institutions—an attractive example for France! Moreover, Anglomania had made such progress among us that the minister could expect the support of a numerous and powerful party. But there was one obstacle that only time could overcome: the repugnance of the king for everything on the other side of the Channel, the English customs, legislation, and way of life. An English system could be realized among us only by waiting for the Estates General. Necker had no doubt of his influence in the coming assembly. Nevertheless, he thought it wise to satisfy the Third Estate in advance by granting it the increase of numbers that it asked for, and then to obtain a voluntary agreement among the three orders by persuading the two higher ones to grant willingly the requests of the Third.[24]

Also, it was important for the director general of finances not to

---

[24] The example of the estates of Dauphiny, where, as we saw above, the nobility had willingly conceded the doubling of the Third and vote by head, encouraged the hopes of those who desired that the same would follow for France as a whole.

make enemies of members of the future upper house, if he was to preserve the majority that supports or overthrows ministries in a representative government.

All these expectations of Necker's were disappointed. Working with false observations, he inevitably made his policy take the wrong road. The course he chose proved to be the worst.

He persuaded the king to reassemble the old Notables convoked by Calonne and to consult them on the composition of the Estates General and the mode of election of deputies.

These Notables all belonged to the privileged classes by birth, function, or office. What chance was there that a body so constituted would agree to concede to the Third Estate a means of destroying the privileges without a blow?

But Necker, in proposing the doubling of the Third, had no intention of granting the vote in common and by head. Then what would be the importance of the number of deputies, if each order preserved a veto on resolutions of the two others?

It is unbelievable that the minister was so uninformed as to cherish any such illusion. Loménie had stirred up public opinion, which continued to grow, and the convocation of the Notables to deliberate on a matter already accepted by the great majority of the French could only re-arouse opinion and broaden the agitation indefinitely. It was bound to result in augmenting the irritation that already existed between the Third Estate and the other two orders. And this is what happened.

As for the agitation, it manifested itself in a prodigious increase in the production of pamphlets.[25] It was at this time that Sieyès published his famous tract with its epigraph, "What is the Third Estate? Everything." The comte d'Entraigues brought out an even bolder effort, whose first sentence was a consecration of republican government and an anathema against monarchy.[26] He took as his epi-

[25] "All France was agitated. From this moment, public affairs were the only subject of conversation. They were talked about even in the smallest towns, even in the villages. The effervescence was fed by innumerable pamphlets." *Histoire du règne de Louis XVI*, by M. Droz.

[26] "It was no doubt to provide a homeland for the most heroic virtues that heaven wished republics to exist; and perhaps to punish the ambition of men it allowed great empires, kings and masters to arise." Extract from the tract by the comte d'Entraigues. We may add that the comte d'Entraigues later expressed the most bit-

graph the formula of the old cortès of Aragon: "We who as individuals are as great as you, and together are more powerful than you, etc." He declared that "in the people the whole national power resides, by it the whole State exists, through it alone the State ought to exist."

What was becoming of the monarchy of Louis XIV, when his second successor had to listen to such things and let them be published? It was impossible not to foresee that the Third Estate, lifted by the ever-rising flood of passionate discussions, would use its advantage to establish its preponderance on the ruins of what stood in its way.

The Assembly of Notables met on November 6. Its deliberations were prolonged until December 12. All its bureaus voted against double representation of the Third, except the bureau presided over by Monsieur, and even here the majority in favor of doubling was only by one vote. In the whole assembly the vote was 112 to 33.

The middle class was exasperated by this result. It let its revenge be taken later by the common people, only to become itself victim to the people whose fury it had aroused. The men of this time were occupied only with the present; eventualities of the future did not enter their minds.

The Notables showed the same lack of foresight. They might have prevented the dangers they saw in a doubling of the Third if they had specified that only the highest taxpayers should qualify as its deputies. The aristocratic part of the nation would thus preserve its supremacy. But instead of calling for property qualifications in different degree for the right to vote and the right to be elected, they required no such qualification at all for the right to vote. In their view, to be a voter it was enough to be inscribed on the tax roll, however trifling the amount of tax paid, and anyone paying a tax equivalent to a silver mark could be elected as a deputy, though in a two-step process.

No more had been required, it was said, for election of deputies to the Third Estate in former times. But in those times the Estates General had been limited to submitting their supplications to the

ter regret for this writing. [The comte d'Antraigues (as the name is usually spelled) (1755–1812) became a royalist secret agent and counter-revolutionary polemicist in the 1790s.]

king. They had expressed no positive will of their own and they took no decisions. It was evident that the progress of ideas would change all that. In 1788 it could no longer be doubted that the nation aspired to new institutions and that the Estates would have to make pronouncements on these institutions. Their deliberations would assure the rights either of large property or of the multitude. The alternative would depend on the composition of the third chamber. Given the disposition of the people, no illusion was possible on the role of the Third in the Estates General. Yet the Notables seem not to have understood this.

Indeed, on another point they were favorable to democracy. The order of the clergy in the ancient Estates had been composed of deputies named by the bishops, the holders of large benefices, and the canons of cathedrals. The Notables decided that any ecclesiastic provided with any benefice whatever might be elected. The door to the Estates was thus opened to simple curés, who arrived in great numbers. They were expected to follow the wishes of their bishops blindly, and the same submission was expected of ordinary benefice holders. No one imagined that they would hasten to make common cause with the Third Estate, thus greatly adding to its strength.

The system adopted by the Notables, if we may suppose that they had a system, seems to have been to keep the Third Estate weak by refusing it the advantage of numbers, and in the Estates General to compose the Third of men accustomed by habit or interest to follow in the way traced for them by the upper class.

It was self-deception, taking appearances for reality.

[The Parlement of Paris tries to recapture its lost popularity and on December 5, 1788, modifies the terms of its ruling of September 25, declaring now that the form of the coming Estates General is still an open question and calling again for the guarantee of certain constitutional liberties.]

Just as the Parlement seemed to give up its opposition to the wishes of the Third Estate, another sign of conflict with grave consequences for the future made its appearance. The princes of the blood presented the king with a memoir in which they set forth the dangers menacing the State.

"Sire, the State is in peril. Your person is respected, and the virtues of the monarch assure him the homage of the nation. But, Sire, a revolution in the principles of government is being prepared by the fermentation of opinion. Institutions hitherto regarded as sacred, by which this monarchy has prospered for so many ages, are now converted into problematic questions or even denounced as unjust. Writings appearing during the Assembly of Notables, communications addressed to the undersigned princes, demands issued by various provinces, towns, and organized bodies, all announce and demonstrate a systematic insubordination and contempt for the laws of the State." The princes went on to protest against the doubling of the Third in the Estates General, and even suggested the possibility of a secession if the king granted double representation. "In a kingdom where there have long been no civil dissensions we pronounce the word 'secession' with regret, yet it must be expected if the rights of the two higher orders are subject to alteration; in that case one of these orders, or perhaps both, might refuse to recognize the Estates General or to confirm their own degradation by appearing in such an assembly." Monsieur and the duc d'Orléans abstained from signing this protest, the former out of respect for the king, the latter from concern for his own popularity.

This published protest remedied nothing, but it inspired in the nation a hatred for these princes that soon obliged them to emigrate. When this hatred was softened by time, there yet remained indestructible prejudices, so deep was the resentment. A bitter memory was transmitted from father to son, so that the reign of Charles X was received with cold distrust, because that prince was believed to be still the protector of privilege and inequality of ranks. The revolution of 1830 inspired regrets, but it had no adversaries.

A little later, the peers of France published a declaration abandoning their fiscal privileges, both for themselves and in the name of the whole French nobility. But the nobles were unhappy that the peers should claim to be their interpreters, and the bourgeoisie saw no more than a pathetic ruse in their declaration. It was by this time not merely the pecuniary privileges that caused the trouble.

Finally, on December 27 the government announced its action. Called simply the "result of the council," it granted the Third a number of deputies in the Estates General equal to the other two orders combined. But at the same time, it announced that the king intended no changes in the institution of separate deliberation by the three orders. A report by M. Necker, published with the ordinance, gave the reasons for these two provisions.

The public showed itself more logical than the minister. It found a striking contradiction in the two rulings, and from this moment the idolization of Necker disappeared.

Opponents of the Revolution have severely criticized Necker for the doubling of the Third Estate. But refusal was no longer possible. Not only did the king and queen regard it as the best means of overcoming the opposition of the privileged bodies, but we have seen how the general excitement had reached its height. The Third Estate, if the king had refused to grant it double representation, would have seized it anyway in the elections that were soon to come. An admission let slip in 1797 by Duport, a former counsellor in the Parlement and a leader in the organizing club of late 1788,[27] throws a great light light on the course of action, premeditated and adopted, to be followed if double representation should be refused.[28] "I said to Duport that the revolution was decided by the king's granting of double representation. 'Not at all,' he replied; 'if it had not been granted we would have taken it by force, along with the merger of the orders and the vote by head. Here was our plan: In each electoral assembly the Third would put in its *cahier* an article insisting on the doubling and would have authorized the alternate deputies to take their seats if necessary. At the meeting of the Estates General the first act of the Third would have been to bring in these alternates, and so the doubling would have been achieved.' "

So we see that revolution was being hatched in the middle class. Passions had been aroused by clumsy and ill-timed opposition. The royal power, pulled in all directions, indecisive and without confidence in itself, never took soon enough the measures that circumstances required. It allowed itself to be overwhelmed by the wave of popular opinion. At the head of affairs was a minister who viewed the general agitation with composure, persuaded that it would end in the adoption of his system of government. He supposed that the

[27] In this club were Mirabeau, Target, Roederer, Talleyrand, etc. [This is what historians know as the Society (club, committee) of Thirty. There may be some doubt in Sallier's recollection.]

[28] The conversation of which we quote a part took place between Duport and Sallier, who reports it in his *Annales françaises*.

waves would be calmed by his voice and that he would retain enough power to appease the storm.

The Third had as its chiefs and leaders men whose talents were to shine a little later in the first of our national assemblies. These men wished for a destruction of privileges, but not of society. Later, when society was attacked at its foundations, its collapse brought on their ruin. A scaffold was being prepared for them. Already we see violent language, in still guarded tones, used by writers who would later invoke murder as the best and surest of revolutionary measures. Meanwhile, the people needed a capable tribune. Mirabeau was at hand.

The fermentation did not stop at the walls of the capital. It rapidly spread to the *pays d'états*, whose old constitutions gave a pre-eminence to the two higher orders. Brittany distinguished itself in the general effervescence by inaugurating civil war.

While the municipalities of this province sent addresses to the government to obtain double representation, the nobility protested against the second convocation of the Notables and especially against the doubling of the Third, on which the government sought the Notables' advice. The Breton nobility formed a compact mass. Every gentleman had the right to sit in the provincial estates, so that a coalition of all of them was not without its importance. To oppose the nobility, someone thought of a coalition even more formidable in energy and activity: a coalition of bourgeois youth of the leading towns in the province. The first meeting took place at Rennes, where six hundred young men organized themselves into a kind of patriotic battalion with its own chiefs, of whom one of the most important was Moreau, later so famous for his military talents. The association soon entered into correspondence with the young men of other towns, so that similar associations were established.

The year 1788 came to an end, and 1789 began with its parade of calamities. At midnight on January 1 the thermometer fell to 19 degrees below zero. Grain was scarce because of the bad harvest and because the rebellious spirit throughout France interfered with the free circulation of provisions. The poor in their attics suffered from hunger and severe cold at the same time. In vain was relief given in the capital; charity, however extensive, was insufficient to the needs.[29] Food shortages came to the aid of troublemakers and gave them the means to excite popular feelings that had hitherto been latent. Combining with the effervescence over doubling of the Third, they soon led to bloody scenes.

The estates of Brittany had opened in late December 1788. At their first session the town deputies who formed the Third Estate declared that they would take no part in the deliberations until the higher orders agreed to a redress of certain grievances, especially the abuses in assessment of a hearth tax, called the *fouage*. The nobility replied that it would attend to the requests of the Third after dealing with the affairs of the province. Discontent became extreme. A violent irritation estranged the three orders so recently united in opposition to the royal will.

Learning of these disputes, the ministry ordered the suspension of the Breton estates. The Third obeyed with joy. The two higher orders obstinately continued with their work and drafted remonstrances. Both sides prepared for hostilities. The nobles felt sure of the working class to which they gave employment. The rebellious young men called on those of Nantes for assistance. The youth of Nantes started for Rennes. There was a riot in which several young men were beaten up by the populace. But the volatile popular feelings soon found another target. The tocsin sounded. The crowd surrounded the hall where the nobles were sitting. For three days the nobles were held prisoner, and they were finally reduced to breaking out sword in hand. Blood flowed; one gentleman was wounded, another killed. The young men from Nantes arrived at Rennes and entered the city against a prohibition by the governor, so great was the contempt for authority. The disorder continued, and ended only with the departure of the nobles, most of whom left the city.

These deplorable events aroused no concern in the government. "I spoke to M. de Montmorin," says M. de Bouillé in his memoirs; "he was my friend and relative; I told him frankly and freely that it was necessary to put a prompt stop to these disorders by royal au-

---

[29] The king and queen engaged in immense charities. Some rich persons ordered great fires to be lit at the street crossings, and food was distributed to the poor. The archbishop of Paris (Juigné), after giving all the money he had, borrowed 400,000 francs for distribution to the needy.

thority and military force. He replied, to my great astonishment, 'The king is too dissatisfied with the nobility and parlement of Brittany to protect them against the bourgeoisie, which is rightly irritated by their insolence and vexations. Let them arrange matters themselves. The government will not be involved.' "

At Besançon, while the provincial estates were sitting there, an insurrection broke out with demands for doubling the Third Estate and for vote by head. The houses of two members of the parlement were pillaged, and their owners saved themselves only by flight. In Provence riots followed each other at Aix and Marseilles. Everywhere the agents of the government were powerless to prevent disorder; and the parlements, overwhelmed by the force of public opinion, dared not act with vigor.

A decision now had to be made on where the district elections should be held and where the Estates General should meet. Necker gave a new proof of the vain self-assurance that blinded him to the dangers facing the monarchy. He felt no fear in proposing to convoke the assembly in the capital. Paris was the heart of intrigue and the center of agitation, but Necker had no doubt that his influence would keep passions under control and that the Estates, protected by his popularity, would enjoy the freedom needed for their deliberations. Wiser heads wanted them to meet in some city where factions would not be stirred up by concocted opinion, the clubs, and the press. To this it was objected that the court would be inconvenienced by a meeting of the Estates at a distance, so that the city of Versailles was chosen; it might as well have been the capital, as Necker wished.

It was decided that election of deputies should take place in the chief town of each *bailliage*, in each of which the principal judicial officer would preside over the meeting of the Third Estate.

The victory of the bourgeoisie was henceforth assured. How would it use that victory? What institutions would it give to France? The polemic in the press changed its goal. All the pamphlets discussed the constitution to be established, and conversations were full of the same subject. Those favoring an English form of government insisted on having two legislative chambers. A single chamber, they said, would abuse the powers derived from election, and despotism would simply be shifted from one place to another. Instead of the authority of one man, we would have a collective tyranny, the more to be feared since individual responsibility would be shrouded in numbers. Such an assembly would take all power to itself, and a fatal antagonism would arise between the legislative and executive, and perhaps even the judicial, power.

What was needed, therefore, was a counterweight to maintain a balance. This necessary and indeed indispensable counterweight would be found by creation of a second chamber having the power to approve or reject the resolutions of the first.

But herein lay an immense difficulty. How or by whom would a second chamber be composed? If elected like the first, it would have the same passions and prejudices. Liberty would no longer be secure. If named by the chief of state, and if privileged persons formed a majority, such a chamber would have its special interests to defend. Disunion would soon break out between the two legislative bodies, and the one that owed its existence to election would excite popular opinion against the other.[30]

In earlier Estates General the three orders had balanced each other. Also, as already said, their powers were limited to submitting requests to the crown, which could accept or reject them. In 1789 the Third was determined in advance to absorb the two higher orders into itself and to leave them no political power as separate entities.

While these grave concerns agitated the whole nation, a royal ordinance proclaimed January 24 as the date for opening the elections and set May 4 for the meeting of the Estates General. Each district electoral body, after chosing its deputies, was authorized by ancient usage to give them instructions, which were called *cahiers*.

A prodigious movement followed this signal from the government. Ambitions were awakened; passions became even more lively; everyone tried to influence public opinion in the elections in favor of his opinions, his prejudices, his caste, or his vanity. Yet for many these motives were secondary to a love of the public good. A real patriotism then animated much of the nation. It lacked only the knowledge drawn from experience. A smiling liberty charmed all

---

[30] This difficulty has been resolved by time. Since the clergy and nobility no longer have privileges or political existence, they have been able to enter into a senior chamber or chamber of peers without arousing mistrust in the nation.

hearts. Blessings were invoked on the king for allowing his authority to be replaced by the power of law. New institutions were to open an era of felicity by protecting the country against despotism and preserving it from anarchy.

Unfortunately, these magnificent hopes concealed vices that were developing behind the scenes: cupidity seeking satisfaction in disorder, pride eager to raise itself by overthrowing all that existed, and resentments born of inequality in the burdens felt by people of differing conditions. Able but factious men took advantage of these bad feelings. And since simple ideas are best understood by the multitude, they began by reducing all these reasons for animosity to a single word—*aristocrats*. Aristocracy was the enemy of liberty, the oppressor of the people to be pursued without limit and exterminated without remorse;[31] every weakness of mind was exploited by these agitations. Fear of scarcity was aroused in the urban populace by accusations of hoarding and a thousand rumors were accepted by the credulous, however absurd. These men knew that rioting is an enjoyable spectacle for those who take part in it and that it is in human nature to look for a factitious importance when your lot puts you in an inferior position. The more the individual is habitually obliged to obey, the more the populace in mass enjoys the pleasures of command.[32]

From the great centers of population emissaries went into the countryside to sow hatred and arouse vengeance. The burden of taxes, the heavy charge of feudal dues and the tithe, and the humiliation produced by certain seigneurial rights were the text expounded to excite popular wrath. Unfortunately, too little had been done to spread education in the rural areas. Ignorance stood in the way of discernment. Instead of awaiting legislation for the relief of wrongs that were harmful to general prosperity, many individuals were disposed to attack them by violence. The greater the ignorance, the closer it is to barbarism.

[31] For sixty years all parties in France have tried to stigmatize their adversaries by epithets condemning them to public disapproval.

[32] The headquarters of the Revolution was at cafés of the Palais-Royal; in its gardens improvised orators harangued the crowd, principally a marquis de Saint-Huruge, who was lost in debt, and Camille Desmoulins, who later called himself the attorney general of the lantern and who, along with Danton, was brought to death by Robespierre for not being terrorist enough.

In 1789 the French nation was divided as follows: at the top, an excessive degree of civilization in a society with no foresight of the future; at the bottom, a long-suppressed indignation ready to transform itself into scenes of carnage; in the middle, an educated and enlightened bourgeoisie which, in aiming at the topmost rank, was willing to use the weakness of the former and excessive energies of the latter. While the horizon still seemed calm, an appalling storm was taking shape, whose repercussions would soon shake France and resound throughout Europe.

The primary assemblies were less well attended than expected. Many were kept away because of the severity of the weather or because they did not understand the new rights that they were to exercise. Yet these assemblies named electors, who then met to choose the national deputies and draw up the *cahiers*. Almost all *cahiers* of the nobility accepted abolition of pecuniary privileges while maintaining the honorific ones. Those of the clergy were imbued with maxims of tolerance. All *cahiers* of the Third Estate required their delegates to demand, as a constitutional principle, the doubling of the Third in the future and the vote by head in the present. At the same time, they forbade any consent to taxation until the basis for new institutions was laid. . . .

In summary, the elections were favorable to the popular and democratic cause. Of 300 members representing the clergy, 208 held no ecclesiastical dignity and were mostly curés. Among 600 deputies of the Third Estate were counted 374 advocates, attorneys, or officers of subordinate law courts, and a certain number of obscure literary men without property. In the noble order, 80 gentlemen professed principles of liberty and desired to create corresponding institutions.

Anyone can see the added strength that a body already equal to two others in numbers would derive from the support of men who, without belonging to it, were united with it by a community of opinions or background. Would not such strength be employed to give the Third a complete preponderance in affairs, without consideration for the necessary and legitimate rights of the monarchy? Therein lay the danger. Many of the best observers were disturbed by it. They saw the best way to avoid it in a return to the ideas of Malesherbes, who had insisted that the crown should seize the initiative for changes demanded by the majority of the population and not leave the credit for such changes to the assembly. Malouet, who had connections with Necker and Montmorin and was one of the most distinguished members of the Estates General, explained emphatically to these two ministers the dangers facing the State and urged the only measure that seemed likely to conjure it away. "Do not wait," Malouet said to them, "until the Estates General makes demands and issues orders. Offer without delay what the best minds desire within reasonable limits of authority and recognition of national rights. You have their *cahiers* and their mandates; take note of the wishes of the majority and let the king take the initiative in his opening address to the Estates General. Be forceful and candid in your plans and concessions. Take a stand, for you have not done so yet."

Cicé, archbishop of Bordeaux, and La Luzerne, bishop of Langres, both of whom were deputies, supported Malouet in this opinion. But Necker, still counting on the gratitude of the Third Estate, was convinced that if the representatives should not agree, they would all come to him and request his mediation. He rejected the salutary advice that he was given. "I would see too many disadvantages," he said, "for the king to make such advances without being certain of success. If the concessions seemed inadequate to deputies of the Third Estate it would be dangerous to offend them. It would be dangerous for the monarch if he were to yield too soon, and on his own initiative, on those privileges of the nobility and clergy that are burdensome for the people; for to do so would alienate two powerful classes."

Malouet replied: "The privileged classes have lost all credit. To save them from total destruction you must be careful not to speak and act under pressure from them. Propose what is useful and right; if the king hesitates and the clergy and nobility resist, all is lost."

It could still be hoped that concessions by the crown, though late, might arouse feelings of gratitude that might have prevented many misfortunes. The nobility, forced by the royal will, would have abstained from those acts of resistance that provoked such terrible hatreds against them.

Meanwhile, a disdain for the wishes of the government had already manifested itself in several electoral bodies that refused to observe the regulations decreed by the royal council. The electoral college of Paris led all others in the spirit of insubordination. It began by refusing to recognize M. Angrand d'Alleret, the civil lieutenant, as its chairman, as provided by the regulations. He was a highly respected magistrate who would have been gladly accepted if chosen by election, but the right of imposing him by authority was rejected. The electoral college, called into being simply to name deputies and draft their instructions, continued to meet and deliberate. It censured a decision of the council forbidding circulation of a journal edited by Mirabeau. It went further, and instead of dissolving after the election as it should have done, it declared itself to be a permanent body so long as the Estates General were in session. It became a new kind of club in which affairs of state were discussed and decided upon whenever they affected the capital city. The ministry tolerated everything, believing that neither obtaining obedience nor punishing disobedience was any longer possible.

[Labor riots against the wallpaper manufacturer Réveillon; gossip at that time on their political significance, if any.]

CHAPTER VII

The Estates General until
the Royal Session of June 23. The Fall
of Monarchical Government

ON ARRIVING at Versailles, the deputies were summoned to meet
on May 4, 1789, for a procession and mass of the Saint-Esprit,
which was to precede the opening of the Estates. They assembled at
the parish church of Notre-Dame, where the king and queen and
whole court were to receive them. A huge crowd thronged the sides
of the street by which the procession marched from the Church of
Notre-Dame to the Church of Saint-Louis. The deputies walked according to the precedence of their order: first the clergy, then the
nobility, and finally the deputies of the Third Estate. Loud acclamations saluted their passage, and resounding cries of *Vive le roi!*
were heard. The face of Louis XVI showed the serenity and satisfaction that he felt at being in the midst of representatives of his people. It could not be so with the queen. This princess, already
wounded by slanders of which she later became the victim, received
no testimonies of good feeling, and she returned from the ceremony
sad at heart and with thoughts filled with dark forebodings.

In fact, the prestige that for centuries had surrounded and supported the royal authority was undermined among most deputies of
the Third. They had been influenced by the declarations shouted in
clubs and spread abroad in pamphlets. Many of them felt jealousy
and prejudice against the sovereign authority and the privileged
bodies; they already sensed the coming power of the Third, whose
strength had been revealed in the discussion so ineptly provoked
over double representation. It was thus in vain that the king flattered
himself in supposing that the Estates General were motivated by a
disinterested zeal for the public good, and in assuming that his deal-
ings with them would bring the happiness that he so ardently
longed for.

An incident during the religious ceremony showed how far, from this first day, the respect for the king's person and for religion had declined. The bishop of Nancy mounted the pulpit and in the course of his sermon dwelt on the evils produced by the salt tax. The assemblage burst into applause just as the holy sacrament was being raised. Never had such an impropriety occurred in the presence of our kings or in a church during divine service.

On the next day, May 5, the three orders met together for the opening session. To the right of the throne sat the deputies of the clergy, to the left, those of the nobility; the Third Estate was seated on benches facing the throne. The king delivered the following speech in a firm and resonant voice:

"Messieurs, the day that I have awaited with heartfelt anticipation has at last arrived, and I find myself surrounded by representatives of the nation that it is a glory for me to command.

"A long interval had passed since the last holding of the Estates General; and although these assemblies seemed to have become obsolete, I have ventured to restore a custom from which the kingdom may derive new strength and which may provide the nation with a new source of happiness.

"The debt of the State, already immense on my accession to the throne, has become even greater during my reign; a costly but honorable war was the cause; an increase of taxes has been the necessary consequence and has made their unequal incidence more keenly felt.

"A state of anxiety, an exaggerated desire for innovations, has made itself evident and in the end would lead all opinions astray unless brought under control by wise and moderate counsels.

"It is in the confidence of such an outcome, Messieurs, that I have called you together; and I have seen this confidence justified by the willingness shown by the two higher orders to renounce their pecuniary privileges. My hope that all three orders, united in sentiment, will work with me for the general good of the State will not be disappointed. . . ."

The keeper of the seals, Barentin, spoke next. He said that the king "in agreeing to double representation, had no intention of changing the old form of deliberation and wanted no vote by head except by consent of the Estates General and with the approval of His Majesty." This remark alienated the Third order from him instantly and forever.

Necker, following him, read a speech three hours long on the financial situation. He began by trying indirectly to turn his hearers' thinking toward forms of deliberation as practiced in the British parliament. "You will readily see," he said, "that deliberations entrusted to two or three orders have great advantages for maintaining an established system and discouraging innovations."

As minister of finance, he went on to explain that the difference between receipts and expenditures was only 56 million, so that the deficit could be met without new taxes by economy alone. Hence the needs of the treasury had not been the motive for the royal decision to convoke the Estates General. The king had yielded to the wishes of his people in a desire to unite himself more closely with the nation.

Louis XVI was welcomed on his arrival and acompanied at his departure with unanimous cries of *Vive le roi!* with which a few cries of *Vive la reine!* were mixed.

On the next day, May 6, the three orders met in their separate chambers to proceed with the verification of powers of their members. The thoughtlessness that for some time had characterized all the acts of the government now had unfortunate effects. The Third felt humiliated by the simplicity of the costume assigned to it compared with the sumptuous dress accorded to the nobility. But another fact heightened the sense felt by the Third of its own importance, for it received for its deliberations the great hall in which the royal or plenary session had just been held. If the king were to appear again before the Estates General, it would be the Third that admitted the other two orders to its meeting place, as if it were the principal part receiving separated fractions. Also, this hall, built to accommodate 1,200 persons, was much too large for the deputies of the Third, who numbered no more than 600. Would not the seats remaining unoccupied suggest that the representives of 24 million had the right to require the presence of deputies of only a million of the privileged? This claim to supremacy grew all the more rapidly since it already existed among the men of true talent who directed the deliberations of the Third during the early period of the Estates General.

Moreover, the great size of the hall led to an unforeseen but very important new development. Persons unconnected with the deputies came in and took the empty seats, and the sessions of the assembly, which had been secret in former times, now became public. From this moment, the crowd began to influence the decisions of the deputies by its applause or its murmurs.

There are two dangers in politics. One is to underestimate the small causes that too often influence great events. The other is to apply in public affairs the inflexible rules of logic. Nothing is more logical than that the wishes and interests of the few should submit to the wishes and interests of the large number; and yet the experience of all ages suggests that liberty perishes and tyranny begins when the affairs of state are delivered over to a single power.

From the first sitting, the Third and the nobility each showed its dominant thought: the Third, its desire to draw the other two orders to itself so as to obtain legislative omnipotence; the nobility, its determination to present a firm opposition to any attempt at fusion. The nobility saw the vote by head as an inevitable consequence, which would lead to the destruction of its order as a political body.

The higher clergy was of the same opinion as the nobility. But the mass of curés was undecided, so that the ecclesiastical order was disposed to play a conciliatory role.

The court was greatly alarmed. The queen, who had favored the doubling of the Third, felt frightened by its aggressive projects. But neither the court nor the nobility appreciated the state of weakness into which they had fallen. They were under the illusion that they could successfully oppose a public opinion that became more heated every day and more ready for a general overturn.

Making haste to organize itself, the nobility appointed a committee to verify the powers of its members.

The Third expressed surprise that the clergy and nobility were unwilling to proceed in common. Since it was of equal interest to all (so they argued) to be assured that none could vote without regular powers, it was evident that verification should take place in the general assembly. The Third sent a delegation to the clergy and nobility to announce that it awaited their appearance in the great hall of the Estates to effect the verifications.

By a majority of 195, the nobility declared itself organized. The clergy held back and proposed the appointment of a committee of conciliation. The three orders accepted this proposal. But the members chosen by the nobility for this committee were instructed to make no concession on the question of verification in common. Tempers mounted; orators declaimed against usurpation by the Third; the interests of the order, the fundamentals of the monarchy, the forms of the constitution were said to be at stake; firmness was necessary; principles and old usages must be followed. As in the days of the Fronde, the women took part with their natural vehemence, making resistance a point of honor.

Calmly and firmly, the Third awaited the further action of the nobility with a calculated inertia. It sent a few of its members to the other two orders to inform them of its willingness to have a joint committee. Target, their spokesman, said "that the deputies of the *commons* of France have named persons charged with attending the conferences proposed by the clergy; that these persons would present themselves on the day most convenient to the gentlemen of the clergy and the nobility."

The expression "deputies of the commons," never heard until then, was a kind of advance claim of the Third to represent the totality of the nation,[33] although the speaker would perhaps not have been unhappy to see the two higher orders consider combining into an upper chamber, as Necker wished. But the astonishment was great and aroused the indignation of d'Eprémesnil, who cried that the Third Estate was giving itself an unconstitutional title.

On May 26 the nobility decided, by a margin of 200, that "for this holding of the Estates General the credentials will be verified separately, and that an examination of the advantages and disadvantages of this procedure will be postponed to the time when the three orders take up the forms of organization of the next Estates."

By this declaration, all means of conciliation were rejected. The Third sent a deputation to the clergy, with Target again as the spokesman, who said: "Messieurs, the deputies of the commons in-

---

[33] "It is certain that by this name the commons laid the basis for their subsequent conduct. There is no concealing the fact that this question of a name and of verification of powers, seemingly of small consequence, underlay all the great questions of unity of the National Assembly" (*Mémoires de Bailly*). [The 600 deputies of the Third, refusing to organize themselves as a separate order, had no president or chairman but elected the astronomer and academician Bailly as a "dean" to preside over their discussions. He soon thereafter became the first mayor of Paris and wrote his memoirs shortly before his death on the guillotine in 1793.]

vite those of the clergy, in the name of the God of peace and the national interest, to join with them in the hall of the general assembly, to advise on measures to bring about the agreement so necessary at this moment for the public good." The clergy were moved, but requested twenty-four hours to consider the matter.

During this interval the king wrote to the three orders, urging them to renew the conferences on conciliation in the presence of the keeper of the seals and a few others whom the king would name. This proposal was accepted. The Third voted to send "a solemn deputation to the king to present the respectful homages of his faithful commons, the assurance of their zeal and love for his sacred person and for the royal family, and their warm sentiments of gratitude for His Majesty's tender solicitude for the needs of his people."

But despite these grateful and submissive words, distrust of the king's personal inclinations was growing. The court, it was said, knew the tendency of many of the clergy to accede to the wishes of the Third, and the king's letter was only designed, in the interest of the nobility, to prevent union of the orders.

Imbued with this idea, the Third soon began to express sentiments of superiority not only over the other two orders but over royalty itself. The royal family at this moment (June 4) experienced the first misfortune that seemed to presage those that would afflict it later. The dauphin died at Meudon in the eighth year of his age after a long illness. The precocious intelligence of the young prince had aroused great hopes; the grief of the king and queen was extreme; during the last moments before the dauphin's death, and for several days thereafter, the king preferred to see no one. Nevertheless Bailly, who then presided over the Third, rudely insisted on admission to the king's presence to deliver the address voted by the assembly. Louis XVI wearily agreed, sighing, "These people then have no children." Bailly soon put forth a new claim, demanding the power, in the name of the assembly, to communicate without intermediary with the chief of state. The assembly was thus tending to put itself first on a plane of equality with the crown and then, aided by the ever-growing popular effervescence in the capital, exploited by agitators, to obtain a superiority before which everything had to yield. It could be seen that the conferences with the keeper of the seals would have no result, which is what happened. The conferences came to an end, and Necker thereupon proposed a new means of reconciliation: (1) each of the three orders would verify its powers separately and report to the others; (2) disputed cases would be taken up by committeemen from the three orders, who would report to their respective chambers; (3) cases on which there was still disagreement would be submitted to the king, who would make the final decision.

The clergy accepted this arrangement without restriction. The nobility accepted it on a condition that was thought to make it ineffective and which gave a pretext to the Third to refuse it. The royal intervention was inconsistent with the sovereignty to which the Third aspired.

A deputation from the clergy arrived on June 6 to propose to the Third the naming of a joint committee to consider measures for relief of the sufferings of the poor, but the proposal only aroused suspicion. It was seen as a dilatory tactic to postpone the union of the orders. The only thought of men who regarded themselves as representing the commons of France was to absorb the clergy and nobility into their own compact majority. The Third, instead of discussing the request of the clergy, did no more than renew its proposal, already made so many times, for a meeting of all in the common hall.

Finally, on June 10, on a motion of Abbé Sieyès, the deputies *of the commons of France* decided to settle the question as if by sovereign power, by sending a delegation to the clergy and nobility to make the following declaration:

"Messieurs, we are charged by the deputies of the commons of France to inform you that they can no longer postpone the obligation imposed on all representatives of the nation. It is surely time that those claiming this status should recognize one another by a common verification of their powers, or at last begin to concern themselves with the national interest, which alone, and apart from all particular interests, constitutes the great purpose to which all deputies should direct their efforts. Consequently, and in view of the need for all representatives of the nation to become active, the deputies of the commons beg you again, Messieurs, and their duty requires them to issue a summons to you individually and collectively, to appear in the hall of the Estates, to be present, take part, and subject yourselves to a common verification of powers. We are charged also to warn you that a general roll-call of all *bailliages* will begin in one hour, after which the verification will proceed, and those not appearing will be considered in default."

Bailly, as presiding officer of the commons, was charged with presenting the resolution of June 10 to the king and explaining the reasons for it. He was admitted on the thirteenth. The king replied: "I will make known my intentions to the chamber of the Third Estate concerning the message from it that you present to me."

It was apparent from the terms used by the king that he disapproved of the title "deputies of the commons." They were undeterred. The resolution of June 10 was already being acted upon. The roll-call of the *bailliages* had begun on the twelfth and continued on the thirteenth; no one from the clergy or nobility appeared. But on the fourteenth three curés from Poitou presented themselves for verification of their powers, and this first accession to the commons was hailed with joy. On the next day six more curés imitated their example, among them Abbé Grégoire, later so sadly famous in the Convention. Soon the number reached nineteen. It was certain that many others would follow.

The chamber had now to organize itself. But under what name? The term "order of the Third Estate" was repudiated; the expression "deputies of the commons" seemed too explicit; several titles were debated for some days. At last, on June 17, the words "National Assembly" were adopted, proposed by a deputy named Legrand and supported by Sieyès. The Third issued the following declaration:

"The Assembly, in a deliberation following the verification of powers, recognizes that this assembly is composed of representatives sent by ninety-six one-hundredths of the nation.

"Such a mass of deputations cannot remain idle because of the absence of deputies from a few *bailliages* or of a few classes of citizens, since the absentees whose names have been called cannot prevent those present from exercising the plenitude of their rights, especially when the exercise of these rights is an imperative and pressing duty.

"Moreover, since such a power belongs solely to representatives

certified to concur in the national will, and since all certified representatives should be in this assembly, it is necessary to conclude that
it is for this assembly, and for it alone, to interpret the will of the
nation.

"There thus cannot exist between the throne and the Assembly
any veto or negative power.

"The Assembly declares, therefore, that the work of national restoration can and should be initiated without delay by the present
deputies, and that they should carry it forward without interruption
or obstacle.

"The name of National Assembly is the only one appropriate for
the Assembly in the present circumstances, because the members
who compose it are the only legitimate representatives publicly certified and known, or because they are sent by almost the totality of
the nation, or because, since representation is one and indivisible,
no deputy, in whatever order or class he may have been chosen, has
the right to exercise his functions separately from this assembly.

"The Assembly will never lose the hope of receiving in its body
all deputies who may be absent today, etc. etc.[34]

"The National Assembly orders the reasons for the present resolution to be put in writing and presented to the king and the nation."

The title of National Assembly corresponded exactly to the
claims that had developed among deputies of the Third. It expressed the integrity of the legislative power. The two other orders
became outsiders, unable to legitimize themselves for lawmaking
except by uniting with the body representing the nation. It is to be
noted as well that, in rejecting the right of veto by the crown, the
Assembly also struck down the royal authority and reduced the
monarch to a passive role.[35]

[34] [The "etc., etc." represents Hervé de Tocqueville's omission of a few words
from the text of this declaration, which he may have taken from Buchez and Roux,
Histoire parlementaire de la Révolution française, 40 vols., Paris, 1834–1838, vol. I, pp.
469–470. The omission has no significance.]

[35] "The Assembly was well aware that this act by which it constituted itself took
a bold and extraordinary form, which might provide powerful means for attacking
it. The court and the two orders had an equal interest in doing so. It cannot be denied that the destruction of the orders was implied in this act. By indicating that it
might do without them, the Assembly asserted their useless and abusive character.
The government could not avoid seeing that this act seized an authority that had

No sooner was the Assembly constituted than the deputies swore an oath for the faithful discharge of their functions.

But it seemed that a more conspicuous act was necessary to establish the sovereignty that the Assembly intended to exercise. Hence:

"The Assembly declares the levy of taxes illegal and consequently invalid in their creation, extension, or continuation.

"It consents provisionally for the nation, however, to the collection in the same way as in the past of taxes and contributions however illegally established and levied, but only until the date of the first disbanding of its members from whatever cause.

"After that date, the Assembly intends and decrees that any levy of taxes and contributions of any kind not freely and formally granted by this Assembly shall entirely cease in all provinces of the kingdom, whatever their form of administration."

The purpose of this declaration was not only to prove the omnipotence of the Third but also to make its dissolution impossible.

Before ending its session, the Assembly decreed protection of creditors of the state by the honor and honesty of the French nation.

Even before these last resolutions of the Third Estate, the government was deeply disturbed by its pretentions. All means of conciliation had failed. Necker told the king that it was time for the royal authority to be used. "The king," he said, "cannot remain indifferent in so great a dispute without compromising the majesty of the throne, the reputation of the supreme rank, and his personal prestige." All the ministers were agreed on the need for a royal session at which the monarch would announce the concessions that he was willing to make to the legitimate desires of the French, and at the same time would determine the relationships among the three orders. The royal session was set for June 22. Necker had asked for it to be held a fortnight sooner, before the Third Estate became strong enough to make demands on the crown instead of receiving its favors.

During the morning of June 20 heralds of arms announced the royal session at Versailles. The deliberations of the three orders were suspended during the work necessary for preparation of the

hitherto been royal alone, to put it in the hands of legitimate representatives of the nation" (*Mémoires de Bailly*).

hall of the Estates General. The hall was surrounded with troops under orders to let no one enter.

The news spread through the city and provoked general excitement. The deputies shared in the agitation. They were persuaded that the aim of the royal session was dissolution of the Estates General. They were seen to cluster in large groups in animated discussions.

The destiny of France pushed it on to inevitable revolution. All the acts of the government were faults or blunders. The presiding officers of the three orders should have been officially notified on June 19.[36] M. de Brézé, the grand master of ceremonies, who was not the proper person to transmit royal decisions, had written to M. Bailly; but his letter was not sent until June 20, and when it reached Bailly, the information in it was common knowledge.

The irregularity of the communication and the unwarranted delay gave a pretext to Bailly to refuse obedience. He replied: "I have not yet received, monsieur, any order from the king for a royal session or for suspension of our meetings, and my duty calls me to the one scheduled for this morning at eight o'clock. I have the honor to be. . . ."

He went immediately to join the deputies who were waiting outside the hall and, marching at their head with the secretaries of the assembly, requested entrance. The officer of the guard, faithful to his orders, politely refused it. Bailly protested and rejoined his colleagues.

After a short and impromptu discussion in the open air it was decided that the assembly should not interrupt its sessions. But where should it meet? Guillotin suggested a tennis court; the others agreed, and soon all the deputies were gathered there. They adopted the following resolution:

"The National Assembly, considering that it has been called upon to settle the constitution of the kingdom, effect the regeneration of public order, and maintain the true principles of the monarchy, and considering that nothing can prevent the continuation of its deliberations in whatever place it may be obliged to establish itself, since

---

[36] When the king wished to make something known to the Parlement, he wrote personally to its first president, informing him of his intentions.

wherever its members are gathered the National Assembly is in being,

"Resolves that all its members shall immediately take a solemn oath never to separate but to meet in any place that circumstances may require, until the constitution of the kingdom shall be laid and established on solid foundations; and that after the swearing of this oath each and every member shall confirm this indefeasible resolution by his signature."

Thus was sworn by all members this famous oath that resounded throughout France and all Europe as the death knell of royalty.

While all this was happening, at Versailles Louis XVI consulted with his council on the form and content of two declarations to be made to the Estates General. Necker had written a draft in which he carefully avoided putting the language of absolute power into the king's mouth. Its first article provided that during the present Estates General the three orders should deliberate in common on all general affairs and that in the separate chambers each should discuss only subjects of particular interest to its order. The king would also:

Proclaim the abolition of pecuniary privileges;

State his refusal to accept an organization of the Estates General in less than two chambers;

Set forth at length and in detail his views for the public good and his personal feelings in favor of the people.

Examined and debated, this draft was about to be adopted when the king adjourned the meeting until the following day, June 21.

On that very day the duc de Luxembourg, president of the nobility, arrived to protest, in the name of his order, against the titles assumed by the Third Estate on June 10 and 17.

The council met again, but it was not the same council as on the day before; the king's two princely brothers attended, and four magistrates were added. The king's inclinations had changed: persons near to him had aroused his scruples on sacrificing the interests of his faithful nobility; his duty now obliged him to respect ancient usages; the public interest required him to ward off the danger to which a preponderance of the Third, already so powerful by numbers and audacity, would expose the State.

One understands the repugnance of the nobility to consent to the abolition of a political privilege that it had enjoyed for ages, but one cannot but be astonished at its ignorance of the mood of the French people. The noble order relied on the court; the order of the Third Estate was supported by the rest of the nation. The throne thus ceased to be national by embracing the interests of the privileged, and it ran the risk of being dragged down in their fall. The danger passed unnoticed by all, even by the sovereign; and those who urged him on were too obtuse to see it.

The council met again, reinforced as we have said by new members, and reviewed the projected declarations. It proposed various changes and the discussion was prolonged, but nothing was definitely settled on the evening of June 21. The royal session had to be postponed to June 23.

This delay was another mistake, for it gave the National Assembly the chance to confirm its resistance by a new action, in which its presumption was heightened by the accession on June 22 of a majority of the clergy.

There had been no meeting on the twenty-first because of the religious ceremonies on Sunday, but on the twenty-second the deputies met in the nave of the Church of Saint-Louis without interference from the civil or ecclesiastical authorities. A large table was brought in, and the president sat facing it, with the secretaries on both sides. At his right were seats destined for deputies of the clergy, at his left those for deputies of the nobility, while members of the Third Estate were seated before him.

Soon the grills of the choir opened, and 148 members of the clergy came forward, announcing that they were ready to proceed with the verification of their powers in this assembly. They took the places reserved for them.[37]

Necker had strongly opposed the changes proposed in the two projected declarations. He obtained a private audience with the king, in which he did not conceal that the fidelity of the troops was doubtful, that according to information reaching the ministry they would not march against the National Assembly. His efforts were fruitless. He was unable to prevent the king's speech and the two

[37] The majority of the clergy uniting with the assembly was composed of five prelates (the archbishops of Vienne and Bordeaux and the bishops of Chartres, Rodez, and Coutances), two grand vicars, six canons, a commendatory abbot, and 134 curés.

declarations from taking on the peremptory and absolute tone of a *lit de justice*.

Louis XVI appeared on June 23 in the hall of the Estates General in all the pomp and panoply of royalty. The three orders awaited him. The Third Estate was irritated by being made to stop at the door while the grand master of ceremonies seated the members of the nobility and clergy. Their indignation was the greater because of their sense of their importance. It reached such a point, after a while, that they told M. de Brézé that they would leave unless the hall was opened immediately.

The king was received by the two higher orders with acclamations. The Third, in its injured dignity, kept silent. Stools were placed on both sides of the king as seats for the ministers. It was noted with surprise that one was vacant. Necker was absent.

The minister had excused himself from accompanying the king. His vanity could not bear the rejection of his advice on the wording of the two declarations. He was convinced also that the absolute language assigned to the monarch would have a deplorable effect. He preferred to compromise his master by showing opposition through absence, rather than risk his own popularity by ostensible adherence.

For a moment the king seemed disconcerted by the aspect of the assembly, but he regained his composure and delivered the following speech:

"Messieurs, I thought that I had done all in my power for the good of my peoples when I made the decision to call you together, when I overcame the difficulties involved in your convocation, and when I met the wishes of the nation by showing in advance what I desired to do for its welfare.

"It seemed that you had only to complete my work; and the nation awaited impatiently the moment when, by a conjunction of the benevolent views of its sovereign with the enlightened zeal of its representatives, it would enjoy the prosperity that such a union would procure.

"The Estates General have been sitting for almost two months and have not yet been able to agree on the preliminaries of their operations. A full understanding should have arisen purely from love of country, but a fateful disagreement is now cause for alarm. I would like to think that the French have not changed, but I now see, with reproaches to no one, that dissensions, debates, and exaggerated claims have been brought on by the length of time since the last Estates General, the agitation that preceded the present meeting, the purpose of the convocation so different from the days of your ancestors, the limits set by constituents upon your powers, and various other circumstances.

"I owe it to the common welfare of my kingdom, and I owe it to myself, to put an end to these divisions. It is with this in mind, Messieurs, that I assemble you again in my presence as a common father to all my subjects. It is as defender of the laws of my kingdom that I come to recall to you its true spirit and to suppress the dangers that menace it.

"But, Messieurs, after clearly establishing the respective rights of the three orders, I expect from the patriotic zeal of the two higher orders, I expect from their attachment to my person, and I expect from their knowledge of the urgent evils afflicting the State, that in matters concerning the general good they will be the first to propose a union of minds and sentiments that I regard as necessary in the present crisis to save the State."

The keeper of the seals then read the first declaration, which was listened to with pained surprise by most of the deputies. There were a few bursts of applause from the ranks of the nobility. We extract here the most important articles of the declaration:[38]

"The king wishes that the ancient distinction of three orders of the State shall be preserved in its entirety as essential to the constitution of the kingdom; and that the deputies freely chosen by each of the three orders, forming three chambers, deliberating by order, but empowered with the approval of the sovereign to deliberate in common, shall be considered as the body representing the nation. Consequently, the king nullifies as illegal and unconstitutional the resolutions adopted by the Third Estate on the seventeenth of this month, as well as those following thereupon.

"His Majesty, having exhorted the three orders for the welfare of

---

[38] [Hervé de Tocqueville omits about half of this declaration as printed in Buchez and Roux, *Histoire parlementaire*, II, pp. 13–15. Important among the points omitted was the king's annulment of the mandates by which nobles in the *bailliages* forbade their deputies to merge with the Third Estate.]

the State to meet together during this holding of the Estates General, but only to deliberate in common on matters of general concern, wishes to make known his intentions on how they are to proceed.

"Explicitly excepted from affairs to be treated in common are those regarding the ancient and constitutional rights of the three orders, the form in which future Estates General are to meet, feudal and seigneurial properties, and the useful rights and honorific prerogatives of the higher orders.

"The specific consent of the clergy will be necessary for all arrangements concerning religion, ecclesiastical discipline, and regulation of secular and religious orders and bodies.

"Decisions to be made by the three orders in common, in disputes over credentials with which interested parties may be provided for the Estates General, will be taken by the plurality of votes; but if two-thirds of those voting within one of the three orders protest against the decision of the assembly, the case will be referred to the king, to be settled definitively by His Majesty.

"If, with a view to facilitating the union of the three orders, it should be desired that the decision to meet in common should require two-thirds of the vote, His Majesty is willing to authorize this procedure.

"Matters decided in assemblies of the three orders meeting together will be reconsidered on the following day if a hundred members of the assembly so request.

"The good order, propriety, and freedom of voting require His Majesty to forbid, and he does expressly forbid, any persons not members of the three orders of the Estates General to be present at their deliberations, whether occurring in common or separately."

After this reading the king spoke again, pronouncing a few words as a preface to the second declaration. This second declaration was a list of the concessions and ameliorations accorded by the crown.

"The necessity for the Estates General to consent to the levy or continuation of taxes.

"Examination of the finances by the Estates and assignment of amounts to each government department.

"The debt entrusted to the honor of representatives of the nation.

"The king will approve decisions by the clergy and nobility concerning their renunciation of pecuniary privileges.

"Abolition of the *taille*, to be replaced by a tax distributed in equal proportions without distinction of estate, rank, or birth.

"Suppression of the right of *franc fief*.[39]

"Respect for properties, including tithes, *cens*, *rentes*, and feudal rights and obligations.

"The Estates General to determine which government offices and employments confer nobility.

"The Estates General to find the most suitable means for replacing *lettres de cachet*.

"They will consider how to reconcile freedom of the press with respect for morals, religion, and the honor of citizens.

"In every province or *généralité* there shall be established a provincial assembly in which two-tenths of the members shall be of the clergy, three-tenths of the nobility, and five-tenths of the Third Estate. Some qualification based on tax-paying may be required. Members of these assemblies will deliberate in common.

"The Estates General are invited to consider the best use to be made of the royal domains, and to realize the project for carrying tariff barriers to the frontier.

"They will consider the deleterious effects of the salt tax.

"A thorough examination of the excises and other taxes.

"Abolition of the *corvée*.

"Suppression of fees for *mainmorte*.

"Easing of the lottery for militia service.

"The king wishes that all provisions for public order and for the welfare of his peoples that His Majesty will have approved, among others, those concerning personal liberty, equality under taxation, and the establishment of provincial estates [sic: should be "assemblies"?], can never be changed without the consent of the three orders taken separately.

"The king most expressly declares that he wishes to retain in its entirety, and without the least impairment, the training of the army, as well as all authority, police regulation, and power over the military such as French monarchs have constantly enjoyed."

[39] [See the Glossary.]

Louis XVI closed the session by a third speech:

"You have how heard, Messieurs, a summary of my intentions and my views. They reflect my keen desire to promote the public good. But if, by a fatality far from my thoughts, you abandon me in this great enterprise, I will work alone for the benefit of my peoples; I will consider myself alone to be their true representative, and knowing the content of your *cahiers*, knowing the complete accord between the most general will of the nation and my benevolent intentions, I will have all the confidence that such a rare harmony must arouse, and I will march toward my goal with all the firmness and courage that it must inspire.

"Remember, Messieurs, that none of your projects, none of your decisions can have the force of law without my specific approbation. I am the natural guarantor of your respective rights, and all orders of the State can rely on my fair-minded impartiality. Any mistrust on your part would be a great injustice. I am the one who until now has worked for the good of my peoples, and it is rare, perhaps, that a sovereign's only ambition should be to persuade his subjects to agree on accepting the benefits that he intends.

"I order you, Messieurs, to separate at once, and each of you to proceed tomorrow morning to the chamber assigned to your order, and there to resume your sessions. I therefore order the grand master of ceremonies to prepare the halls."

This speech was received with the same coolness as the two before it. The king's good intentions might have touched a responsive chord, but they came too late. The deputies of the commons wanted all that he offered, and still more. Since they felt strong enough to achieve these objectives without the monarch's assistance, they preferred to reserve the merit for improvements exclusively for themselves in the eyes of the nation. Hence the consent of the royal authority made no sense, and the form of sovereignty in which this consent was asserted contravened the sovereignty of the nation that they represented. The first declaration, moreover, which had so ineptly been read before the other, had greatly irritated the deputies. Even many friends of the existing order felt uneasy.

During the session many handwritten notes had been passed out to the public with news of what was happening within. The king emerged through an immense crowd that was dejected and silent. He returned to the château deeply discouraged.

After the king's departure the two higher orders complied with his orders and withdrew. The commons remained in their place, motionless and silent. The grand master of ceremonies approached the president, M. Bailly, and said: "You have heard the king's orders." Bailly replied: "Monsieur, I cannot dismiss the assembly until it has debated on its adjournment." Then, turning to his colleagues: "I believe that the nation when assembled cannot be given orders." But what constitutes sovereign power in an assembly if not the universality of representation, and by what right does only a portion of the deputies call itself the nation?

Mirabeau let fire the exclamation that has remained famous: "Go and tell those who sent you that we are here by the power of the people, and nothing but the force of bayonets can drive us hence!" The deputies all cried, "That's the will of the assembly! That's our decision!" The grand master of ceremonies retired.

Several representatives, including Camus, Barnave, and Sieyès, then spoke excitedly. Sieyès, on returning to his seat, made his famous remark: "You are today what you were yesterday." The assembly unanimously, despite the royal order, rejected the name of Third Estate and reaffirmed the title of National Assembly. It decreed the maintenance of all its preceding resolutions that the king had just declared null and void.

During this discussion workmen came in to remove the throne and draperies with which the hall had been ornamented. When they began to make a great noise, the president ordered them to depart, and they obeyed.

The session was on the point of ending when Mirabeau moved a decree of inviolability for the deputies. When Bailly and a few others expressed hesitation, Mirabeau replied forcefully: "You do not realize what you are exposing yourselves to. If you do not pass this decree sixty deputies will be arrested this very night." The Assembly accepted Mirabeau's opinion and decreed as follows:

"The National Assembly declares that the person of every deputy is inviolable; that any individual, corporation, tribunal, court, or commission that may dare, during or after the present session, to prosecute, search for, arrest or have arrested, detain or have detained a deputy on the ground of any proposal, statement, opinion, or speech made by him in the Estates General, as well as all persons who might use their office to promote such attempts, by whomever they might be ordered, are to be branded as infamous, traitors to the nation, and guilty of a capital crime. The National Assembly decrees that in such cases it will take all necessary measures to have the authors, instigators, or executors thereof found out, prosecuted, and punished."

It cannot be doubted that a great many members were devoted to the monarchy and the king. How, then, did it happen that, in proclaiming their disobedience, they arrived at a unanimous vote to maintain decrees that the king had declared null and void? The explanation lies in what had become the dominant thought in the whole nation on the need for a new constitution. The *bailliages*, in their *cahiers*, had imposed this obligation on their mandatories. A constitution had to be written with the king, without the king, or despite the king. The Assembly was composed of two parties, one that directed opinion and kept it excited, and another that was pushed by this same opinion to go beyond what their own judgment and reason would advise. Malouet, who showed himself to be one of the most courageous defenders of monarchical institutions, nevertheless observed in a report to his constituents: "After the royal session we had no other course than the one we had taken in the tennis court. Whether the other orders combined with us or remained separate, we owed France a constitution; and France would owe its happiness and glory to us if this constitution guaranteed the rights of all."

When the marquis de Brézé reported to the king that the deputies of the Third would yield only to force, the king reflected for a few moments and then gloomily answered: "Oh, well! If they don't want to leave the hall, let them stay." This unfortunate prince had lost the courage to act and took refuge in the passive resignation that gives strength to endure anything, even death.

A strange scene occurred on the evening of June 23. Necker had sent his resignation to the king, and on hearing of it, a crowd gathered beneath the windows of the château, crying *Vive Necker! Vive le tiers état! A bas les aristocrates!* The queen, alarmed by the clamor, rushed to the king's apartment. Necker was summoned, and the royal couple, feeling their weakness, urged him not to abandon his post. He yielded to their wishes. But instead of returning to the controller general's rooms by going through the château he flung himself into the arms of the people, who carried him off in triumph. Soon a good many deputies came to congratulate him. The royal power had sunk into contempt, while Necker remained popular.

The Assembly had performed the act of disobedience with impunity. Its power rose above the king's, and it would march on in this same path. It possessed sovereignty; Louis XVI, a name without power. His reign ended; the reign of the national representation began, which is not our subject. Writers of great talent have treated this period of our history; we end our story at this point. The constitution later restored some of his prerogatives to Louis XVI. It is well known that on the first occasion when he attempted to use them, he was besieged in his palace, taken prisoner, conducted to the Temple, and then to the scaffold.

Conclusion

LOUIS XVI was not deceived. He had felt power slipping from his hands into those of the people. But meanwhile, an antagonism was arising against these men who called themselves representatives of the nation. Clubs and open-air meetings insisted on governing the assembly that took it upon itself to govern France. After the session of June 23 the excitement in the capital became extreme. Orators at the Palais-Royal hurled their menaces without sparing the person of the king. Weakness, after provoking scorn, led to insults.

The king hastily contradicted his declaration of June 23. He wrote to the clergy and nobility, urging them to join with the Third Estate. The duc de Luxembourg, president of the nobility, hurried to the king to make his remonstrances: "An unlimited power exists in the Estates General," he said; "but division into three orders checks their action and preserves yours; combined, they acknowledge no master; divided, they are your subjects. Your faithful nobles now have the choice of doing as Your Majesty invites, by sharing legislative power with their co-deputies, or else of dying in defense of the prerogatives of the throne. Their choice is not in doubt; they will die, and they ask no reward for doing their duty; but in dying they will save the independence of the crown, and they will reduce to nothing the work of the Assembly, which surely will not be thought complete when a third of its members are consigned to the fury of the populace and the guns of murderers."

The king's reply revealed his character. "M. de Luxembourg, my thoughts are formed; I am determined to face any sacrifice; I do not wish a single man to perish in my quarrel. Say, then, to the order of the nobility that I beg them to join with the two others. And if that is not enough, I order them as their king. It is my will."

Meanwhile, the court took courage, pressing the king to use armed force. He agreed, because they persuaded him that it was more important to overawe than to take action. Certain regiments were ordered to approach Versailles, but several of their units marched to the cry of *Vive la Nation!* The Assembly pretended to more alarm than it felt. Its leaders judged that the moment had arrived for an explosion. They were assured that the regiment of the Gardes françaises was at their disposal. The riotings of July 12, 13, and 14 took place and remained triumphant. The Revolution was consummated.

After these events the character of the various segments of French society underwent a notable change. All felt a hitherto unknown energy, glorious and grand when guided by honor, ferocious when it expressed hatred, pride, and revenge.

Some, with an instinct for crime, sought to inflame the lowest class to make it their instrument. This class, obtaining liberty without knowing the duties and prerogatives that it imposes, saw in it only a right to satisfy resentments and a desire for vengeance. In the sudden and profound revolutionary commotion, the force of law was suspended. The restraints of religion had been destroyed in advance. In several provinces the peasants in their hatred of feudalism attacked and burned the châteaux.

The lower elements in the towns, excessively credulous, were enraged by the slanders to which some persons were subjected. They thought they achieved higher status by becoming judges, and degraded themselves by becoming executioners. Murders multiplied; the pavements of the capital were red with blood; heads fixed on the ends of pikes were paraded through the streets, horrible trophies of the power of the multitude. At Caen, women turning into furies made a hideous feast of the heart of Belzunce, whose body they had dismembered.[40]

In the course of our recital we have observed that, in all the disordered exaltation of mind, a true patriotism developed. The youth of France rushed to the frontiers to repel the foreigners who invaded their country's soil. From the population in arms came a profusion of great captains. They defeated the enemy, and our flag soon

[40] [Belzunce was a young officer of dragoons. This episode at Caen is described at more length by Droz, *Histoire du règne de Louis XVI*, II, pp. 374–375. Droz concluded by saying, ". . . his body was mutilated and torn to pieces, and some accounts present his murderers, without metaphor, as cannibals." Thus Hervé de Tocqueville, while barely mentioning the incident, adds more affirmative and gruesome detail.]

floated over the territory of princes who fought against us. A victorious France was enlarged by several new provinces.

If we consider those opposed to the Revolution, we find the same vigorous courage that was typical of the time. The emigration has been blamed as a political error, but justice has been done also to those of the French, formerly so frivolous and so futile, who abandoned the country of their birth and the fortunes by which they lived, renouncing the dearest ties of the heart to go where they thought honor called them.[41]

History transmits the story of the peasants of the Vendée, admired even by their enemies. A victorious philosophy had closed the temples of the true God and proscribed his ministers. The Vendéans claimed the right of a free people to worship in the way of their ancestors. It was refused to them, and they flew to arms. Gentlemen of the province were called on to lead the Vendéan cohorts. All marched in this upheaval under the orders of a peasant who became their general and led them to victory. The Vendéans raised the white flag because under it the Catholic religion had always been respected. Suppressed in the end, but not subjected, they rose as intrepid warriors against the oppression that crushed them or which they feared.

The French clergy, and especially its great dignitaries, have been reproached for the laxity of their morals and the weakness of their faith. The bad times came, they were persecuted, the stain disappeared, and conscience alone prevailed. Prelates as well as simple priests, facing death, resigned themselves to exile rather than betray their religious duties. After amazing the world by their courage, they edified foreign nations by their piety.

We have said that the revolution suspended the force of law. Anarchy and an atrocious tyranny ensued. The scaffold was set up permanently. Youth, maturity, old age, women, girls hardly more than children mounted it with the same courage; it is hard to find even a few cases of weakness among the victims.

Humanity at last reappeared. The Revolution showed the world what crimes, but also what great virtues, so prodigious an upheaval

---

[41] It must be agreed that a sense of terror prompted a certain number of women and old men to flee beyond the frontiers. But almost all the men of active age obeyed what was seen as a demand of honor.

can produce. It quieted down; but a need was felt for an authority to sweep away the ruins and restore the soil. A man favored by victory presented himself. He was accepted as master, but on condition that his favors would go preferably to new men, for no one in France intended to tolerate the superiority of birth. On this condition, and dazzled by a brilliant administration and by glory, the nation submitted to the most absolute authority for the first fifteen years of this century. Then liberty, a secondary and almost extinguished passion, made a dramatic reappearance, but the fear of losing equality slipped in with it and prepared the way for a new revolution.

Characters were enfeebled by the imperial despotism. Military courage did not fail, but the energies of civilian life had been seriously crippled. There was a gradual transformation for the worse. Greed replaced the spirit that prevailed in 1789, and society was threatened by a shameful dissolution, brought on by selfish and sordid calculation of personal interests.

Alexis de Tocqueville

Chapters and Notes for His Unfinished
Book on the French Revolution
(mostly 1857)

Alexis de Tocqueville in 1850. From a portrait by Théodore Chassériaux.
Courtesy Beinecke Library, Yale University

[IN 1856, as he completed and published his *Old Regime and the Revolution*, Tocqueville began to think about its sequel, which in his mind was not so much a sequel as a continuation of the same work. In this year 1856 he wrote two notes to remind himself of his long-range plan.

From the first note it is clear that Tocqueville still had a study of Napoleon I and the First Empire as his ultimate aim. He had expressed this intention as early as 1850, when casting about for a subject on which to write a book.[1] For him, Napoleon and the Empire were phenomena within the French Revolution as a whole. On this great subject he hoped to write a new kind of history, something "grand and original if it is well done."

On the margin of this first note Alexis penned a passing thought that is puzzling and indeed questionable if taken as a statement of historical method. It declares that contemporaries of a great event understand it better than later historians, who may be more successful in filling in details. This marginal note becomes more understandable if we remember that Tocqueville thought of the French Revolution as a continuing process still at work in his own day, so that he himself was one of its contemporaries feeling its "last tremors." He would therefore not attempt a detailed history of the Revolution, but rather an account of its general impact and significance, leaving the details to be filled in by posterity.

In the second note, which he called "first gropings" and dated November–December 1856, we see Tocqueville narrowing down his plan, at least temporarily, to a consideration of the Revolution within the usual chronological scope of the word. In these "gropings" he expected to concentrate on the first period of the Revolution, beginning with the meeting of the Estates General on May 5, 1789. He would then analyze and judge the work of the Constituent Assembly. During 1857 he accumulated materials on the Revolutionary years, and from October through December of 1857 he drafted the seven chapters translated here.

[1] See below, pp. 150 and 227–228.

If we compare these seven chapters with his "first gropings," we see another of Tocqueville's traits, a tendency toward a kind of infinite regression in the focus of his efforts. Back in 1851, he had set out to write a book on Napoleon I as a means of understanding the seizure of power by Napoleon III. He had begun with a study of the situation *preceding* Napoleon's coup d'état of 1799 and had composed in 1852 two fairly finished chapters on the state of France under the Directory.[2] This led him to think that he must go further back into the Revolution itself, of which the result was a whole book on what *preceded* the Revolution—his *Old Regime and the Revolution*, published in June 1856. He now thought that he must turn again to the Revolution, and, as shown in his first gropings, he would begin with the meeting of the Estates General. But the seven chapters that he succeeded in writing dealt entirely with what happened *before* the meeting of the Estates. On what happened *at* the meeting—the transformation of the Estates General into the National Constituent Assembly (which Hervé de Tocqueville had treated at length in 1850, and others before him)—we have from Alexis only a few brief comments and longer summaries of his readings.

There are similar notes, mostly bits and pieces, among Alexis's papers on the following years of the Revolution. But, although published by André Jardin, they are too disjointed and sporadic to be put together in any connected form, and they are not translated in the present book.[3] He clearly intended to treat the Constituent Assembly at length; but how he would have presented it is unclear, since he sometimes said that its work was noble and far-reaching, and sometimes that it was impractical and short-sighted. There is even less in his notes on the climactic years of the Revolution. There is nothing on the flight of Louis XVI and his repudiation of the Constituent Assembly, nothing on the war and invasion of 1792, nothing on the Jacobin club and its radicalization, nor on the Committee of Public Safety and its revolutionary dictatorship, which re-

[2] These two chapters, along with notes on the Revolutionary years, as edited by Jardin, are in OC II, 2, pp. 171–350.

[3] Selections have been translated by John Lukacs in *The "European Revolution" and Correspondence with Gobineau*, New York, 1959, pp. 89–116.

pressed popular revolution and aristocratic and royalist counter-revolution alike. Tocqueville's great theme was the continuance of centralized power from the Old Regime through the Revolution into the First Empire (and then the Second), with the depressing corollary that the quest for liberty seemed always unsuccessful. In the needs of war and revolutionary government he might have found understandable (if unpalatable) reasons for this centralization. He seems not to have seen them. He once referred to the years of the Revolution as "a transitory and fairly uninteresting period separating the administrative Old Regime from the administrative system created by the Consulate and which still rules us."[4] Or, as he put it in another undated jotting, "It was by *moeurs*, not by ideas, that centralization was re-established."[5] It was as if the French simply reverted to centralization from habit, with or without cause or reason.

It is to be observed also that in his preliminary notes Tocqueville suggests the importance of individual persons (he refers to Napoleon, Louis XVI, and Mirabeau) but that in the seven draft chapters he hardly mentions anyone by name except in passing. It was indeed fundamental to Alexis's thinking in all his work, both in his writings and in his political career, to insist on the importance of moral qualities in men of action. Yet there is nothing in these seven chapters like the character sketches of Louis XVI, Necker, Calonne, and Brienne attempted by Hervé. The one place where Alexis expands on an episode involving an individual, and where he adopts a narrative mode, is his account of the arrest of Duval d'Eprémesnil in the hall of the Parlement of Paris. He presents it as an example of liberal resistance to arbitrary power. The contrast in the treatment of d'Eprémesnil by Alexis and by Hervé (see pp. 88 and 171) reveals the difference between their points of view: Alexis sees d'Eprémesnil as a hero of liberty; Hervé regards him with more reservation as a troublesome young man opposing a clumsy but benevolent government.

Tocqueville's two preliminary notes follow.]

[4] André Jardin, *Alexis de Tocqueville, 1805–1859*, Paris, 1984, p. 463.
[5] OC II, 2, p. 200.

I

Original Idea
Earliest General Feeling for the Subject[6]

To be reread from time to time to put me back
on the general course of my thinking (1856)

My subject is:

1. A true portrayal of the man [Napoleon Bonaparte], less a great man than an extraordinary one, whom I take as my object and who until now, it seems to me, has not been portrayed with either accuracy or depth. New side of my subject.

Everything that reveals him in his thoughts, his passions, in his true *self* should attract my particular attention.

2. The advantages for himself that he found in the state of facts and opinions at the time.

3. The means that he used.

But what I want above all to depict, the better to understand him, is the great Revolution in which he played such a principal role. To judge and depict that Revolution with a freer spirit than those who have dealt with it until now, and making use of the light cast on it as it still goes on; that can be grand and original if it is well done.

What I want also to do is to portray the features of the French character in this general revolution or in this phase of humanity: what this Revolution takes from the national character and what the national character adds to it. A new view if I bring to it the freedom of mind of which I am capable, especially today when, no longer actively involved in my time and my country, I feel no urgency to embellish or change anything, and no ardent feelings except to find and report what is true.

[Tocqueville's note in the margin of the last two paragraphs:] We are still too close to the events to know the details (this seems strange, but is true); the details become known only by posthumous revelations and are often unknown to contemporaries. What contemporaries know better than posterity is the movement of minds and general passions of the times of which they feel the last tremors

[6] Ibid., p. 29.

in their own minds and hearts. It is the true relationship between the principal actors and the principal facts, and between the great historical movements, which those close to the times described perceive better than posterity. It is for posterity to write the history of details. Those close to the events are better placed to trace the general history and general causes, the grand movement of facts and current of opinion of which men who are placed too far away cannot form an idea because such things cannot be learned from memoirs.

II

First Gropings[7]

(November and December 1856)

I think that in the first part of a history of the Revolution, which is the part on which the most has been written, it is best to say as little as possible on details of fact. I should be lost in the immensity of it all. But what general features or questions should I choose?

What place to assign to persons? They certainly played a great part at the beginning.

Louis XVI; especially the court; Mirabeau.

My mind is drowned in details and can't see any leading ideas.

I shall not extricate myself if I wish to write a history of this first phase, even of a philosophical kind, or try anything except a few considerations. But what shall they be?

Why did Reform turn so fast into Revolution?

How explain that an apparent and real agreement was followed by violent dissension? How could the Revolution have been made by a riot? Paris. How could the people become suddenly enraged and the most powerful element on the scene?

How explain the powerlessness of individuals? Or the impossibility of civil war? . . .

The first thing to depict is the first period from the meeting of the Estates General to the fall of the Bastille and the formation of the Constituent Assembly. From that moment the Revolution was a fact.

[7] Ibid., pp. 173–174.

Here is the beginning and the most difficult part of the whole book. It is in this short period that I must first concentrate my attention. I can write nothing *a priori*; perhaps the leading ideas will come from an examination of the details.

Choose for this first stage the questions that led to the formation of the Constituent Assembly.

Then judge the work of this Assembly. Distinguish what in its work was true, grand, and durable; then show how it nevertheless threw everything into confusion and failed. This will be a major part of my book.

Apparent unanimity; good dispositions; general love of liberty. First scene. . . .

When I come to an analysis and judgment of the work of the Constituent, the horizon clears; on the one hand, show the grandeur, honesty, and beauty of its principles; on the other, the lack of practical wisdom that ends up in general disorganization. . . .

How the Old Regime fell all of a sudden into Revolution.

Perhaps put this great question first of all: could the Old Regime have fallen without Revolution?

The Violent and Uncertain Agitation of the Human Mind on the Approach of the Revolution[8]

DURING the ten or fifteen years preceding the French Revolution the human mind throughout Europe was gripped by strange, incoherent, and irregular movements, such as had not been seen for centuries, symptoms of a new and extraordinary illness by which contemporaries would have been frightened if they had been able to understand them.

The idea of the greatness of man in general, the omnipotence of his reason, and the unlimited extent of his understanding had penetrated and absorbed everyone's thoughts. With this grand notion of humanity in general was mixed an unnatural contempt for the time in which one lived and the society to which one belonged.

There was an absurd pride in humanity and a singular humility with regard to one's own time and place. Throughout the continent, among the enlightened classes there was less and less of the instinctive love, or almost involuntary respect, usually felt by men of all countries for their own institutions, their traditional customs, or the wisdom or virtue of their fathers.

Everywhere the talk was of the inadequacy, incoherence, and ridiculous features of institutions, the vices of contemporaries, the corruption and rottenness of society.

—All this is evident in novels. That insipid philosophical novel, *Woldemar*, written by F. H. Jacobi in 1780, which despite its interminable twaddle made a great impression at that time, is full of diatribes against the present and predictions of coming catastrophe.

"To me the present state of society seems like a dead and stagnant sea, and that is why I would welcome any inundation, even by bar-

---

[8] [Tocqueville's note written on the jacket containing the draft of this chapter:] A sketch barely roughed out, though written with pains. Do all this over at one rewriting.

barians, to sweep away these infected marshes and uncover a virgin land."

The speaker's friend, Hornick (an earthy man, the butt of the novel), expressed his alarm at hearing such words, and indeed with reason. I think the author would have been even more alarmed if he had really believed in this sweeping away by barbarians.

A little further along: "We live in the ruins of forms and institutions, a monstrous chaos presenting everywhere an image of corruption and death."

This was written in a pretty country villa by a rich man keeping open house, a literary salon where people passed the time in philosophizing without end, exhibiting their tenderness, their excitement, their enthusiasm, and pouring out daily torrents of imaginary tears.

Nothing shows better how far the whims of an idle, agitated, literary society (passion for philosophizing, analyzing sentiments, creating subtleties, sensibility, overheated style) had been diffused all over Europe. The book exaggerates in the heaviness and awkwardness of a German setting the faults in the French spirit of the time.

No great social change was anticipated by princes, ministers, administrators, or those who under different titles conduct human affairs. To them it seemed an absurd chimera to suppose that men could be governed otherwise than the way they were, that what had lasted so long could be replaced by what did not yet exist except in the minds of a few writers, or that the order they saw with their own eyes could be overthrown in an attempt to establish a new order in the midst of disorder and ruin. The possible, for them, went no further than a gradual improvement of what existed. It is curious to see, in the administrative correspondence of the period, able and foresighted government servants drawing up their plans, adjusting their policies, and arranging for the use of their powers in advance for times when the government they worked for, the laws they applied, and the society in which they lived would no longer exist.

It is a common error of men called wise and practical to go on judging, by rules, men whose aim is precisely to change and destroy the rules. But in times when passions take over in human affairs, we should attend less to what experienced people think than to what occupies the imagination of dreamers. . . .

—Cosmopolitanism here (a new word instead of patriotism), the love of humanity replacing the love of country—[9]

We are not to think that this kind of aversion for one's own time and country, which had so strangely affected almost all inhabitants of our continent, was a mere superficial and passing feeling. Ten years later, when the French Revolution had afflicted Germany with all kinds of transformations, accompanied by ruin and death, one of those Germans who . . . [a blank space] reflecting on the past, cried out in a confidential effusion: "What used to be is now in ruins. What new edifice will rise? I do not know. What I can say is that the most horrible outcome would be for the old times of lethargy and effete manners to be born again from this time of terror. You don't perform a play by repeating the first act. So then, forward!"

"Yes," replied his companion, a noble, "the old society ought to perish."[10]

The ten or fifteen years preceding the French Revolution were a time of great prosperity almost everywhere in Europe. The useful arts developed; the need for material enjoyments spread; the commerce and industry to provide for them became more extensive and improved. It may seem that, with life filled with such satisfactions, the mind would turn away from the abstract sciences of man and society to concentrate more on small daily affairs. This is what we see all too much of today, but it is the opposite of what then happened. In all Europe, almost as much as in France, philosophizing and dogmatizing occupied the enlightened classes. Even the classes whose habits and business normally removed them from such discussions took them up passionately whenever they had the leisure. In the most commercial cities of Germany, at Hamburg, Lübeck, and Danzig, men engaged in trade and industry would meet, after

[9] [Note by André Jardin: A new theme that might have followed the theme of distaste for one's own time, as announced above.]

[10] [A note by André Jardin: Tocqueville's notes show that he was quoting from a biography of the German Clemens Theodore Perthes. There is a blank page in the manuscript here, where Tocqueville perhaps intended to insert a passage on England, as indicated in the following note:]

England did not escape from this universal epidemic, but it experienced it in a way suited to its own temperament.

the day's work, to agitate the great questions of the existence of man, his condition, and his happiness. Women, surrounded by their small household tasks, sometimes dreamed of the great problems of our existence.[11]

It was as if everyone was trying to escape at times from his private affairs to interest himself in the great concerns of humanity.

As in France, the pleasures of literature occupied a large place in the busiest lives, and the publication of a book was as great an event in the smallest towns as in the capital cities. Everything was a matter for curiosity, a subject of emotion. It seemed that everyone had a treasure of feelings that he wanted to spread abroad.

A traveler who had been around the world attracted general attention. When Georg Forster, one of the companions of Captain Cook, appeared in Germany in 1774, he was greeted with a kind of craze. There was no small town where he was not fêted. People crowded about him to learn of his adventures from his own mouth, but they especially wanted to hear him tell of the unknown countries he had visited and the customs of new peoples among whom he had lived. They asked whether the simplicity of savages was not worth more than all our riches and our arts, whether their instincts were not better than our virtues. . . .

A certain excommunicated Lutheran priest, an ignorant and quarrelsome man and a drunkard, named Basedow, a kind of caricature of Luther, imagined a new system of schools, which he said would change the habits and ideas of his contemporaries.[12] He touted it in vulgar but vehement language. He was careful to say that his aim was to reform not only the Germans but the human race. He had a simple and easy method by which all men could become enlightened and virtuous without difficulty. All Germany was excited; princes, ministers, nobles, bourgeois, and free cities lent their aid to the innovator. The greatest lords and ladies wrote to Basedow with modest requests for his advice. Mothers hurried to give his books to their children. Throughout Germany the old schools founded by Melanchthon were deserted. A college called the *Philanthropinum* was founded to instruct these reformers of the

---

[11] [Marginal note:] Describe this more fully. Quotations if possible. They give life to the picture.

[12] [J. B. Basedow (1723–1790), well-known educational theorist and reformer.]

human species; it made a great sensation for a while, then disappeared. The enthusiasm collapsed, leaving dismay and confusion. That such a man could produce such effects would be inconceivable if we did not know that, in times of revolution, the influence of innovators comes less from themselves than from what they chance to find in the crowds about them.

It is well known that on the eve of the French Revolution, Europe swarmed with peculiar associations and secret societies, which were then quite new and whose names have long since been forgotten. There were the Swedenborgians, Martinists, Freemasons, Illuminati, and Rosicrucians; the men of strict observance; the sectaries of Mesmer; and many others that were only varieties of these.[13]

The purpose of several of these sects was originally only the private interest of their members. But all now were concerned with the destinies of the human race. Most, at first, were purely philosophical or religious; but all now turned to politics and gave it their full attention. Their methods differed, but all now had a common goal of regenerating societies and reforming governments. Physicians tell us that during epidemics all particular illnesses end up by showing the symptoms of the prevailing malady. The same phenomenon now showed itself in the world of ideas.

There is something else worthy of notice. It was a time when the sciences, in becoming more well defined and certain, discredited the marvelous and made the inexplicable seem simply false, when reason claimed to take the place of authority in all things, putting the real in the place of the imaginary and the free search for knowledge in the place of faith. This was indeed the general direction of thought; yet hardly any of the sects I have just mentioned did not somewhere touch on the invisible, and all bordered in one way or another on the chimerical. Some gave nourishment to mystical imaginings; others believed they had found the secret for changing some of the laws of nature. It was a time when there was no enthusiasm that could not pass for science, no dreamer who could not get himself heard, no impostor who could not be believed. And nothing shows better the troubled agitation of the human mind at that

[13] [In a long note Tocqueville gives details on these groups, and also mentions the Cabalists and Cagliostro.]

time, running this way and that like a hurried traveler who cannot find his way and who sometimes abruptly retraces his steps instead of going forward.

In our time it is poor workers, obscure artisans, and ignorant peasants who ordinarily fill up the secret societies. At the time I am speaking of it was princes, great lords, capitalists, men of trade, and men of letters. When in 1786 the secret papers of the Illuminati were seized on the premises of their chief, Adam Weishaupt, they were found to contain several notably anarchical principles: individual property was said to be the source of all evils, and absolute equality was demanded. These same archives of the sect also contained a list of its adepts; it included only the best-known names in Germany.

Many contemporaries, unable to fathom the general causes producing the strange social upheaval that they witnessed, attributed it to the action of secret societies. As if specific conspiracies could ever explain the sudden destruction of all existing institutions!

The secret societies were assuredly not the cause of the Revolution, but they must be considered one of the most obvious signs of its approach.

It would be wrong to believe that the American Revolution aroused a deep sympathy only in France. Its fame resounded to the extremities of Europe; it was seen everywhere as a signal. Professor Heinrich Steffens, who took part in the rising of Germany against France thirty years later and served it as a soldier right up to the occupation of Paris, tells us in his memoirs of recollections of his early childhood. His father, a doctor at Elsinore, coming home one evening, related incidents of the American war to his children, who were then very young, Heinrich being only seven or eight years old.

"I was then," Steffens writes, "already enough aware of the importance of the American war to be interested with my whole soul in a people who so bravely defended their liberty. . . . I recall vividly what happened in the harbor at Elsinore on the day when news arrived of the peace treaty assuring the triumph of liberty. It was a fine day, and the harbor was filled with ships of all nations. We had awaited the occasion with great impatience. All the ships were dressed as for a holiday; the masts were decorated with long pennants; flags were everywhere; the weather was calm, with just enough wind to flutter the pennants and spread the flags; the firing of cannon and the joyful cries of the crews on the decks added to the air of a festival. My father had invited some of his friends to dinner. They celebrated the victory of the Americans and the triumph of the liberty of peoples, but their joy was mixed with obscure presentiments of the great events that would ensue. It was the bright and gentle dawn of what became a bloody day. My father wished to impress upon us a feeling for political liberty. Contrary to his usual custom he brought us to the table; he tried to make us understand the importance of the event we had been watching, and had us drink with him and his guests to the health of the new republic."

Among such men, in the farthest corners of Europe, who were so moved on hearing of the deeds of a small people of the new world, there were none who understood the deeper and secret cause of the emotion that they felt. They listened to this distant sound as to a sign, without knowing what it portended. It was like the voice of John the Baptist crying in the wilderness that new times were close at hand.

Do not look here for particular causes in all these facts that I have related; they were all only symptoms of the same social malady. Everywhere the old institutions and the old powers were poorly adjusted to new conditions and new needs.

Hence came that strange malaise that made their condition seem intolerable even for great personages and men of the world. Hence that universal idea of change, coming over everyone without being sought and with no one imagining what the change would be. An internal movement, with no motor, seemed to be both disturbing the public life of societies and shaking everyone's ideas and habits on their foundations. People felt that they could no longer hold up as before, but they had no idea which way they would fall. And all Europe offered the spectacle of an immense mass oscillating before collapsing.

How This Vague Agitation of the Human Mind Suddenly Became a Positive Passion in France, and What Form it Took at First

(War on absolute power; Notables)

IN THE YEAR 1787 this vague agitation of the human mind that I have just described, and which had long been disturbing all Europe without any settled direction, suddenly became in France an active passion with a precise goal.

But, strange to say, this goal was not at first the one that the French Revolution would attain; and the men who felt the new passion first and most keenly were the very ones that the Revolution would devour.

In the beginning it was not equality of rights but political liberty that seemed to be aimed at. Those among the French who were the first to act, who shook up society and began the Revolution, belonged not to the lower classes but to the upper. Before descending to the common people, this new hatred of absolute and arbitrary power was felt by the nobles, the priests, the magistrates, and the most privileged of the bourgeoisie, in short, by all those who, standing first in the state after the master, had better means than others to resist him and some hope of sharing in his power.

I shall not relate how financial embarrassments brought Louis XVI to call to his side an assembly of members of the nobility, the clergy, and the high bourgeoisie, and to submit the state of his affairs to this Assembly of Notables. I am discussing history, not narrating it. . . .[14]

Henry IV had used this device to postpone the calling of the Estates General and to give a kind of sanction to his wishes in their ab-

[14] [Marginal note:] Say a word on the composition of the Notables. [See the note at the end of this chapter.]

sence. But times had changed. In 1596 France was emerging from a great revolution; it was weary and uncertain of its strength; it sought only for calm and asked of its chiefs only the semblance of deference. The Notables could then make the country forget the Estates General. In 1787 they reawakened the memory.

In the time of Henry IV the princes, great lords, and rich bourgeois called together and consulted by the king were still the heads of society; they could thus check whatever they set in motion and support royalty even while resisting it. These same classes, under Louis XVI, retained only the externals of power; we have seen how they had already lost the substance of it forever.[15] They were now like those resounding hollow bodies easily broken by a single blow. They could still agitate the people but were unable to guide them.

Since this great change had occurred gradually and secretly, no one yet perceived it clearly. Those who had the greatest interest in it were unaware that it had happened; even their adversaries[16] hardly suspected it. The whole nation had been kept apart from its own affairs and now had no more than a troubled view of itself.

Hardly had they assembled when the Notables, forgetting that they were appointees of the prince, chosen by him to give him advice and not lessons, acted as representatives of the country. They asked to see the accounts, censured the actions of the government, and attacked most of the measures of which they were asked merely to facilitate the execution. The government requested their help, and what it got was opposition.[17]

Public opinion was soon aroused and threw its weight to their side. All talk and writing supported the Notables. There was thus the strange spectacle of a government trying to become popular by measures favorable to the country's interest and yet remaining un-

[15] [Alexis refers here to his *Old Regime and the Revolution*, published over a year before.]

[16] [Alternate version:] the innovators.

[17] [Marginal note to this paragraph:] Depict this more fully, I think, and lead up to it with a passage containing this idea: already for a long time all the malaise that people felt seemed to come together in discontent with the ruling power and change into a spirit of opposition.

[Note by André Jardin: Tocqueville probably decided against introducing this passage because it would have repeated what is said at the end of the chapter.]

popular, and of an assembly resisting the same measures while enjoying public support.[18]

The government proposed to reform the *gabelle* that weighed so heavily and cruelly on the people. It wanted to abolish the *corvée*, reform the *taille*, and suppress the *vingtièmes* from which the upper classes had managed in part to exempt themselves. In place of these abolished or reformed taxes it proposed a land tax on the same basis as our real estate tax today. It pushed out to the frontiers the internal tariffs that hampered commerce and industry. Finally, alongside and almost instead of the intendants who administered each province, it wished to create an elected assembly charged not only with supervising the conduct of affairs but also in most cases with conducting them itself.[19]

All these measures were in the spirit of the time, but all were opposed or put off by the Notables. Yet it was the government that was unpopular and the Notables who had the public voice on their side.

Fearing that he had been misunderstood, the minister Calonne explained in a public document that the effect of the new laws would be to relieve the poor of a part of the tax burden and transfer it to the rich. This was true, and yet he remained unpopular. "The priests," he said in another place, "are citizens and subjects above all else. They should be subject to taxation like all others. If the clergy has debts, it should sell some of its property to pay them." This was to touch one of the most sensitive areas of public opinion, which, however, seemed to feel nothing.

To the reform of the *taille*, the Notables objected that it could not be realized without adding a surcharge on other taxpayers, and in particular on the nobles and clergy whose privileges in the matter of taxation were already reduced to nothing. Against abolition of internal tariffs, they peremptorily raised the principle of provincial rights in the levying of certain taxes, which must be dealt with only with great caution. While approving in principle the creation of provincial assemblies, they desired that, at the least, instead of the three orders being mixed together in these small local bodies, they

[18] [Marginal note:] What I lack are sufficient notions on what passed in this first Assembly of Notables.

[19] [Marginal note:] Verify this as soon as possible.

should be kept separate and always have a gentleman or a prelate as president. "For," said some of the bureaus, "these assemblies would tend toward democracy unless directed by the superior understanding of the two higher orders."[20]

Yet the Notables kept their popularity until the end. They even increased it. In their resistance they were pushed on in the struggle with loud cries. And the king, in hurriedly dismissing them, felt obliged to offer them his thanks.

Several of them were said to be amazed at this public favor and the sudden power that it revealed.

They would have been even more amazed if they had been able to foresee what was to follow. For what they fought against with such popular favor, the new laws that they rejected or tried to delay, rested on the very principles that were to triumph in the Revolution. The traditional institutions through which they blocked the novelties proposed by the government were precisely the institutions that the Revolution would strike down.

What made the Notables popular was not the form of their opposition but the fact of opposition itself. They criticized the abuses of the governing power, censured its wastefulness, and demanded an account of its expenditures; they spoke of the constitutional laws of the country and of fundamental principles limiting the power of the king. Without exactly calling on the nation to regulate its own affairs in the Estates General, they persistently revived the idea of that institution.

It was enough.

The government had long suffered from an ailment, the ordinary and incurable malady of a power that has undertaken the command in everything, to foresee everything, and to do everything. It had become responsible for everything. However different their complaints, all now joined in blaming it; but what had hitherto been only a general inclination now became a universal and impetuous passion. All the unexpressed pain born of frequent contact with ruined institutions, whose wreckage interfered with habits and ideas in a thousand ways, all the repressed anger arising from class divisions, disputed conditions, and ridiculous or oppressive inequali-

---

[20] [Marginal note:] Verify.

ties, now combined against official power. These feelings had long groped for a way to come out into the light of day. When a way opened, they pressed into it blindly. It was not their *natural* route, but it was the first that was offered. The hatred of arbitrary authority thus seemed for a moment to be the sole passion of the French, and the government the common enemy.

[NOTE RELATING TO CHAPTER II]

[TOCQUEVILLE's separate note concerning the composition of the Notables:]

1. about 9 peers of France
2. 20 nobles without rank
3. 8 councillors of state
4. 4 masters of requests
5. 10 marshals
6. 13 bishops or archbishops
7. about 18 first presidents of parlements
8. various other magistrates, attorneys general, or presidents of sovereign courts
9. about 22 municipal officers of principal towns
10. about 12 deputies from the *pays d'états* (Burgundy, Languedoc, Brittany, Artois)

about 125 or 135 persons, counting the princes of the blood and magistrates other than first presidents.

[Marginal note:] An assembly too numerous to be an effective council, and without sufficient authority to render support.

[Tocqueville was more concerned with the effectiveness of the Assembly as a consultative body than with its composition or representativeness. Since a conflict between bourgeoisie and aristocracy was one of his principal themes, it is surprising to find him taking so little note of it in this connection. His figures above may be compared with those given by Hervé de Tocqueville (see p. 65 above). Hervé's list is exactly copied from Droz's book of 1839 (see above, p. 8*n*), which in turn derives from the proceedings of the Assembly of Notables as officially published in 1788: *Procès-verbal de l'Assemblée des Notables tenue à Versailles en l'année 1787*, Paris, Imprimerie royale, 1788, pp. 3–28. Both Hervé de Tocqueville and Joseph Droz comment on the monopoly of the privileged classes in the Assembly and the underrepresentation of the bourgeoisie. As Hervé said, "almost all the representatives of the Third Estate held municipal offices conferring nobility." Joseph Droz, who had himself been born in 1773 into an old family of *parlementaires* at Besançon, made the same point: "The list of notables consisted of 144 names, almost all of which belonged to the two higher orders. The Third Estate was not really admitted . . . to the discussions." (See his *Histoire du règne de Louis XVI*, Paris, 1839, vol. 1, pp. 470–471, and note that Droz's figure of 144 has been used by historians ever since.)

Alexis made no such comments, and his list obscures the preponderance of the nobility. His bishops, marshals, presidents of parlements, and others were nobles. His category of "nobles without rank" was hardly lacking in rank, since it was composed of one prince, four dukes, seven marquises, eight counts, and one baron. This may be seen in Buchez and Roux, from whom Alexis took his list of members of the Assembly. In Buchez and Roux the term *noblesse sans rang* refers not to rank but to the seating arrangements in the hall where formal sessions of the Assembly met and for which they appended a diagram. While princes of the blood, peers of France, and a few others had seats reserved for them individually, those of the *noblesse sans rang* sat in the place reserved for them as a group but without order of precedence among themselves. (See P. J. B. Buchez and P. C. Roux, *Histoire parlementaire de la Révolution française*, 40 vols., Paris; 1834–1838, vol. 1, pp. 482–485.)]

How the Parlement Overturned the Monarchy by the Use of Precedents

(Struggle of the Parlement against the court, from the end
of the first Notables to September 1788)

THE FEUDAL government, in whose ruins people were still living, had been a government in which the arbitrary and the violent went along with much liberty. Under its laws, actions were often compelled, but speech was almost always proud and independent.[21]

The kings had always exercised legislative power, but never without control. When the great political assemblies ceased to exist in France, the parlements took their place in part. When a new law was proclaimed by the king, the parlements, before entering it in their own law books, would explain their objections to him and offer their advice.

There have long been researches on how it first came about that part of the legislative power was usurped by the judicial power.[22] We need look no further than the general customs of the time, which could neither endure nor even conceive of an absolute secret power or an obedience on which at least some discussion was not permitted. The practice was not at all premeditated. It came spontaneously from the habits and ideas of contemporaries, including the habits and ideas of the kings themselves.

An edict, before it was put into effect, was brought before the Parlement. The king's agents set forth its principles and advantages; the magistrates discussed it; all took place in public and in spoken discourse with the virility that characterized medieval institutions. It often happened that the Parlement sent a deputation to the king, sometimes repeatedly, to beg him to modify or withdraw an edict. Sometimes the king came to the Parlement in person; he would let them debate his own law in his own presence with vivacity or even

[21] [Marginal note:] The only good thing here is the wording.
[22] [Variant:] by the Parlement.

166

with violence. But when he had finally expressed his will, every-thing returned to an obedient silence, for the magistrates recognized that they were only the first officers and representatives of the prince, charged with informing and enlightening him but not with forcing him to any course of action.

In 1787 the procedure only followed these ancient precedents of the monarchy. The old machine of government was set in motion but was soon to seem driven by a new and unknown kind of engine, which, instead of making it operate, was about to break it down.

The king, as was the custom, had his new edicts brought to the Parlement, and the Parlement, conforming to usage, remon-strated.[23]

The king replied, the Parlement insisted. Matters had proceeded in this way for centuries, and the nation had heard this sort of polit-ical colloquy between the prince and the magistrates going on over its head from time to time. It had been interrupted only for a while during the reign of Louis XIV. What was now new was the subject of the debate and the nature of the arguments.

This time the Parlement announced that before registering the edicts it must have documentation to support them, and so required communication of the financial accounts, or what would be called a state budget in times when France has had a government under which one could breathe freely. When the king refused, with rea-son, to turn over the whole government to an irresponsible body that had no mandate or to share the legislative power with a court of justice, the Parlement declared that only the nation had the power to grant new taxes and asked that the nation be assembled.

It was a way of capturing the hearts of the people, but only for a moment.

The arguments used by the magistrates were as new as their de-

---

[23] [Note by André Jardin: Reference here is to the edicts of June 1787, listed by Tocqueville as follows in his working note]:
     1. For freedom of the grain trade
     2. Conversion of the *corvée* to a money payment
     3. For provincial assemblies
     4. Territorial subvention or land tax
     5. Stamp tax.
The parlements accepted the first two without objection and the third with amend-ment; they refused the last two.

mands: the king being only the administrator and not the possessor of the public fortune, the representative and chief officer of the nation and not its master, sovereignty resided only in the nation itself; the nation alone could decide on its great affairs; its rights did not depend on the will of the prince but had their source in the nature of man and were as indestructible as that nature itself.[24]

When the Parlement was sent into internal exile by the king, it declared in its protest that freedom of action and speech was an inalienable right of man and, short of tyranny, could be taken away only by regular forms of law.

We must not think that the Parlement presented these principles as innovations. On the contrary, it drew them industriously from ancient depths of the monarchy. Its statements bristled with historical quotations, often in a barbarous Latin of the Middle Ages. It dwelt on capitularies, old royal ordinances, decrees, and precedents from the dim recesses of the past.

It is a strange sight to see these ideas that had hardly been born so wrapped in ancient swaddling clothes.

It was an old tradition of the monarchy that the Parlement in its remonstrances might express itself with a manly candor bordering on rudeness. The Parlement habitually made much noise to obtain little. Words went normally beyond ideas, and a kind of exaggeration of language was permitted. The most absolute rulers had allowed the Parlement this freedom because of its very impotence; they were sure of its obedience, knew that they could hold it within limits, and so gladly left it the consolation of speaking freely. Thus in this well-settled society a sort of solemn comedy was acted out before the country. But now the play had changed and had a different audience.

The Parlement now carried its freedom to a point of license unprecedented in its history, for a new fire burned in it and unconsciously inflamed its language. I dare to say that among governments of our time, although most of them rest on force in greater

---

[24] [Marginal note:] Bring in and accumulate and present together all the new theories expressed by the parlements in this conflict; clothe them insofar as possible in the revolutionary words then already in use; in short, show the philosophy of the eighteenth century and a republican spirit poking its head through the tattered rags of the monarchy.

or lesser degree, there is not one that could let its ministers or its measures be attacked so furiously without falling.

It was especially against taxes and fiscal officers that the judicial bodies, even in calmer times, had the habit of expressing themselves with particular vehemence. Their language would seem inconceivable if it were now used for the first time. But they only repeated what had often been said on the same subject. Since in the old monarchy most taxes were collected by private contractors or their agents, who "farmed" them by a concession from the government, the usual view for centuries had been to see in taxes only a profit made by certain persons, not the common interest that they represented. They were regarded as odious exactions whose evils were evident and whose burden was exaggerated; those who collected them were called public robbers who grew rich by impoverishing everybody else. The government itself, which had granted such powers to the farmers, took the same attitude. It was as if the affairs of the tax-farmers were no business of the government, or the government hoped to escape the outcry that pursued its agents.

Thus when the Parlement said . . .[25] it only followed its general habit and only repeated what had already been said a hundred times. The play was the same but the audience was much larger. The uproar, instead of remaining as usual within the classes whose privileges made them least sensitive to taxation, was now so loud and widely repeated that it reached those who suffered the most and filled them with frenzy.

The Parlement and the king came together on only one point. They agreed on the edict creating new local powers to be called provincial assemblies.

When we reflect on the importance of such a law and the strange revolution in the whole of government that it implied, we cannot but be astonished at the agreement on this occasion between the two most ancient powers of the monarchy, the one in presenting it, the other in accepting it. Nothing makes us understand better how in this country, where everyone including the women spent time in discoursing on government, the science of human afairs was un-

[25] [Note by André Jardin: A blank in the manuscript here, no doubt to make room for a quotation.]

known and how the government, by plunging the nation into such ignorance, ended up by falling into it itself.

—Here show by a rapid analysis how the edict on provincial assemblies managed to demolish the old political system of Europe from top to bottom, replace all at once what was left of feudalism by the democratic republic, aristocracy by democracy, royalty by the republic.—[26]

I am passing no judgment on the value of the change. I say only that it was an immediate and radical change in all the old institutions and that if the Parlement and the king so deliberately took this path together, it was because they did not see where they were going; they were holding hands in the dark.

If the Parlement used new arguments to restore its ancient rights, the government used arguments no less novel to defend its ancient prerogatives.

—Here bring together whatever I find in the replies of the king and his ministers and in works published by their official supporters, which tend most positively to raise the rich against the poor [the poor against the rich?], the unprivileged against the privileged, the bourgeois against the noble. Then say:

It seems, in short, that the king and the Parlement had divided their roles so as to give the quickest and most convenient education to the people, the Parlement undertaking to teach it the vices of royalty; the king, the crimes of the aristocracy. The Parlement attacked a power that it had no wish to destroy; the king insisted on odious rights that he had no wish to exercise.

While the very principles of government were thus under discussion, the daily work of government threatened to come to a halt. Money was lacking. The Parlement had repulsed the tax proposals; it refused to authorize a loan. In this extremity the king tried to force it, being unable to persuade it. He proceeded to its hall and there, before commanding obedience and being less eager to exercise his rights than to affirm them, he allowed the edicts to be discussed again in his presence.

—Here a very brief account of this session, limited to explaining

[26] [See Note 1 at the end of this chapter.]

the principal truths that the king allowed to be expressed for eight hours on this day.—

Meanwhile, after allowing a debate in his presence over the most generally recognized and least feared of the royal rights, the king tried to revive one of the most contested and unpopular of these same rights. He himself had opened the mouths of the speakers; now he would punish them for having spoken. A scene now took place that would make the mildest authority seem like a tyranny.

Two men in particular had called attention to themselves by their bold language and revolutionary dispositions: Goislard and d'Eprémesnil. A few days after the royal session it was decided to arrest them. Forewarned, they fled from their homes and took refuge at the Parlement, which was about to assemble; they put on their judicial robes and mixed in with the crowd of magistrates that formed this great body. Soldiers surrounded the Palace of Justice and guarded the exits. Their commander, the vicomte d'Agoult, entered the *grand' chambre* alone. The whole Parlement was assembled and sitting in its most solemn form. The number of the magistrates, the venerable antiquity of the court, the gravity of their costume and manner, the extent of their powers, the very majesty of the place so filled with all the memories of our history, all made the Parlement the most august and respected object in France after royalty.[27]

At the sight of this assembly the military officer was at first disconcerted. He was requested to state his mandate. He replied gruffly but nervously that he had come to seize two members of the court, and asked that they be pointed out to him. The Parlement sat motionless and silent. He withdrew, then returned, and withdrew again. The Parlement remained unmoving and mute; it neither resisited nor yielded.

Night fell. The soldiers lit their fires outside the Palace as if outside a town under siege. A crowd of people surrounded them but did not press. Troubled but not yet menacing, and looking on from afar by the lights of the bivouac, the crowd only contemplated a spectacle so new and strange in the monarchy: how the oldest gov-

---

[27] [Marginal note:] The difficulty and danger in what I say here is that I cannot enter sufficiently into the narrative of events to interest the reader in the facts, and yet what little narrative there is retards the development of the idea.

ernment in Europe could take it upon itself to teach its people to defy the majesty of ancient institutions and violate the most revered of old powers in their own sanctuary.

It was approaching midnight when d'Eprémesnil at last arose. He thanked the Parlement for its efforts to save him and said that he wished to abuse their patience no longer. He commended the public cause and his children to them, descended the steps, and gave himself up. One might suppose that he left this place to mount the scaffold; he was indeed to mount it, but at another time and under other authorities.

The only witness of this strange scene still living today[28] has told me that on hearing him many wept. One would suppose that it was Regulus leaving Rome for the nail-studded barrel awaiting him in Carthage. The maréchal de Noailles was heard to sob. Alas! how many tears would soon be shed for even higher destinies than these!

These woes were exaggerated but not feigned. In the first days of a revolution emotions go far beyond facts, as at the end they fall far short of them. . . .

It is well known that France was then divided into thirteen judicial areas, each under a parlement. All these parlements were quite independent of one another, all equal in prerogatives, all equally enjoying the power to discuss a legislative order before submitting to it. This seems natural if we remember the time when most of these courts of justice had been established. The different parts of France then differed so much in their interests, outlook, habits, and customs that a uniform legislation could not be applied to all at the same time. The law was usually specific to each province, and it was natural that in each province a parlement should be charged with its "verification." Since then, the French people had become more alike and the laws more uniform, but the power of verification was still divided.

So when a royal edict had been accepted in one part of France, it could still be contested or differently applied in twelve others. Such was surely the case in law, but no longer in usage. A kind of tacit accord had arisen, for men are ordinarily wiser than laws. The particular parlements generally now contested only the acts designed

[28] [E. D. duc de Pasquier (1767–1862).]

especially for their own provinces. Most often, they accepted general laws without debate, or after the parlement [of Paris?] had approved them. But now each parlement wanted to assert itself by its own contribution to a common resistance.

A provision in an edict accepted in Paris might be resisted in a province, or one accepted in a province might be opposed in Paris, so that the government, blocked on all sides at the same time by all kinds of adversaries using all sorts of weapons, looked about in vain for a place where it might overcome the resistance by a single blow.

But what was remarkable was not that the attacks were simultaneous but that they expressed a common spirit. Each of the thirteen courts took a different way, but they all converged on the same point. Their remonstrances, which were published at the time, would fill several volumes. Everywhere in them I have found the same ideas in almost the same words.

All complain. . . .

—Here quotations or at least a concise analysis.—

Listen to the clamors of these magistrates all over France and you will suppose it the confused noise of a crowd; listen attentively to what they say and you will hear a single voice.

The union of parlements was not only a means of the Revolution but also a sign of its coming. It implied that the nation was already one, despite the multitude of institutions that seemed still to divide it into a thousand parts; that no part any longer had a life of its own, but that the whole nation already led a common life, had the same interests, and entertained the same ideas.

—Perhaps, after showing the multiple yet united action of the parlements striking from all directions at once with the same aim,[29] explain how this judicial insurrection was more dangerous than other insurrections for the government, even military mutiny, because it turned against the government all the regular, civil, moral force that is the habitual instrument of power. A government can put down a disturbance from time to time by using the army, but it defends itself every day through the law courts. Disorders in justice,

---

[29] [An alternate version:] This unity of mind, showing for the first time through a diversity of actions, not only announced a revolution but was the certain sign of a revolution already accomplished. Which is to say . . . and announced a new and very dangerous malady.

or its suppression, are enough to engender a state of affairs that no regular government can endure.

The result of this kind of resistance was less the damage that the courts did themselves to the governing power than the damage that they *let be done*. For example, they established the worst of all liberties of the press, a liberty arising not from a conceded right but from the non-execution of the law and paralysis of the right to repress excesses—[the liberty] of meeting, which allowed the members of each order to raise for a moment the barriers that separated them and meet together in common action. The same as between the orders. . . .[30]

Six edicts were then issued simultaneously.

—Analyze them perhaps in very few words to show that they were not bad in themselves, indeed that they realized several of the most useful and important reforms (separation of powers, equality of taxation[31]) that the Revolution was to achieve.

The time had not yet arrived when despotism can get itself excused by democracy by providing order and equality. Without delay, the whole nation rose up. . . .

It was the nobility that entered first and most boldly into the common struggle against the absolute power of the king.

It was by displacing the nobles that absolute government had been established. The nobles were the ones most inconvenienced and humbled when some obscure delegate of the central power, called an "intendant," came every day to regulate their small local affairs without them and often in spite of them. The ruinous state of society stirred up a variety of angry feelings that combined into one common resentment against the government, and it was this common resentment that moved the nobles to action, quite apart from their particular grievances. This may be seen in the nature of their attacks. What they complained of was not that their own po-

---

[30] [At this point André Jardin, in assembling Tocqueville's somewhat chaotic notes and fragments, expresses uncertainty as to how Tocqueville intended to proceed (OC II, 2, p. 68n1). After a gap, in Jardin's reconstruction, Tocqueville mentions the edicts of May 1788, of which he made long and careful analysis (see Note IV, pp. 185–187 below). Presumably, at this point in the present chapter he would have explained the edicts more fully if he had ever been able to revise.]

[31] [Note by André Jardin: Tocqueville is in error here.]

litical privileges were violated but that the common law was being trampled underfoot, freedom of the press curtailed, personal liberty threatened, the provincial estates abolished, the Estates General suspended, the nation treated as a child, and the country deprived of the government of its own affairs.

In this first period of the Revolution, when the war between classes had not yet been declared, the language of the nobility was like that of other classes,[32] except that it went further and adopted a higher tone. Their opposition had traits of republicanism, with the same ideas and the same strong feelings animating hearts more proud and minds more accustomed to looking at human greatness face to face.

—Here bring together all the facts belonging to this period before withdrawal of the edicts that illustrate what I have just said *by their actions*: their meetings, their writings, their hesitation in leading soldiers against demonstrators, the nobles of Brittany ready to arm the peasants in a struggle against the royal power! Then resume:—

The opposition of the clergy was no less decided, though more discreet. It naturally took a form characteristic of that body.

—Try to determine the particular character of this clerical opposition, what it had that was special in language and actions; show the particular features of the clergy in all this excitement, the speeches before the parlements, especially at Troyes, the instructions issued by bishops, the assembly of the clergy which *I think* was of this period.[33]

At the beginning of the struggle the bourgeoisie was timid and uncertain. It was on the bourgeoisie that the government counted for relief in its distress without losing its ancient rights. It was the particular interests and feelings of this class that the new measures were intended to satisfy. But the bourgeoisie, long accustomed to obey, joined in the resistance apprehensively, with circumspection, still deferential to the government even in opposing it, recognizing its rights while objecting to the use made of them, tempted in a way by its favors, and ready to accept the absolute power if only given some role in it. Even where the bourgeoisie took the lead, it would

[32] [Variant:] the bourgeoisie.
[33] [Note by André Jardin: Tocqueville is in error here.]

not risk going alone but advanced as if sheltered by the upper classes. It marched under their protection, sharing in their angry excitement but filled also with feelings of its own as expressed by its own spokesmen.

Then, as the struggle was prolonged, the bourgeoisie became more excited, bolder, more aroused, and moved on ahead of the other classes, taking the leading role which it held until the common people came upon the stage.

—Here strengthen this portrayal with facts. I am inclined to think that in this first part of the struggle the upper classes (whether sword nobility or robe nobility) were always ahead of the bourgeoisie in both language and action, and that the bourgeoisie came to the fore and took the lead, as I have said, only when the problem was the meeting of the Estates General and the class question came into the open. Until then, the bourgeoisie followed rather than led (but see the episode in Dauphiny, where, it seems to me, even at this early stage, the bourgeoisie is in the lead, yet never venturing to act alone). It benefited from the agitation of the upper classes to gain concessions for itself much more than it incited them.—

In this first phase of the struggle no trace of class war.[34] One single passion is evident, building up into a common spirit of opposition.

—Rapid and lively description of this spirit as expressed in both large and small matters, appearing everywhere and taking all forms, even those that distort it.—

Some in this struggle against the government appealed to what was left of old liberties . . . [several lines blank].

One man claimed some old privilege of his class, another some long-recognized right of his occupation. In the ardor of attack on the government all kinds of weapons were resorted to, even those that were awkward. It might seem that the aim of the coming revolution was not the destruction of the Old Regime but its restoration. So difficult is it for individuals caught up in great social movements to recognize the true motive force among the causes that impel them! Who would have said that what produced the appeal to

---

[34] [Marginal note:] Quotation to establish this. Reciprocal compliments.

so many traditional rights was the very passion that led on irresistibly to the abolition of them all!

In all this tumult of the upper classes let us try to hear the sound of the storm that begins to agitate the broad sea of the people.

I can see no sign, at our present distance from these events, that shows the population of the countryside to be yet aroused. The peasants go silently about their affairs. This huge part of the nation is mute and as if invisible. The common people in the towns show little of the excitement of the upper classes and remain at first indifferent to the commotion going on over their heads. But when they begin to act, they are clearly moved by a hitherto unknown spirit.

I have said in another part of this work that under the Old Regime nothing was more common than riots; the government was both so strong and so . . . [blank] that it purposely let these passing outbursts run their course. But the moment had come when old things took on new characteristics, riots as well as everything else.

—Here study the facts. Show these shouts in the night, these executions in effigy, this unexpected resistance; something violent, wild, and cruel revealing itself.

Paris, which a hundred thousand men can hardly hold down today, was then kept in order only by the watch (define this). This time, the watch was insufficient.—

At the sight of such a new and widespread opposition the government was at first surprised and troubled rather than defeated. It tried all its old arms in turn, and it forged new ones, but this time in vain: admonitions, *lettres de cachet*, exiles to the provinces, employing enough violence to irritate but never enough to intimidate. In any case, a whole people is not to be intimidated.

It sought to arouse the feelings of the people against the rich, of the bourgeoisie against the nobility, of the lower organs of justice against the upper. It was the old game, but now played in vain. It offered favors of money, but men were too aroused to be venal. It appointed new judges, most of whom refused to serve. It tried to distract public attention, which remained fixed. Unable to stop or even limit the freedom of the press, it tried to make it serve its own purpose, going to great expense to have little things written in its defense, and the result was to elicit a thousand pamphlets that attacked it.

At last came an incident that precipitated the crisis. The Parlement of Dauphiny had resisted like the others, and had been punished like the others. But nowhere had the cause it upheld found such unanimous support and such vigorous defenders.

—Specific situation of the province. The *taille réelle*.—[35]

The former estates [unfinished sentence].

Class grievances perhaps more acute at first than elsewhere. But the common passion silenced all particular passions for a moment.

But where in most other provinces the different classes carried on the war against the government separately and without agreement, in Dauphiny they joined politically together to prepare their resistance. For centuries in the past, Dauphiny had had its own meetings of estates. A few nobles, a few ecclesiastics, and a few bourgeois, after coming together spontaneously at Grenoble, boldly dared to call a meeting of the provincial estates that had been suspended since [blank, actually 1628]. They incited the nobility, the clergy, and the Third Estate to assemble in a château situated [blank] and called Vizille, and give an air of regularity to what was a disorderly proceeding.

—Since I should give importance to these facts in Dauphiny, I must study them better and find what lies beneath them. Thus it seems to me that most of the gentlemen at the assembly of Vizille had a somewhat doubtful right to attend the estates, so that their liberalism was mixed with a kind of relatively democratic spirit.

But, of the clergy, I think that there were hardly any at Vizille except the curés, that is, ecclesiastics who (doubtless) would not have the right of entry into the old estates.

Take care, in making these fine distinctions, not to lose sight of the main point to be emphasized, namely the momentary union of classes and its immediate result of making the absolute power helpless.

Get to know Vizille, its appearance, its location, the château built by Lesdiguières, the great *feudal* château. (Try to see pictures of Vizille, or Vizille itself if possible.)

---

[35] [The *taille*, the oldest continuing regular tax of the French monarchy, was *réelle* where it fell on the status of the land (not of the person), so that it was paid even by nobles who possessed non-noble land or *terre roturière*. So far as nobles possessed such land, they enjoyed less privilege by way of tax exemption.]

Narrate as best I can the affairs of this assembly after re-reading all the notes I have on it. Then say:—

The assembly of Vizille had a great impact throughout France. It was the last time that an event occurring outside Paris exerted so much influence on the general destiny of the country.

The government feared that what had been done so boldly in Dauphiny would be imitated elsewhere. It finally despaired of overcoming the resistance and admitted its defeat. Louis XVI discharged his ministers, abolished or suspended the edicts, and recalled the parlements.

—Make the reader realize that this time it was not merely a matter of concessions on details. It was absolute government that was renounced. It was a sharing in government that was accepted, and for which assurance was given by serious promises of the Estates General.—

It may be said that from this moment the Revolution had triumphed, though it had not yet shown its true colors.

We often find authors writing before the end of 1788 using such expressions as "things happened in such-and-such a way before the Revolution." We are surprised, since we are in the habit of hearing about the Revolution of 1789. But if we consider the significant actions and public innnovations of this year 1788, we see that for centuries there had been no such great change in class relationships or in the government of the country. It was indeed a very great revolution, but one that would soon be lost in the immensity of the one that followed, and so would disappear from the view of history.

We may wonder at the number and the magnitude of the mistakes that the government of Louis XVI had to make before bringing public affairs to the condition they were now in. Yet, arrived at this point, its yielding cannot be seen as a crime. The government abdicated its absolute authority because it had no means of defending it. It could not take shelter in the laws; its own courts were against it. It could not prevail by force; its army chiefs viewed its aims with repugnance. In the old France the absolute authority had never been of a crude kind. It had not been born on the battlefield and had never been maintained by arms. It was essentially a civilian despotism founded less on violence than on art.

The king had been able to create this unrestricted authority only by dividing the classes, isolating each within its own prejudices, jealousies, and hatreds, so as never to have to deal with more than one of them at a time and so be able to bring against that one the full weight of all the others.

When the French who formed these different classes, breaking through the barriers that had been raised against them, met together in common resistance if only for a single day, it was enough to put the absolute government at their mercy. It was bound to be vanquished on the day when they agreed. And so it was.

The Assembly of Vizille was the material signal, visible to all, of this new union and what it could produce. Thus an event happening in a small province in a corner of the Alps was decisive for all of France. A particular incident suddenly became a principal fact. It revealed to every onlooker what had been visible only to some, it showed everyone where the decisive force lay, and so in a flash determined the victory.

[NOTES RELATING TO CHAPTER III]

[I]

KING'S PROJECT for provincial assemblies presented to the Notables of 1787:
1. Elective assemblies
2. Elected every three years
3. From all estates without distinction.

The first level of these assemblies to be in rural parishes and towns; the second, in districts formed from a certain number of parishes and towns of the area; the third, a meeting of the whole province.

So that there are to be three kinds of assemblies:
1. Provincial [sic: clearly meaning "parish"] and municipal assemblies composed of property owners.
2. District assemblies formed by deputies of towns and parishes.
3. Finally, provincial assemblies whose members are deputies from the districts.

Obviously this plan was a far cry from the Old Regime. Shifting society abruptly to a new footing, it meant the radical destruction of the old order of things as formed in the Middle Ages and of which traces still survived. It was a whole administration of the country without nobility and clergy.[36]

When we see the king, for no compelling reason, putting forward such a plan, we may conclude:

1. How far the old society was dead at the back of men's minds without their realizing it.
2. How the ideas appearing in connection with the Estates General were a natural growth.

[II]

[The Tone of the Remonstrances of the Parlement of Paris]

REMONSTRANCE OF JULY 24, 1787: AN OUTSPOKEN LESSON FOR THE KING.

The general tone of these remonstrances is to lecture the king rather rudely in both form and substance. In this there was nothing absolutely new. Even under the most powerful kings, before Louis XIV, the parlements had used language whose firmness reached the point of rudeness. But on the one hand, the king could tolerate such language because he was well established among solid and uncontested institutions, and on the other hand, the Parlement that addressed and admonished him so roughly was his principal support against the powers that he feared the most: the nobility and the church. He was therefore not sorry to see the Parlement adopt a tone of independence that strengthened an instrument in his own hands.

Hence there had grown up a kind of tradition of speaking freely, of a bold and even exaggerated style in addressing the king, which had no connection with any corresponding action in the minds of

---

[36] [Tocqueville's note on this note:] According to the project, an income of 600 livres a year was needed to vote in the parish. It was ARISTOCRATIC but not nobiliary. [Tocqueville's inattention to money and numbers is apparent here. An income of 600 livres a year was modest by eighteenth-century standards. A skilled artisan might earn as much, but even if it came to a nonworking owner of property it would hardly make him "aristocratic."]

the king, the nation, or the Parlement itself. It was a kind of empty noise authorized by custom. The king willingly let his Parlement say things that would have bordered on high treason if said by an assembly of nobles or a *grand seigneur*.

These habits of an old feudal society transported into a democratic society in which the people were to play the leading role, instead of producing an empty noise, could not fail to produce revolution. In our own day there is no sovereign power, even in the freest state, that would not find itself in a conflict or a revolution if it allowed language to be used against it such as the Parlement of Paris used against the king in the document that I am analyzing. In its language and conduct there was an anachronism that passed unnoticed but would soon be revealed by the consequences. . . .

The inflation of sentiments, the exaggerated words, the incoherence of images, the references to antiquity that characterized the language of the Revolution were all already in the national way of speaking.

It was impermissible to have calm feelings about anything. It was a necessity, even a commonplace, to refer to the passion at the bottom of one's heart even in cases where it was not felt. Nothing could be talked about simply. Expression had always to go beyond the idea or feeling to be expressed.

MARCH 11, 1788, ETC. NEW REMONSTRANCES ON LETTRES DE CACHET.

[Since November 1787 the duc d'Orléans had been sent into internal exile and two members of the Parlement of Paris imprisoned.]

We see the struggle changing its character. It is no longer a question of registering laws, but a direct struggle against the royal power and existing institutions.

The despotism of *lettres de cachet* painted in the most frightful terms. "It seems inconceivable to dispose of men without judging them, or even hearing them, to plunge them and keep them in darkness where the light of day cannot penetrate, nor any considerations of law, the cry of nature, or the voice of friendship be heard."

PHILOSOPHICAL AND LITERARY LANGUAGE. The *lettres de cachet* are contrary to the laws of nature, man is born free. Philosophical and very abstract discussion of the meaning of human liberty. . . .

The *lettres de cachet* are incompatible with the use of reason, repugnant to human nature, a menace to the rights of man, contrary to the highest principles of the human race.

DEMOCRATIC LANGUAGE. The *lettres de cachet* are used against the poor in favor of the rich. Two citizens are imagined facing each other in an oratorical style. One of them concludes: "Is poverty then a crime? Is simple humanity no longer a title? Is a poor man without credit no longer a citizen?"

THE BASTILLE DESIGNATED IN ADVANCE FOR POPULAR FURY. "Why can Your Majesty not question these victims of arbitrary power, confined and forgotten in impenetrable prisons where injustice and silence reign?" . . . who have been put there "by intrigue, greed, jealousy of power, thirst for vengeance, fear or hatred of justice, or the simple convenience of one man?"

IS THIS DOCUMENT GENUINE? I wonder whether this remonstrance may not be apocryphal. If it is genuine, we should not be surprised at the strength of passions at the time, which make people lose their common sense in attacking so violently an abuse they have tolerated for 150 years without saying a word.

MAY 3, 1788. EXTRAORDINARY SESSION OF PARLEMENT; NEW REMONSTRANCES; MANIFESTO OF CIVIL WAR [after Brienne's failure to obtain financial relief and his decision to reorganize the judiciary].

The government prepares a coup d'état; the Parlement, forewarned, meets and adopts a true bill of rights in which, in the name of *imprescriptible laws* of the nation, it includes the voting of taxes by the Estates General, the irremovability of magistrates, the right of Parlement to register laws, individual liberty and the right to be judged only by one's natural judges. In addition, each member engages himself not to become a member of any other court.

In the preamble the Parlement states that the only cause of the dangers that menace it is its refusal to surrender the public fortune or go along with the old, wasteful habits.

All this was meant to be read and posted in public.

When we see such acts, what surprises us is not that they led to agitation and insurrection but that they did not produce them sooner. The only explanation is the old habit of obedience and failure to understand revolutions.

MAY 4. REMONSTRANCES OF THE PARLEMENT, confirming the resolution adopted the day before. This remonstrance is hardly a judicial document, rather a political one. It speaks the language of civil war, it is a rolling of drums, and all the grand, big words of the Revolution are in it. We are menaced by an "excess of despotism." . . . "Slaves substituted for subjects."

The past and the king's predecessors are attacked in an inflamed style. "Richelieu and his cruelties, Louis XIV and his glory, the Regency and its disorders, the ministers of Louis XV and their indifference, had forever blotted out the very name of the nation; all the stages through which peoples pass on the way to self-abandonment: terror, enthusiasm, corruption, indifference, none were neglected by the ministry to bring on the nation's fall."

"If the Parlement did not oppose, the government would in the end declare itself the co-owner of its subjects' property and master of their freedom."

[III]
[The King's Appeal to Anti-Aristocratic Opinion]

APRIL 17, 1788. THE KING'S REPLY TO THE PARLEMENT.

"If a plurality of my courts were to force my will, the monarchy would be only an aristocracy of magistrates. It would be a strange constitution in which the lawmaking power was subject to as many wills as there are courts of justice in the kingdom."

The king, in calling them "aristocrats," had found the sensitive spot in the nation. So we note that the Parlement became almost furious at the word.

"Ministers see in us no more than ambitious aristocrats when we refuse to share in their despotism."

The word ARISTOCRAT, so often used since, is now taken in this [unfavorable] sense:

"No, Sire, no ARISTOCRACY in France, but no despotism either." Note:

1. The hidden power of this democratic element in the nation, when men, without seeing it clearly, have a confused sense that the most wounding blow that the king can deliver to his adversaries (1788) is to call them "aristocrats."

2. The mistakes of the upper classes, the general confusion and profound ignorance of all the laws of politics, shown in the phrase "no aristocracy" pronounced by men who from any point of view were the greatest partisans of aristocracy and who, if they wanted anything, wanted to found liberty on old institutions saturated with aristocracy.

A PROTEST OF THE THIRD ESTATE TO THE KING AFTER THE EDICTS OF MAY 8.

One of those pamphlets attributed to writers hired by the [royal] court.

The attempt here is to prove that the Parlement is aroused only by the threat to privileges, that they wish to preserve the right of not paying taxes. What is happening, according to the author, is a formidable alliance of the nobility of the sword and nobility of the robe, under pretense of liberty, to go on humiliating the Third Estate, which only the king defends and wants to raise up.

A premature effort, but worth being considered, at that union of democracy and absolute power to destroy privileges and aristocracy for the benefit of despotism. An effort so often and happily repeated since.

[IV]
[The Edicts of May 1788]

MAY 8, 1788. LIT DE JUSTICE.[37] The Parlement is commanded to appear at Versailles, where a *lit de justice*, the last of the monarchy, is held.

HOW THE KING ENTERS FULLY INTO THE SPIRIT OF THE TIME AND EVEN THE COURSE OF THE REVOLUTION, AND YET CANNOT MAKE HIMSELF POPULAR.

1. Justice made more accessible. An organization such as we have today, but still not winning popular favor.

a) *petits bailliages* (presidial courts) with an increased range of final jurisdiction.

b) *grands bailliages* judging criminal cases as courts of last resort and civil cases involving less than 20,000 livres.

[37] [See the Glossary for this and other untranslated words.]

c) parlements for appeals of cases involving more than 20,000 livres and special cases involving privileged persons. It is evident that these are our courts of first instance and appellate courts.[38]

The Parlement, left in existence with reduced powers, is obviously supernumerary, maintained so as not to shock the sovereign courts too violently, but a useless piece due to disappear at some convenient future time.

2. SUPPRESSION OF ALL EXCEPTIONAL COURTS. Contentious issues handled by such courts transferred to the presidials, the *grands bailliages*, or the parlements according to the matter in question.

This great reform reflected all the new ideas on simplification and unity of justice. It destroyed a multitude of offices, as was universally demanded.

It was essentially liberal in transferring to the ordinary courts all disputes in which the government had an interest.

This aspect of it was less striking to contemporaries than it is to us. Since judges in the exceptional courts were irremovable and independent, contemporaries complained that justice was badly administered, where we would blame it above all for not being impartial.

3. REFORM OF THE PENAL LAW.

a) Death sentences to be followed by a period of delay during which recourse may be had to the king.

b) Abolition of the penitent's stool, which shamed the accused before any conviction.

c) Judges required to give their reasons for decisions in criminal cases.

d) The *question préalable* abolished.[39]

e) Indemnities to be paid to accused persons if acquitted.

---

[38] [Tocqueville's note:] On September 25, 1788, at the opening session of the Parlement, the attorney general, Séguier, delivered a critique of the edicts, and especially this one, in which he raised the most imaginary objections, denouncing as impracticable what has existed easily and without interruption since 1789. Curious to read and perhaps useful to say.

[39] [This was the kind of *question*, or torture, used against persons condemned to death to extract information on accomplices. The *question préparatoire*, or torture to force confession, had been abolished in 1780 and had fallen into disuse before that date.]

All this was strongly demanded by public opinion, was in the spirit of the new age, and has been realized since, except for the last item.

4. REDUCTION IN THE NUMBER OF POSITIONS IN THE PARLEMENT. A natural result of the reduction of its business. The king says, with reason, that the principle of irremovability applies only to individuals and cannot prevent the suppression of functions.

Precautions to ease the situation of those whose offices are suppressed; their costs immediately reimbursed; they have a right to new appointments.

Absolutely nothing here of which anyone except the Parlement could complain.

5. ESTABLISHMENT OF A PLENARY COURT. This was the most direct blow against the parlements. They lose the power of registration and hence the right of remonstrance, which is transferred to a single body on which they are generously represented but which takes political power out of their hands.

Grounds for the edicts in the spirit of the time. The reasons given by the king were excellent and conformed to the secret passion of the time for unity and uniformity in the law. Yet it was all seen as a triumph of absolute government. The measure had the following disadvantages:

a) It struck at the *whole* magistracy and not merely at the Parlement of Paris.

b) Yet it left the parlements still in existence.

c) It was useless if there was a real desire to convene the Estates General. It produced a huge and unnecessary agitation, for the arrival of the Estates General would in fact put an end to administration by magistrates.

d) And finally, it created a single powerful body which in certain circumstances might have become formidable.

6. ALL THE PARLEMENTS ARE PUT ON VACATION. Suppression of justice throughout the kingdom. It would be impossible to offer a program more effective in arousing all classes and inflaming their worst imaginings simultaneously.

The Estates General should have been summoned immediately.

[V]

[The New Character of Riots]

FIRST INSURRECTION IN PARIS. THE PEOPLE REAPPEAR ON THE
SCENE. THE MONSTER SHOWS ITS HEAD.

[After Brienne's dismissal and Necker's return to office, August
1788:]

Learning of these events, the people of Paris engage in tumultuous and joyful demonstrations, explode fireworks, burn the minister in effigy, insult the guard. They are put down violently, as in
the past, but this time they take to arms, burn guardhouses, disarm
soldiers, try to set fire to the hôtel Lamoignon, and are checked only
by the Gardes françaises.

I think this is the first riot involving bloodshed since the days of
the Fronde [since 1648].

NEW SPIRIT IN RIOTING. There had always been grain riots in
France. But they had been the work of unorganized crowds without
objective or capacity for resistance. Now we see rioting as we have
known it since, that is, involving a violent crowd with some organization and aim entering knowingly into civil war and breaking
down opposition.

The terrible genius of the Revolutionary riots is already present,
but it is still a child.

A pamphlet of the time, signed "Charon" (an unknown person),
well written and even-tempered, divides the population into the
public, the *populace*, and the *rabble*. He says that in this riot the public
encouraged the populace and the populace incited the rabble. It is
the story of all great riots. How many of them we have seen since!

CAUSES TURNING THE POPULAR JOY INTO VIOLENCE. The same
author says: "How many evils have come from the suspension of
the law courts? They have affected all classes. They have combined
with the troubles of our workshops brought on by the trade treaty,[40]
the shortage of raw materials, the scarcity of money due to fear, and
the general stoppage of circulation."

PARTICULAR CAUSES TURNING THE REVOLUTION TO POPULAR
VIOLENCE. Independently of the general causes of a revolution and

[40] [The free trade treaty of 1786 with England. See above, p. 66.]

of a popular revolution, we must consider the economic crisis, which, in the Revolution of 1789 as in modern revolutions, was one of the most effective among secondary causes.

FERMENTATION ALREADY AT WORK. REVOLUTIONARY SPIRIT DEVELOPED BEFORE THE REVOLUTION IN THE MINDS OF THE PEOPLE. Everything that had happened for two years, while not yet bringing the people into the streets, was preparing them for it and making them revolutionary before the Revolution.

The author tells, I think truthfully, of a conversation with his shoemaker, who said that food prices were too high and entirely out of proportion to wages—that the royal court was too expensive—that people were overwhelmed with taxes—that everything was going up. Although you pay us six or seven livres for a fancy shoe, we earn much less than when prices were lower. All that will change only when the Estates General meet.

ANOTHER CAUSE OF POPULAR AGITATION. YOU MIGHT BE LISTENING TO ONE OF OUR CONTEMPORARIES, AND THIS IS BEFORE THE CONSTITUENT ASSEMBLY. Since the confusion of ranks and status, says this author, nothing is respected except enough income to meet the pressing needs of ordinary well-being. Every man at the lower levels of his occupation wants to get out of them. The general dissatisfaction keeps everybody in a state of continuous instability—materialistic artisans—no more good fellowship—much poverty and many efforts to overcome it—tendencies to insubordination (without much success)—unbridled freedom in the lower social ranks—demoralizing and often libelous performances in the cheap theaters.

This is all the more remarkable since the author is very hostile to the government and its measures, happy at the fall of the minister that caused the riot, and extremely indulgent to the rioters in almost siding with them against the watch.

How the Parlements, Just as They Thought Themselves Masters, Suddenly Discovered They Were Nothing[41]

WITH THE DEFEAT of the royal authority, the parlements at first thought that they were the ones that had triumphed. They returned to their bench as if after a victory, not an amnesty; and as victors, they supposed that the delights of victory would now be theirs.

The king, in annulling the edicts creating new supreme judges, had ordered that at least the decisions they had rendered should be respected. But the parlements declared void whatever had been decided without them. They arraigned before them the insolent magistrates who had aspired to take their place, and finding medieval language for such a novel offense, they declared them "branded with infamy." One could see throughout France how the friends of the king were punished for having obeyed him and learned by an experience not to be forgotten that obedience henceforth gave no safety.

The intoxication of the parlementary magistrates is easy to understand. Never had Louis XIV in all his glory been the subject of such universal adulation, if that is the right word for laudatory excesses inspired by genuine and public-spirited feeling.

—Here put all the titles bestowed on them: senators, heroes, etc.—

When the Parlement of Paris was exiled to Troyes (August–September 1787), all the official bodies of the town came in succession to lay their homage at its feet, as if it were the sole sovereign in the country.

—They came bearing the incense of hyperbolic praises: "Their fate plunges us into grief and consternation. . . . They are generous citizens, compassionate and virtuous magistrates. . . ."

[41] [See the translator's note, pp. 194–195 below.]

The officers of the mint at Troyes: "Our descendants will know that this temple (the Palace of Justice)[42] became the sacred place of your oracles (the place where you handed down your decisions); they will know that their forefathers were witnesses to your patriotic decrees." (I doubt it!)

"You arouse a determination to die for their country in all French hearts. . . . You console the nation in its woes. . . . Your actions are sublime acts of energy and patriotism. . . . The Parlement is an august senate. . . . The principles it upholds are those by which the monarchy is constituted. . . . The cry of the nation recognizes the councillors of the Parlement as its fathers. . . . We do homage to your patriotic virtues and adorn your brows with civic crowns. . . . All Frenchman look upon you with tenderness and veneration."

The Church itself came with its compliments. The cathedral chapter of Troyes: "As much as other orders in the state we have seen with pain . . . this universal mourning of the nation as you are deprived of your functions and removed from the bosom of your families . . . ; in all of which we beheld a spectacle of shame, and while these august halls resounded with the accents of public sorrow, we betook our own sorrows and supplications into our holy temple." (In ordinary style: while others came to the Palace of Justice with their compliments, we prayed for you and your cause in our churches.) "We will follow you with our benedictions, and will no longer conceal the extent of our veneration and our love under cover of our duties of hospitality. Our country and our religion call for a lasting monument to you and what you have done."

Even the university came in its robes and square caps to present its homage in bad nasal Latin:

"Illustrissimi senatus princeps [*sic*: principes?] praesides insulati, senatores integerrimi: we share in the general emotion and testify to the keen sentiments of admiration aroused by your heroic patriotism and constancy in defending the interests of the people. . . . Olden times esteemed only the military valor that made legions of heroes rush from their homes. . . . Today we see heroes of peace in the sanctuary of justice. . . .

---

[42] [The phrases in parentheses here and in the next paragraphs are Tocqueville's ironic comments on these quotations.]

"The nation watches you with enthusiasm. You are under the eyes of a Europe made attentive and touched by the spectacle that you offer. . . .

"The palace in which your oracles once re-echoed (the Palace of Justice) has heard only the cries and groans of the citizens since your departure. The nation will raise altars to this august senate, for peace has its heroes as well as war. . . . They are fathers of their country who carried the truth into the palace of kings and pleaded there the cause of the people. . . . Like those high-minded Romans who after defeating the enemies of the state were honored by a triumph before the eyes of their fellow citizens, you will enjoy a triumph (the king had just withdrawn a tax) that will assure you an immortal memory."—

It would be impossible for a judicial body not to be elated when it found itself so suddenly bathed in the delights of political popularity. The first president replied to each address like a king, in a few words, assuring the speaker of the benevolence of the court.

In several provinces the arrest or exile of magistrates had led to riots. In each case their return produced almost insane manifestations of popular joy. In France there are hardly any strong emotions without a bit of absurd exaggeration, or deep concerns that do not degenerate into a bit of a show.

—Principally what happened in Dauphiny and at Bordeaux.[43] The scene at Bordeaux would be excellent if it could be recounted quickly and naturally, yet clearly. But how to make the reader feel the comedy in the crowds swarming around the carriage blocking the door, and pursuing the first president into his own house?—

Only a few days had passed when the commotion ended, enthusiasm collapsed, and solitude engulfed them. Not only did the public become indifferent, but all the grievances ever expressed against them, including those that the government had tried to exploit, were now thrown in their faces.

They had been called lawgivers and fathers of their country; now they were not even wanted as judges.

—Here all the reproaches against them at this time.—[44]

[43] [See Tocqueville's note, pp. 196–197 below.]
[44] [See Tocqueville's note below, pp. 198–199.]

For the Parlement of Paris, this fall from popular favor was especially sudden and terrible.

—Portray the isolation, impotence, despair, and sadness so well reproduced in the memoirs of Pasquier, the haughty vengeance of royal power, the nullifying of d'Eprémesnil, their amazement and inability to understand. . . .[45] They question one another to find out what. . . .—

These magistrates could not see that the flood that had raised them was the very one that now drowned them.[46] How often in my time have I seen with my own eyes a spectacle like what I have just described!

—Develop the reasons for this.—

Originally the Parlement had been composed of jurisconsults or lawyers chosen by the king from the most capable in their profession. Merit had opened the way to the highest honors of the magistracy for men born in the most humble conditions. The Parlement, then, like the Church, was one of those powerful democratic institutions born and implanted in the aristocratic soil of the Middle Ages, which it penetrated with a kind of equality.

Later the kings, to obtain money, put the right of rendering justice up for sale. The Parlement filled up with rich families that considered the national administration of justice to be their particular privilege. Soon, and with increasingly jealous care, they kept out all others, obeying that singular impulse that seemed to push every particular body into becoming more and more a little closed aristocracy, just as the ideas and habits of the nation made society incline more and more toward democracy. Rules that would never have been accepted in feudal times required that judges in the high courts of justice must be gentlemen.

Surely nothing could be more contrary to the ideas of the time than a judicial caste that had purchased the exclusive right to render justice. No institution, in fact, had been criticized more often and more bitterly for a century than the venality of office.

These judges, whose principle of organization could not be maintained, nevertheless had a rare merit that our better constituted tri-

---

[45] [See Tocqueville's note below, pp. 197–198.]
[46] [See Tocqueville's note below, pp. 200–201.]

bunals today hardly possess. They were independent; they obeyed no passions but their own.[47]

After all the intermediate powers that could balance or moderate the unlimited power of the king had been overthrown, the Parlement alone remained standing.

It could speak when others were silent. It could hold firm for a moment, when all others had long been obliged to bend. Hence it became popular as soon as the government ceased to be so. And when the hatred of despotism became the ardent passion and common sentiment of all the French, the Parlement appeared as the only avenue of freedom remaining open for the country. The faults for which it had been blamed now seemed to be a kind of political guarantee; its very vices offered a shelter. Its spirit of domination, its pride, and its prejudices provided arms to be used by the nation.

But when the absolute power had been definitively overcome and the nation no longer needed a champion to defend its rights, the Parlement became again what it had been before: an old, deformed, and discredited institution handed down from the Middle Ages, and it again took the place it had held in public detestation. To destroy it, the king had only to let it triumph.

[NOTES RELATING TO CHAPTER IV]

[CHAPTER IV illustrates Tocqueville's difficulty in combining a narrative with an analytic treatment. From his own notes written under the chapter titles it is clear that he thought of Chapter III as extending to September 1788 and Chapter V as reaching from September 1788 to the elections in the early months of 1789. Chapter IV has a more analytic purpose: to emphasize the transition in the late summer of 1788 as a sudden change occurring within "only a few days." In Tocqueville's analysis the Revolution really began at this time. That is, the general attitude toward the Parlement turned abruptly from adulation to vilification, the demand for liberty (as

---

[47] [Variant:] As a court, the Parlement had rare merits that history should recognize. Its judges were always independent and often enlightened. But however impartial and enlightened, a justice rendered by a small closed aristocracy that had purchased the right to judge was assuredly. . . .

against the monarchy) turned into a demand for equality (as against the privileged orders), and a movement led by the aristocracy began to draw its strength from the bourgeoisie.

But in this conceptual clarity the dynamics of the situation are made less clear. The chronology is confusing. At the beginning of Chapter IV we are in August 1788; the government has just abandoned or postponed its reform program (the May edicts, involving judicial reorganization, the Plenary Court, etc.), Brienne is resigning, and the Parlement is victorious. Tocqueville accumulated notes on the rejoicings in the provinces at this time. (See the following Note I.) But what he put in his draft chapter was an assortment of quotations showing the praises lavished on the Parlement of Paris a year before, during the weeks of its "exile" at Troyes, although the reader has not been told why the Parlement of Paris was then at Troyes (only the barest allusion has been made in Chapter III). Then, in Chapter IV, the weakness of the Parlement is explained by two paragraphs on how it had become more aristocratic since the Middle Ages. An important immediate cause of the collapse of its popularity does not appear until Chapter V, where Tocqueville explains how the government announced (in July 1788) the convening of the Estates General for 1789 and invited all interested persons to make known their views on how the Estates should be organized. It is only in a fragment (Note III below), apparently relating to Chapter IV, that Tocqueville mentions the action taken by the Parlement on September 25, when it ruled that the Estates should meet in three separate orders, as in 1614. It was at this point that the Parlement definitely lost the support of the bourgeoisie, or of the medley of bourgeois, nobles, and pamphleteers who believed that a new system of representation was desirable. In a narrative presentation these matters would be necessary for an understanding of Chapter IV.]

[I]

[Fêtes Celebrating the Restoration of the Parlements]

[By the May edicts of 1788 the government reduced the powers of the parlements, depriving them of their right of remonstrance and transferring some of their jurisdiction to new courts called

grands bailliages to have final judgment in small cases. Faced with resistance, the government withdrew these edicts and re-established
the parlements with their previous functions. The following are
Tocqueville's notes on the public celebrations that ensued.]

On September 18 [1788] the news of the fall of Lamoignon
reached Grenoble. The messenger was overwhelmed with caresses
and bravos. Women unable to embrace him embraced his horse.
That evening the whole town was spontaneously illuminated. A
mannequin representing the minister was burned. Another, representing the *grand bailliage* of Valence (which had complied with the
edicts of May 8), was dumped on the public road.

On August 29 news had already arrived of the dismissal of the
archbishop of Sens [Brienne]. The streets filled with people who
congratulated and embraced one another. . . .

. . . The first president (M. de Bérulle) [of the Parlement of Dau-
phiny] arrived on October 12. The whole town was in a commotion; the volunteer companies came out to meet and escort him. The
first company of grenadiers in scarlet coats, the second of *chasseurs*
in green, the third in sky blue.

M. de Bérulle, received more enthusiastically than a king, could
hardly make his way through the surrounding country. Everywhere the populations accompanied him in arms; at every halt there
were speeches. He passed under arches of triumph from the top of
which crowns were thrown down at him. Cannon were fired.

At the opening of the parlement (October 20) there were more
demonstrations. It was an endless setting of triumphal arches, ingenious transparencies, magnificent illuminations. . . .

All the corporate bodies paraded before him, offering grandilo-
quent compliments. To all of them the first president replied like a
king, in brief and dignified language. Each group was made to feel
the exact degree of satisfaction or displeasure that its actions since
May 8 had caused. Some received the first president's assurance of
his protection, others of his good will.

Was the Capitol ever so close to the Tarpeian rock?

[And at Bordeaux on October 20, 1788:]

The people unhitch the carriage of the first president [of the
Parlement of Bordeaux] and usher him into his apartments. The

eldest member of the parlement (La Colonie), a man almost ninety years old, cries out: "My children, tell all this to your descendants, that the memory of it may keep alight the fire of patriotism." This man had spent his earliest years under Louis XIV. See what changes in ideas and language can occur among a people during the lifetime of one man!

Magistrates who had wanted to obey the king were hooted; the first president pronounced their public censure.

A mannequin dressed as a cardinal was burned in the public square, which did not prevent the clergy from singing a *Te Deum*.

The parlement, in ratifying the decree that recalled it, took care to disallow all judgments made in its absence and to open the way for appeals for all those judged by the *grands bailliages* as courts of last resort.

[And at Troyes, to which the Parlement of Paris had been exiled a year before, there were the same rejoicings in September 1788 at the news that the Parlement had been re-established in Paris:]

Illuminations, fireworks, general hubbub. . . .

A silly black goose represented M. de Lamoignon, a violet one the cardinal de Brienne.[48] Those who had supported the king were reduced to silence. The town was full of topical verses, for literature and wit were then brought into everything. A certain canon with whom d'Eprémesnil had lodged during the exile of the Parlement put some Latin verses on a transparency in honor of this great man:

> Exilio magnus, legum sed major amore,
> D'Eprémesnil renovat gaudia nostra redux.[49]

What did d'Eprémesnil and the canon think six months later?

[II]
[d'Eprémesnil]

[By the nullifying of d'Eprémesnil, Tocqueville meant his rapid descent from martyr to nonentity, as shown in the following working note:]

[48] [Brienne, though an archbishop, was not yet a cardinal.]

[49] [Great in exile, greater in love of the laws, / D'Eprémesnil on returning renews our rejoicing.]

The same act that brought the Parlement of Paris back into the Palace of Justice gave d'Eprémesnil his liberty. Remember the dramatic scene of his seizure, his words à la Regulus, the tears of his audience, his immense popularity as a Martyr. He was detained at Sainte-Marguerite. He left immediately upon the news of his liberation. On his way, he was at first acclaimed as a great man, but as he advanced he found himself less famous, and on his arrival in Paris no one paid him any attention. On the next day, he was an object of mockery. For him to pass from triumph to ridicule took no more time than was necessary to go 150 leagues posthaste.

[III]

How the Parlement in Its Triumph Buried Itself with Its Own Hands

In its ruling of September 25, 1788, the Parlement decided "to request the king to assemble the Estates General in the form of 1614."

On July 5, 1788, when the king convinced the nation that it would really have the Estates General, he turned its attention to the composition of that assembly and so to the question of class. From that day the affair of the Parlement became secondary, and the true mother passion of the Revolution, the passion of class that the Parlement did not represent, overshadowed the struggle against the royal power, which others would represent better than the Parlement did.

VIOLENT ATTACKS REPLACE THE PLAUDITS.—The ruling with the clause quoted above was dated September 25, 1788. I find a pamphlet dated the twenty-eighth, only three days later, which says that agitators are tearing the Parlement to pieces because of this clause. Why such clamor against it? asks this anonymous defender. Why so many insidious suppositions?

Because up to now you have been the instrument of the dominant passion, and today you put yourselves in the way of a new one.

[Tocqueville then quotes and paraphrases the attacks on the Parlement.]

France is inundated with pamphlets in which the Parlement is not only not praised but is actually vilified; its very liberalism is turned against it, and revolutionaries show themselves more royalist than the Parlement.

"They are judges that understand nothing of politics. They only want to dominate and to use the people for political purposes.

"They agree with the nobility and clergy, and are just as much enemies of the Third Estate, that is, of almost the entire nation. They have thought that this would be forgotten if they only attacked despotism. They make the rights of the nation problematical, even as they defend them, by giving the false color of voluntary concessions to rights born of the social contract." (A pamphlet attributed to Servan, *Glose sur l'arrêté du Parlement*, London, 1789.)

Linguet, in a pamphlet violent and insulting, yet often expressing the truth, calls them a company of the *robe* usurping the right to speak as representatives of the people:

Who authorizes them to act as its interpreters? They have never been more than officers of the king.

They are a *robinesque* aristocracy.[50] What the people demand is a supreme, preponderant, and single authority to defend them against the mummery of miters, noble swords, and judicial caps.

It is by the treachery of the courts, by their self-interested villainy in putting themselves in place of the people for certain rights, that the people have lost the rights that they demand today.

The parlements have obtained the Estates General to their own great surprise and great regret. For they are going to lose the right of registration that they have so abused and so tyrannically applied; they will fall back into the limited and obscure orbit of their natural functions.

What greater abuse than their existence? The right of judging, of disposing of men's goods, life, and honor, sold like the stuff their robes are made of, the symbol of it all.

Your rightful power was to represent the king. At war with the king, what are you?

No more *robinocratic* or ministerial despotism. In this tract all sorts of private views are attributed to the Parlement that it did not have, and the very words that made it popular three months before are turned against it.

[50] [*Robin* was a familiar and mildly contemptuous word for a lawyer; *robinesque* and *robinocratique*, below, are nonce words generated by the controversy.]

199

[IV]

How the Parlements Had Never Been More Powerful, Aggressive, and Seemingly Deep-rooted than at the Moment When They Counted for Nothing

Seeing themselves so popular even with doctrines that were self-interested and contrary to the spirit of the time, how could the parlements not believe themselves to be deeply rooted and a force in their own right?

How could they guess that what made them popular came from a hatred for the very institutions that they represented and defended, a hatred which, by a singular conjunction of circumstances, found them momentarily useful?

It is curious, because it is a history repeated at the beginning of many other revolutions.

Never in the five hundred years that they had existed had the parlements used such harsh language with the king, or spoken to him so much as rivals or even masters, or laid such claim to legislative power. Never had they expressed a theory claiming so much authority for themselves. Never had they proclaimed in a manner so novel yet formidable and authentic the doctrine that all the parlements formed a single body, of which the Parlement of Paris was the head, and that each of them had the right to deliberate on *all* acts of government in *all* of France.

And yet the Parlement was based on nothing. After having served as the great arm of the king against the aristocracy, the Church, and the provincial spirit, it was now no more than an embarrassment and an encumbrance to the royal authority. It had become too heavy an instrument, too defective and dangerous to handle, for the uses that were now to be made of it. It was out of proportion to its object.

As an institution, it was no less outmoded in the minds of the people. The whole political and social state that the Parlement itself had helped to establish, all the ideas that flowed naturally from this state or were derived from it artificially, were contrary to a body of judges who had purchased the right to render justice, who held it by inheritance, who possessed individually or as a body all sorts of privileges, and who, in addition, combined their proper judicial function with political functions that were not their proper role.

But this change in conditions, laws, and ideas which made the Parlement an awkward and dangerous instrument in the eyes of the king and a badly designed instrument in the eyes of the people had produced in the nation a vague desire for innovation, a taste for change, a spirit of independence, and a desire to take control, which on all sides pushed on to resist authority.

This new and irregular power of opinion found in the Parlement the only instrument it could use. It seized on it not to make the Parlement more powerful, not to make it a popular body, but because it was the only body in France that remained sufficiently strong, large, and organized to struggle against the royal power and unsettle a constitution that many wished to overthrow.

As soon as it became possible to create a new instrument of resistance more suited to the new passions in origin, principle, and structure, this old instrument that was good only for shaking up the others became a victim of the common hatred, as if dragged down by its own weight and without anyone, so to speak, having to lay a hand on it. And so a giant that had so recently seemed to have a hundred arms and whose voice had resounded for ten months over all France, suddenly sank back and expired, unable to breathe even a sigh.

How Just as the Absolute Power Was Conquered the True Spirit of the Revolution Suddenly Showed Itself

(from September 1788 to the elections)

THE BOND of a common passion had held all classes momentarily together. They separated as soon as the bond was loosened; and the true face of the Revolution, hitherto veiled, became visible all at once.

With the king defeated, the question was who would benefit from the victory. The Estates General were now to meet, but who would dominate in their assembly?

The king, who could no longer delay the Estates, still had the power to decide the form in which they should sit. No one contested his right, which he could have exercised anyway on grounds of necessity. The Estates General had not met for 160 years.[51] No more than a vague memory of them remained. No one knew exactly what should be the number of deputies, the relationship between the orders, the mode of election, or the procedure for deliberation. Only the king could say. He said nothing.

On these matters his first minister, Cardinal Brienne, had a strange idea, and he persuaded his master to make a decision without parallel in all history. Whether the vote should be universal or restricted, the assembly numerous or small, the orders separate or united, or equal or unequal in rights was treated as a matter for erudite study, and hence an order in council charged all the constituted bodies with undertaking researches on the holding of ancient Estates General and the various forms that had been followed. The order added: "His Majesty invites all men of learning and other educated persons in his kingdom, especially those of the Academy of

[51] [Note by André Jardin: The last Estates General had been held in 1614, hence 175 years before.]

Inscriptions and Belles-lettres, to address all findings and memoirs on this question to M. the Keeper of the Seals."[52]

It was to treat the constitution of the country like a question set by an academy for a prize contest.

The call was heard. Soon everyone wanted to offer his opinion;[53] and since France was the most literary country in Europe, at a time when literature clothed the feelings of the time in the heavy garments of erudition, the land was inundated with writings.[54] All local authorities debated on their reply to the king, all particular bodies made their claims, all classes dreamed of their particular interests and searched in the ruins of the old Estates General for the forms most likely to guarantee them.

The struggle between classes, which was inevitable but which would more naturally have begun later during the meeting of the Estates, in a regular manner, on a limited ground, and on specific issues, now found instead an unlimited field of action and was enlivened by general ideas. It soon took on a character of uncommon audacity and unheard-of violence, which the secret state of feelings makes understandable but which no actual event had laid the way for . . . [a word left blank].

About five months passed between the king's abdication of the royal power and the beginning of the elections. During this time there was almost no change in the facts, but the movement pushing the ideas and feelings of the French toward the total subversion of society became more precipitous and furiously rapid.

At first, all that was considered was the constitution of the Estates General, and big books of raw erudition were hastily written in the attempt to reconcile the Middle Ages to the ideas of the moment. Then the old Estates General were forgotten, the old lumber of precedents was thrown away, and there followed a general and abstract

[52] [In his working notes, Tocqueville comments on this passage:]
Make use of this item, since it shows the state of political education in France. It gives an idea of the prodigious and truly unheard-of incapacity of these poor unfortunates who had the task of guiding affairs at this momentous time. It is also in this connection that a movement that had been liberal up to this point suddenly showed its true character, and the struggle against despotism became a struggle of classes.

[53] [Variant:] There was no one who had written or was able to write who did not attempt. . . .

[54] [Marginal note:] Perhaps a sentence here to characterize these diverse writings.

discussion of what the legislative power ought to be. Views expanded as the argument proceeded; it was no longer a question of the constitution of the legislature alone but of power itself, no longer of the form of government but of changing the very basis of society. At first they talked only of a better balance of powers, a better adjustment between classes; soon they walked, they ran, they threw themselves on the idea of pure democracy. At first it was Montesquieu who was quoted and commented on; at the end, it was only Rousseau. Rousseau became and was to remain the sole teacher of the Revolution in its first stage.

The notion of government was simplified. Numbers alone became the basis for law and right. Politics was reduced to a question of arithmetic. The root of everything to follow was planted in these ideas. There is hardly an opinion professed during the course of the Revolution that cannot sometimes be found in these writings, nor acts of the Revolution not already announced or surpassed.

—Quotations—[55]

The government itself had asked for a discussion of government, but could not limit its scope.

The movement that stirred ideas drove passions toward the same end with furious speed.

At first the Third Estate showed a jealousy toward some of the privileged without violence against persons. Then the language became more bitter; rivalry led to more jealousy and hatred turned into frenzy. Accumulated memories were mixed together into an enormous mass, lifted by a thousand arms to smash the head of the aristocracy. In the beginning, the nobility was blamed for pressing its rights too far. Toward the end, it was said to have no rights at all. At first, its rivals wanted to share power with it. Soon they denied it any power whatever. Not only should the nobles not be masters, they should hardly have the right to be citizens; they were strangers who had imposed themselves on the nation and were finally rejected by it. . . .

[55] [See Tocqueville's working note below, p. 212. He apparently intended to insert here quotations from statements drafted by corporate bodies in Lyon, Bourges, and other towns and from pamphlets by Sieyès, Rabaut Saint-Etienne, and others which he had been reading before drafting this chapter.]

—Quotation from Sieyès—[56]

For the first time, perhaps, since the beginning of the world, we see upper classes so isolated and separated from the others that they can be counted and turned aside like condemned animals in a flock of sheep, middle classes that no longer attempt to mingle with the upper but try carefully to avoid contact; two symptoms which, if they had been understood, would have shown the immensity of the revolution that was to come, or, rather, that had already taken place. . . .

Publications attacking the privileged persons were innumerable; those defending them were so few that it is hard to determine what was said in their favor. It may seem surprising that the classes under attack, which held most of the high public employments and owned most of the land, should have found so few and such feeble defenders when so many eloquent voices have pleaded their cause since they have been vanquished, decimated, and ruined. It is understandable if we think of the extreme confusion into which this aristocracy fell when the rest of the nation, after marching in concert with them, suddenly turned angrily against them. The aristocracy, much surprised, saw their own ideas now used to assail them. Notions fundamental to their own outlook were brought in to destroy them. What had been an intellectual amusement in their leisure was now a terrible weapon turned against them.

Like their adversaries, these aristocrats gladly believed that the most perfect society would be one that came closest to natural equality, where merit alone and not birth or fortune would be the basis of social classification, where the government would represent the general will and a numerical majority would make the law. If interests differed, ideas were the same. What people of all classes knew of politics was only what they had read in books, and always the same books. The nobles might have made the Revolution if only they had been commoners.[57]

[56] [Note by André Jardin: Apparently referring to the following passage in Sieyès's *What Is the Third Estate?*: "Why should we not send back to the forests of Franconia all those families that foolishly claim descent from a race of conquerors and succession to their rights?

"The nation, thus purified, might have the consolation, I suppose, of thinking itself descended from Gauls and Romans."]

[57] The only difference is that their adversaries had an interest in realizing this Uto-

So when they saw themselves suddenly attacked, they were singularly embarrassed in their own defense. None of them had ever thought of what had to be said to justify their privileges in the eyes of the people. They did not know how to explain that only an aristocracy can preserve the people from the oppression of tyranny and the misery of revolutions, so that privileges seeming to benefit only their possessors are the best guarantee of the peace and well-being of those who do not have them. All the arguments so familiar to classes that have long been practiced in affairs and understand the science of government were new and unknown to them. They were reduced to talking about services rendered by their ancestors six hundred years before. They appealed to old claims from a past that was abhorred. They pretended to be the only ones knowing how to handle arms or to maintain traditions of military courage. Their language was often arrogant because they were in the habit of being first,[58] but it was indecisive because they had doubts of their own right. . . .

—Put here or above a discussion of systems for doubling the Third Estate and voting in common. Note divisions inside the parties attacked, show the spirit of rivalry and contention arising even inside the separated groups: nobility against clergy, clergy against nobility, lesser nobles against greater, curés against bishops.—[59]

The discussion provoked by the royal edict, after having gone through the cycle of human institutions, always ended up with the two points that summarized the conflict for practical purposes:

In the Estates General that were about to meet should the third order have a more numerous representation than each of the other two, so that its deputies should be equal in number to those of the nobility and clergy combined?

Should the orders thus constituted deliberate together or separately?

---

pia, they did not. . . .

Unfortunately, one side had everything to gain, the other everything to lose, in the realization of this social improvement.

[58] [Variant:] of looking down on those to whom they spoke.

[59] [Alternate version:] Show how a kind of bewilderment and disagregation reigns. It was not only the bourgeoisie that made war on the nobility, it was lesser nobles against greater, lower clergy against upper! Until the Revolution simplified the division and brought together the diverse occupants of the same compartment.

The doubling of the Third and the vote in common in a single assembly seemed at that time less new and important than they really were. Their novelty and significance were concealed by some minor contemporary or earlier facts.

For centuries the provincial estates of Languedoc had been composed and had deliberated in this way, with no other result than to give the bourgeoisie a greater role in affairs and to create common interests and easier relations between it and the other two orders. Instead of dividing the classes, it brought them together.

The king himself seemed to have pronounced in favor of this system, for he had recently given this structure to the provincial assemblies by the edict establishing them in all provinces that did not have their own estates. It was not yet obvious, though uncertainly foreseen, that an arrangement which, when established in a province, only modified the ancient constitution was bound to upset it violently and from top to bottom as soon as an attempt was made to apply it to the State as a whole.

It was evident that the Third Estate, equal in number to the two others in a general assembly of the nation, would immediately predominate, not merely by taking part in affairs but by becoming absolute master, for it would be united against two groups, each not only divided from the other but also divided within itself—one side having the same interests, passions, and aims, the other having distinct interests, different aims, and often conflicting passions.

One side had the current of public excitement for it, the other against it; and this external pressure on the assembly could not but hold members of the Third Estate together while detaching from the nobility and clergy all those who hoped to heighten their reputation or find a new way to power.[60] In the estates of Languedoc each bourgeois felt the weight of the whole aristocracy, which dominated in ideas and customs.[61] Here the opposite was bound to occur, and the Third Estate could not fail to have a majority even

[60] [Alternate version:] This external force acting on the assembly could not but force a certain number of nobles and priests to join with the Third.

[61] [Alternate version:] In the estates of Languedoc it was usual for some bourgeois to abandon their order and vote with the nobles and bishops, because the existing strength of the aristocracy, still dominant in ideas and customs, made its weight felt upon them.

though in the number of its own deputies it was only equal to the other two.

Its impact on the assembly was bound to be not only preponderant but also violent, for it would meet there with everything that was likely to arouse human passions. To make men with contrary opinions live together is in any case difficult. But to shut up in one arena political bodies already formed, each with its own origin, its own past, its own procedures, and its own individual spirit; to have them constantly confronting one another while working to limit one another's rights; to force them to communicate continuously without intermediaries—all this was to provoke not discussion, but war.[62]

This majority, inflamed by its own passions and those of its adversaries, was all-powerful because it alone was going to determine the law. Nothing could stop or even retard its movements, because nothing remained to restrain it except a royal power that was already disarmed and which could do nothing but yield under the pressure of an assembly consisting of only one chamber.

This was not to change the balance of power gradually; it was to turn it suddenly upside down. It was not to let the Third Estate share in the exorbitant rights of the aristocracy; it was to transfer all power to other hands. It was to deliver up the direction of affairs to one passion, one interest, one single idea. It was to make not a reform but a revolution.

Mounier, who alone among the innovators at this time appears to have had a true idea of free and regular government, Mounier, who later in his definitive plan took care to provide for a division of powers, was favorable to the merging of the three orders into one assembly, and he gave his reason candidly: "Above all, we need an assembly that will destroy what remains of the ancient constitution, the particular rights and regional privileges; this would never be done by an upper chamber composed of nobles and clergy."[63]

In any case it seems that the doubling of the Third and the vote of

----

[62] [Marginal note:] Perhaps eliminate this passage, which is debatable and dangerous. Limit myself to showing the madness of the king, who did everything to lose the game.

[63] [Note by André Jardin: Tocqueville does not quote literally, but summarizes, an essential idea in Mounier's *Nouvelles observations sur les Etats-généraux*, published at this time.]

the three orders in common were inseparable questions. For what good would it do to increase the number of deputies of the Third if the Third was to deliberate and vote separately?

The government imagined that it could separate them.[64]

M. Necker was then directing the will of the king, and briefly serving as the idol of the whole nation. . . . His characteristics have been so forgotten that it is hard to see him distinctly. He was one of those people who never know where they are going because they guide themselves not by what is in their own minds but by what they think is in the minds of others.

It cannot be doubted that Necker wanted both the doubling of the Third and the vote in common. It is very probable that the king himself inclined in the same direction. It was the king that the aristocracy had just defeated. It was the aristocracy that had defied him most openly, raised up the other classes against the royal authority, and led them to victory. He had felt its blows and was not perceptive enough to detect its secret weakness. He willingly delivered it into the hands of allies who became its adversaries. Like his minister, the king therefore was inclined to constitute the Estates General as the Third Estate wanted.

But they dared not go so far. They stopped halfway, not from any clear view of the dangers but because of the vain clamor ringing in their ears. What man or class, occupying a high position, has ever seen the moment when descent was necessary to avoid being forcibly pulled down?

The question of numbers was resolved in favor of the Third, while the question of the vote in common was left undecided. Of all possible options, this was surely the most dangerous.

Nothing, it is true, nourishes despotism so much as class hatreds and jealousies. Indeed, despotism lives on them, but only if they are no more than a quiet and bitter feeling, strong enough to prevent people from reaching agreements yet not strong enough to make them fight. But any government will collapse in a violent conflict between classes once they have begun to collide.[65]

[64] Perhaps here a portrait of M. Necker. Be careful here, but his importance at this time may justify it here.

[65] [Variant:] Any government will perish in a violent class struggle once it can no longer prevent its beginning.

It was late in the day to try to maintain the ancient constitution of the Estates General, even with improvements. If attempted, such a bold move would rely on ancient usage, with the advantage of tradition using the instrument of the law.

To grant both the doubling of the Third and the vote in common would doubtless have been to make a revolution, but a revolution from above. The existing authority, while ruining the old institutions of the country, would have softened their fall. The upper classes would have adjusted in advance to an unavoidable destiny. Feeling the strength against them of both royalty and the Third Estate, they would have seen their own powerlessness at once. Instead of madly fighting to preserve everything, they would have fought not to lose all.[66]

In Dauphiny the assembled estates voted together, in common, in choosing deputies of the three orders to go to Versailles. The assembly in Dauphiny was indeed composed of the three orders, with each order chosen from within itself and representing only itself, but the deputies sent to the Estates General from Dauphiny were chosen by the whole assembly, so that each gentleman had some bourgeois among those who had elected him and each bourgeois deputy had some nobles. The three deputations, while remaining distinct, thus were in a way homogeneous. It may be that if the three orders had been represented in this way at the national level they might have been able, if not to agree, at least to avoid colliding so violently in a combined assembly.[67]

But we must not attribute too much importance to these procedural details. Human affairs are determined by human ideas and passions, not by machinery of the laws. It is always in the depths of the mind that facts are molded as they are then produced in the outside world.

Whatever decision had been taken on the form and regulation for these assemblies of the nation, it must be supposed that the war be-

[66] [Variant:] The upper classes, feeling the weight of royalty added to that of the Third Estate, would have lost hope of keeping the preponderance and would have fought only for equality. They would have become used to the idea.

[67] [Variant:] What was done in Dauphiny could have been done everywhere else. Would orders formed in this way have been able to act in a combined assembly without colliding too violently?

tween classes would have broken out violently. Class hatreds were already too inflamed to make common action possible, and the royal power was too weakened to restrain them. But it must be admitted that nothing that was done could have been better contrived to produce an immediate and deadly conflict.

Try to see whether any art or ingenuity, deliberately employed, could have succeeded better than clumsiness and shortsightedness! The Third Estate had been encouraged to be bold, to be ready for war, to count on its numbers. Its ardor had been increased, and its weight had been doubled. It had been allowed to form all kinds of hopes, then left with all kinds of fears. It had been led to expect victory, then left without it. It had been invited to prevail.

After five months in which the two classes had time to refresh and ripen their old hatreds, to go over again the long history of their mutual complaints and rage against each other to the point of frenzy, they were left in a state of confrontation to debate the question that contained all others, the one question to which it seemed that all others and all their quarrels could be reduced immediately and forever.

What strikes me the most forcibly is not the genius of those who served the Revolution while wishing it but the extraordinary imbecility of those who brought it on without wanting it.[68] When I consider the French Revolution, I am amazed at the prodigious grandeur of the event, at its dazzling message seen to the ends of the earth, at its power, by which all peoples have been affected in varying degree.

Then I think of that court that had so great a part in the Revolution, and I see the most commonplace scenes that history can discover: foolish and incompetent ministers, debauched priests and futile women, audacious and greedy courtiers, a king with only useless and dangerous virtues. Yet I see these petty personages facilitating, pushing, precipitating immense events. They not only play a part; being more than accidents, they become almost primary causes; and I marvel at the power of God, who can move the whole mass of human societies with such short levers.

[68] [Variant:] What strikes me the most in the affairs of this world is not the part played by great men but the influence often exercised by the least important.

[NOTES RELATING TO CHAPTER V]

[I]

Collective Statements Published by Associations, Communities, and Bodies

How, after reading all these papers and seeing the real chasm (covered up only by rhetorical precautions and fine sentiments) that was opening in men's minds between the past and the present, between what was and what they wished to be, between the point of view of the nobles and clergy and that of all others, how, I say, can one not see that the *Revolution* was inevitable, or rather, that it was made in advance.[69]

What strikes me is less the class passions that animate all this polemic, less the jealousies, rancors, and struggle of contrary interests that are evident, than the underlying basis of thinking (to which everything is referred and which produces the final result of revolutions).

Even those showing the most respect for privileges, for particular rights, consider these rights and privileges as completely unjustifiable. Not only the ones of long standing, but particular rights and privileges of any kind. The very idea of a temperate and prudent government, that is, of a government in which the different classes forming society and the different interests that divide it act as counterweights to one another, or in which men count not only as units but according to their property, their patronage, their interest in the general good . . . all these are absent from the thoughts of the most moderate (partly, I think, even of the privileged persons) and are replaced by the idea of a crowd of similar elements represented by deputies, who represent *number* rather than interests or persons.[70]

[69] In the first part of the year [1788] this basic attitude was concealed; it became obvious in the second. Leading idea.

[70] Go further with this thought and show how the Revolution was in this idea more than in the facts of what happened; that it was practically impossible for ideas to be what they were without the facts being as we know them.

[The reader may see here a new statement of the fears of "individualism" expressed in *Democracy in America*: that a democratic society may dissolve into a mass of equal but equally ineffective individuals isolated from one another, each concerned with himself, unable to come together in any action for the public good.]

[II]

[On a separate sheet attached to this chapter:]

Radicalism of the moderates. Emphasize it. It is the moderates who show most clearly what ideas were current. This is also the most original way to take hold of the subject.

[Another note illustrating this point:]

CONVOCATION OF THE ESTATES GENERAL, by Lacretelle. It seems that this pamphlet was quite widely read. Although moderate in language and respectful to persons, it is nonetheless singularly *radical* and *revolutionary* in its conclusions, and nothing shows better the violent current of the time than to find such thoughts and language in such a benevolent and well-intentioned *fool* as Lacretelle.

As in Roederer, all the arguments for forming a government are based on natural law, the rights of man, and metaphysics. Anything else seems to the author so false and even absurd that he does not know how to combat it.

It seems that, like Roederer, he is dealing with the constitution of an ideal people and has no perception of the past or of old influences and interests. It is surprising to see absolutely *nobody* upholding principles in this matter. Thirty years before, there would have been. Montesquieu had defended or at least noted them. No one in 1788 understands them, not even the interested parties; or from political expediency they dare not maintain them. The ideas of Rousseau are a flood submerging for a moment all this part of the human mind and human knowledge.

While saying that reasonable prerogatives of the orders should be respected, Lacretelle reasons as if there should be no order or class of any kind and as if the problem was to represent everyone as completely as possible, with *numerical* majority the rule.

He seems to accept some property qualification for elections and to see some usefulness in two legislative houses. What he cannot understand is that there should exist different orders with a mutual veto, and he indicates clearly that if the king should wish to maintain such an arrangement, the Third Estate should refuse to vote.

How the Drafting of the *Cahiers* Made the Idea of a Radical Revolution Sink Deeply into the Minds of the People[71]

WHAT IS MOST striking in the imperfect institutions of the Middle Ages is that they were so diverse and genuine. They went straight to their objective and gave all the liberties[72] that they seemed to promise. There was no guile or artifice in them.

When the Third Estate was called to take part in general assemblies of the nation, it was granted an unlimited faculty for expressing grievances and submitting petitions.

In the towns designated to send deputies to the Estates General the whole people was invited to give its opinion on abuses to be suppressed and on requests to be made. Independently of the general communal assemblies where affairs were publicly discussed and decided, each guild or group might express its grievances and wishes. Moreover, each particular person had the right to make his complaint.[73] The means were as simple as the procedure was bold. Until the sixteenth century in the towns (even Paris) there was a big box into which people put a paper expressing their grievances. From all these various sources came an organized memoir[74] to include what each and all had to complain of, expressed with a boundless liberty and often an extraordinary asperity of language.

[71] [See Tocqueville's note, p. 217 below.]

[72] [Variant:] all the rights.

[73] [Variant:] No one was excluded from the right of making a complaint; each could express his grievance in his own way. [Tocqueville's idealized Middle Ages to set against the troubles of the eighteenth century!]

[74] [A working note showing an example:] In Paris in 1614, in an accessible and public place in the Hôtel de Ville, a box was set up to receive whatever opinions or ideas were put into it. An assembly composed of the regular councillors of the Hôtel de Ville, 160 notables and a few ecclesiastical deputies, appointed a committee to gather the complaints, wishes, and remonstrances of the people, compile them, and draw up the *cahiers*.

The social and political constitution of that time had such deep and solid foundations that it was in no danger of being unsettled by this kind of popular scrutiny of vices and abuses. There was no question of changing the principle of the laws but only of modifying their practice, nor of breaking the royal and aristocratic powers but only of keeping them within proper bounds. What was then called the Third Estate meant the inhabitants of certain towns; it did not include the lowest class or even the middle class of the countryside. (Such people were thought to be represented by their seigneurs and were not consulted even if the deputies of the Third Estate spoke for them.) Townspeople were left with a complete freedom to express grievances because they were in no position to obtain by force what they might conceive to be their rights. There was no inconvenience in giving them an unlimited use of democratic liberty because everywhere else the aristocracy reigned uncontested. The societies of the Middle Ages were indeed only aristocratic bodies, which contained, however (and this was their greatness), small fragments of democracy.

In 1789 the Third Estate to be represented in the Estates General was no longer composed only of bourgeois in the towns, as in 1614, but consisted of twenty million peasants spread over the surface of the kingdom. These peasants had never been concerned with public affairs. Political life for them was altogether a novelty, without even incidental memories of a former age. Very old liberties were simply extended to a new people, with the result that the attempt to do what had been done three hundred years before produced exactly the opposite.

On a certain day, to the sound of church bells in every rural parish of France, the inhabitants assembled in the public place at the door of the church. There, for the first time since the beginning of the monarchy in France, they went to work to compile what was still called, as in the Middle Ages, the *cahier des doléances*, or list of grievances of the Third Estate.

In countries where political assemblies are elected by a universal suffrage a general election stirs a people to its foundations, unless the right to vote is a fraud.[75] In 1789 there was not only a universal

[75] [Tocqueville refers to the France of the Second Empire of the 1850s, the only country in Europe then having a universal male suffrage.]

suffrage but a general deliberation and universal survey. Each citizen of one of the most populous countries in the world was not only asked what he thought of some particular matter but also encouraged to say whatever he pleased against all the social and political institutions of the country. I think that the earth had never yet seen such a spectacle.

All the peasants of France, at the same time, thus went about recalling and recapitulating all that they had had to suffer on which they had a just right to complain. The revolutionary spirit agitating the town bourgeoisie rushed by a thousand channels through the agricultural population, which, restless and open to outside influences, was thoroughly penetrated by it. But this spirit was not the same as in the towns. It took a particular form more suited to those who felt it. What was general and abstract theory for the town middle classes became here more definite and specific. In the towns, the great question was rights; in the country, it was needs.

When the peasants came to consider their grounds for complaint, they paid no attention to a balance of powers, guarantees of political liberty, or general rights of man and the citizen. Their minds turned first to particular and familiar burdens that each of them had to bear. One man thought of the feudal payment that had taken half his grain crop for the year, another of the *corvée* that had obliged him a short time ago to give his time without pay. One remembered how the lord's pigeons had devoured his seed before it could germinate, another of the rabbits that had eaten his grain before it could ripen. As they became excited in detailing these troubles to one another, it seemed to them that all these evils came not from institutions but from one man who still called them his subjects although he had long since ceased to govern them, who now had only privileges without obligations, and who had no political rights except to live at their expense. They came to agree in seeing him as their common enemy.[76]

Providence, as if to make our passions and misfortunes a lesson to the world at this very moment when our Revolution was begin-

[76] [Tocqueville here restates one of the main ideas in his *Old Regime and the Revolution* (Book II, chapter i), that each peasant's manifold grievances converged against his local seigneur or feudal lord.]

ning, inflicted upon us a great dearth and an extraordinary winter. The harvest of 1788 was inadequate, and the weather was of unheard-of severity during the first months of 1789. Cold such as is known in the extreme north of Europe froze the ground to a great depth. For two months all France disappeared under a thick blanket of snow as in the steppes of Siberia. The air was frigid, the sky empty, dull, and sad. This accident of nature made human feelings harsh and violent. Grievances against the laws and those who enforced them were embittered by sufferings due to scarcity and cold. Jealousies and hatreds were sharpened by the general misery.

And when the peasant left his barely lighted hearth, his cold home, and his starving family to go and talk with some of his fellows about what they should say of their condition, it was not difficult to find an explanation; he thought that it would be easy, if only he dared, to point his finger at the author of these troubles.

[NOTES RELATING TO CHAPTER VI]

[I]

[A note on the jacket containing the manuscript of this chapter:]
This short chapter contains important things that it would be too bad to lose. It prepares the reader for the peasant insurrections and château burnings after July 12. But it may interrupt the flow of thought because it takes the reader into a different theater. He has been living with the enlightened classes; now he finds himself with those that were not, and the following chapter brings him back to the earlier ones.

[A marginal note added later to the note above:]
By substituting the idea of a *revolution* for *revolutionary passion* and postponing the fall of the Bastille, the famine, and the economic crisis until later, I think this chapter may fit.

[And a bit further down:]
I have been unable to make the best use of the winter of 1789, and yet this accident of nature was a big political event.

[II]

[Tocqueville made the following note while examining some official correspondence of 1788–1789. It shows his sense of the importance of rising food prices on the eve of the Revolution.]

In this correspondence we see that as the winter of 1788–1789 advanced, the agitation over food supplies set the common people all over France into motion: disturbances in the marketplaces, crowds forming everywhere, troops of armed beggars roaming through the countryside.

These same symptoms had existed a hundred times before without leading to revolt. They have been forerunners of revolution almost always ever since.

[III]

[In the following notes, taken from pamphlets of 1789, Tocqueville saw evidence of widespread ideas in favor of redistribution of land.]

PEASANT SOCIALISM BEFORE THE MEETING OF THE ESTATES GENERAL [quoting the pamphlet:] "In some provinces the country people are persuaded that they will pay no more taxes and will divide the land of the seigneurs among themselves. They are already having meetings to learn the extent of these lands and equalize the distribution. They look forward to the Estates General only as a means to formalize these innovations."

What a curious piece! How well it shows what is to follow! How the peasant was already exactly the man we see today!

GENERAL THEORY THAT FRANCE HAS TOO MANY LARGE LANDOWNERS, AND THAT FOR THE PUBLIC WEALTH AND COMFORT THERE CANNOT BE TOO MUCH SUBDIVISION OF THE SOIL. Although the author has a horror of democratic violence, we see in his own mind the roots that nourish it and how false economic doctrines support ignorant greed.

The author, like almost all his contemporaries, sees two propositions as evident truths:

1. That there are too many great landed fortunes in France.
2. That it would be desirable for the soil to be divided indefi-

nitely, either in small properties or let out in *farms*, because in this way the land could be made to produce infinitely more.

[In another pamphlet written in 1789 Tocqueville found the same economic doctrine.]

SMALL PROPERTIES DISAPPEARING; LARGE ONES GROWING; THE MORE THE LAND IS SUBDIVIDED, THE BETTER IT IS CULTIVATED.

The author, while citing no facts and in a declamatory style, complains that small properties are being absorbed into large ones that are increasing without bounds. One would think that the author was writing in England. The fact is very false for France.

Like all his contemporaries (not excepting, I think, the large landowners), he also has the idea that large properties are harmful to agriculture, a notion to be explained and justified by what was happening in France, the abandonment of rural areas by large landowners [who preferred to live in towns].

This notion in political economy went well with the rise of democratic passions and contributed to the hatred of the rich so well expressed by the author.

CHAPTER VII

How Hearts were Joined
and Spirits Raised as They Were at Last
to Meet in a National Assembly[77]

TWO QUESTIONS above all had divided the classes: the doubling of the Third, and the vote in common. The first had been decided, the second postponed. The great assembly, which each person had seen separately as an avenue of hope and which all together had sought with the same ardor, was finally about to meet. The event had been long awaited, yet was clouded by doubt. It arrived at last. There was a general feeling of passing from the preparation to the work itself, from words to acts.

At this solemn moment all paused to consider the greatness of the undertaking, being now close enough to action to perceive the magnitude of what they were about to do and to understand the effort that must be made.

Nobles, priests, bourgeois, all clearly saw that it was not a question of modifying such-and-such of our laws but of recasting them all, of introducing a new spirit, changing and rejuvenating institutions, or, as they then said, regenerating France. No one yet knew exactly what would be swept away or what created. But everyone realized that there would be immense demolition and immense new construction.

But their thoughts did not stop here. No one doubted that the destiny of the human race was involved in what they were preparing to accomplish.

Today, now that the hazards[78] of revolutions have humbled us to the point that we think ourselves unworthy of the liberty that other

---

[77] [Notes found with the manuscript of this chapter (see below, pp. 223–224) suggest that Tocqueville had difficulty in writing it. It does, indeed, seem hard to reconcile with the "malady" and the mounting class conflict described in the preceding chapters.]

[78] [Variant:] misfortunes.

nations enjoy, it is difficult to imagine the pride that our fathers felt. When we read what was then written, we are astonished at the lofty opinion that Frenchmen of all ranks had of their country and their race, the simple and untroubled confidence with which they took the French to stand for all human beings. Among all the reform projects that had been devised, at the time when the government seemed to put up the constitution for a prize contest, we find almost none that deigns to imitate what was done in other countries.[79] France was not to receive lessons, but to give them. (This view was favored by the nature of the political ideas in everyone's mind, and which seemed applicable to all peoples.[80]) There was not a Frenchman but was convinced that the coming decisions would not only change the government of France but introduce into the world new principles of government applicable to all peoples and destined to renew the entire face of human affairs, not only for his country but for humankind.

If this sentiment was exaggerated, it was not mistaken.[81] The great enterprise was in truth about to begin. Its grandeur, beauty, and risk could be seen close at hand. At the full and distinct sight of them, the French imagination was entranced. In this vast presence, thousands briefly put aside their own interests to dream only of the common work. It was only for a moment, but I doubt if there has ever been such a moment in the life of any other people.[82]

The enlightened classes then had none of the timid and servile nature that revolutions have since given them. They had long ceased to fear the royal power and had not yet learned to tremble before the people. They were made intrepid by the greatness of their purpose. The taste for comfort that would finally overwhelm all others was still only a weak and subordinate passion. Reforms already made had upset many individual lives; they were accepted with resignation. Inevitable coming reforms could not fail to alter the condition of thousands; no one thought of that. The uncertainty of the future

[79] Perhaps develop this.

[80] [Marginal note:] Idea badly expressed but certainly to be placed here.

[81] [Added in parentheses:] perhaps.

[82] Perhaps turn about and say: class interest seemed for a moment to be in abeyance. (Bad, but the movement may be good.)

had already slowed down the movement of trade and industry;[83] the activity of humble people was troubled or suspended. Distress and suffering did not dampen their ardor.[84] In the grandeur of the common enterprise private miseries were lost and ignored even in the eyes of those who endured them.

Even the passions that had brought the classes so violently to blows seemed suddenly to grow milder at this hour, when for the first time in two centuries the classes were to act together; in a few *bailliages* [electoral districts] the three orders made war on one another, but in almost all there was a sudden harmony, far more than had been expected.

All had with equal ardor demanded the restoration of the great assembly now being born. Each person had seen in the meeting of this great body the means of realizing his dearest hopes. These Estates General, called for by tumultuous and unanimous voices, were at last taking form. A common joy filled hearts that had been so divided and brought them together for a moment before they separated forever.

All were impressed at this moment by the perils of disunion. They made a supreme effort to agree. Instead of considering how they differed, they strove to concentrate on a common aim:

Destroy the absolute power, restore the nation to itself, secure the rights of every citizen, obtain a free press, make individual liberty inviolable, humanize the laws, reaffirm justice, guarantee religious toleration, remove the obstacles to trade and commerce—these are the things that all demanded. They were on everyone's mind, the subject of mutual congratulations, which all talked about as matters of common interest, while they kept silent on what still divided them. Fundamentally they did not agree, but they tried to persuade themselves that they would agree, in a mood of reconciliation in which no explanations were offered.

—Here put facts that may illustrate all this.—

I think that never in history, and nowhere on earth, has there been seen so great a number of men so passionately devoted to the public good, so truly forgetful of their own interests, so absorbed in the

[83] Revolution had gone far enough to disturb the order of trade and industry.

[84] [Marginal note:] Make all this more precise without bothering about money terms.

contemplation of a great purpose, so determined to risk all that men hold most dear and lift themselves above petty concerns. It was the common basis of passion, courage, and dedication, from which came all the great actions of the French Revolution.

It was a brief spectacle, but with incomparable beauties. It will never pass from human memory. All foreign nations saw, applauded, and were moved by it. Try to find a place in Europe so remote as not to perceive it and respond with admiration and wonder; there is no such place. In all the many memoirs that contemporaries of the Revolution have left to us I have never found one in which these first days of 1789 have not left their indelible trace. Everywhere we find the clear, fresh, and lively emotions of youth.

I dare to say that there is only one people on earth that could have produced such a scene. I know my nation. I see its mistakes, faults, weaknesses, and miseries only too well. But I know also what it is capable of. There are enterprises that only the French nation is able to conceive, and magnanimous resolutions that it alone will dare to adopt. It alone, at a favorable moment, can wish to embrace the cause of humanity and be *willing* to fight for it. And if it can precipitately fall, it can soar to sublime heights that no other people will ever attain.

[NOTES RELATING TO CHAPTER VII]

[A note by Tocqueville on the jacket containing the manuscript of this chapter:]

This was the great floodtide of 1789 that continued for a while but has been receding down to our own day.

For this historic moment the reader must be made to realize that, *except for the harmony*, most of the feelings I am depicting did not originate at this time but had been built up since long in the past, and, especially, that they would not cease with the moment itself.

[At the head of a first sketch of this chapter Tocqueville also considered his objective as follows:]

What do I want to describe?

Is it the general outburst that produced the French Revolution and drove on this great wave of feelings and ideas, which has been dying away down to our own time?

The conviction that their mission was to regenerate France and change the world, the enthusiasm born of this great purpose, the devotion to this great course, the scorn for private interest and individual well-being that all this suggested to millions of men[?]

Or, rather, is it not a particular moment, a peculiar accident in the great upheaval of men's minds?

This solemn moment of passage from speculation to practice, from preparation to event, from words to acts, when the French, about to launch on this vast enterprise, seeing clearly the work they are to undertake, bring themselves to a halt, calm down, come together, make a supreme effort to understand one another, to forget private interests and think only of the greatness and beauty of the common task.

A moment of moral grandeur unequaled in history.

[Marginal note:] The *apparent* and sincere coming together of classes is only the principal symptom, though still only a symptom, of that admirable *effort* of the spirit to prepare for the coming task, to be fulfilled by abnegation, sacrifice, and devotion to the great cause. Contempt for comfort, ruin, and life itself was only the final such effort of the spirit.

This whole chapter must turn on this one idea.

Alexis de Tocqueville

Excerpts from His Correspondence Concerning
the Writing of His Unfinished Book
(1856–1858)

Excerpts from Alexis de Tocqueville's Correspondence

[EXCEPT for the first, the following excerpts are all from letters written in 1856, 1857, and 1858, when Tocqueville was at work on the sequel to his *Old Regime and the Revolution*. The first letter, although written at the end of 1850, is included because it shows so clearly what his long-term project was. He had gone in 1850 to Sorrento in southern Italy to recover from the first attack of the pulmonary illness from which he died nine years later. At leisure there, and soon to retire from politics, he shared with his friend Louis de Kergolay the first germ or intimation of what was to become *The Old Regime and the Revolution*. The letter makes clear that he thought of the Revolution as a contemporary disturbance lasting into his own time, and that his first idea was to study the empire of Napoleon I as a particularly significant phase in this great disturbance. It shows also his awareness of the difficulties in writing the kind of history that he had in mind, and which continued to trouble him in his final efforts on the book he was unable to finish.

Much of what he says here to Kergolay in 1850 is repeated in the note he wrote to himself in 1856 (p. 150 above) to put himself back on the track for writing the sequel to his *Old Regime*.]

To Louis de Kergolay   *Sorrento, December 15, 1850*

. . . I think myself now in a better position than I was when I wrote *Democracy* [*in America*] to treat a great subject of political literature. But what should the subject be? More than half the chance of success depends on the choice of subject, not only because one must be found that is of interest to the public, but also because I must have one that excites me and brings out what I have to give. . . . All these reflections and agitations of mind, in the solitude in which I am now living, make me search more deeply and seriously for the master idea of a book, and I want to tell you what I am imagining and ask your opinion. Basically it is only the affairs of our time that interest the public or interest me. . . . But what subject to choose? What would be most original and most suited to my nature and habits of mind would be a collection of reflections and insights on the present time, a freely ranging judgment on our modern societies and forecast of their probable future. . . . I must find somewhere a solid and continuous basis for my ideas, which I can find only by writing history, attaching myself to a period that gives me the occasion to deal with the men and affairs of our day and bring all these detached portrayals into a picture. It is only the long drama of the French Revolution that provides such a period. As I think I have told you, I have long had the thought of choosing, within the great length of time from 1789 to our days, which I continue to call the French Revolution, the ten years of the Empire, the birth, development, decline, and fall of that prodigious enterprise. The more I think of it, the more I believe this period to be well chosen. . . . [He will not write a work such as Adolphe Thiers's *History of the Consulate and Empire*.] Such a work would take many years; moreover, the principal merit of a historian is to know how to weave together the facts, and I do not know whether I have that art. What I have been most successful with until now is to judge the facts rather than narrate them in a history properly speaking. . . .

To this way of envisaging my subject I would add another. It would not be a long book but a fairly short one, perhaps one volume. I would not write a history of the Empire, strictly speaking, but a combination of reflections and judgments on its history. I would no doubt indicate the facts and follow their thread, but my main objective would not be to narrate them; I would try to make the reader understand the principal facts and see the diverse causes that produced them and the consequences that flowed from them; how the Empire came into being; how it could establish itself in the society created by the Revolution; by what means it was built; what the *true* nature was of the man who founded it; what made his successes, and what his reverses; the transitory influence and the lasting influence that he exerted on the destinies of the world and on those of France. It seems to me that there is matter here for a very great book. But the difficulties are immense. The one that troubles me most comes from the mixing of history, properly speaking, with philosophical history. . . . The inimitable model of this genre is Montesquieu's book on the greatness and decline of the Romans. . . .[1]

[1] OC XIII, 2, *Correspondance avec Louis de Kergolay*, pp. 229–234.

[The following excerpts reveal Tocqueville's perplexity as he worked on his unfinished book—his inability to conceptualize the Revolution to his satisfaction and his tragic struggle to carry on through alternating episodes of physical strength and weakness, anxiety and hope, as his lung disease grew worse.

In January 1856 he wrote to his friend Henry Reeve in London, who had translated his *Democracy in America* twenty years before, announcing the completion of his book soon to be published in France, *L'Ancien régime et la Révolution*. He asked Reeve to arrange for an English translation, to be made from the French proof sheets and so published almost simultaneously with the original. Reeve replied that he was now too busy to do it himself but that he would find a competent translator, closely supervise his work, and correct or improve it where necessary. Tocqueville thereupon explained that the book now ready for publication was only the first of what might become two or three volumes.]

To Henry Reeve   *19 place de la Madeleine, February 6, 1856*

. . . I am more concerned with my reputation than with my pocketbook. Do not sacrifice anything just to get a translation at a bargain, and above all don't disappoint the hope you have given me that you will go over the translator's work before releasing it to the public. This is important to me.

There is one fact of which I should inform you. There is a proposal to translate me in America. Does this circumstance affect what I want to do in England?[2]

As for the work itself, I can best answer your very natural question by sending you the titles of the chapters that make it up. The subject of the book is the *Revolution* (and this will perhaps be its title) as seen in its causes, its movement, and its effects, not only in France but in the whole world. The work will have two, perhaps *three volumes*. But as I have told you, the one I am about to publish forms a whole that could stand by itself if the rest should never appear. . . .

. . . In this book there are a certain number of general and ab-

---

[2] John Bonner's translation was published in New York in 1856, shortly after Reeve's in England.

stract ideas that grow out of the huge mass of details, many of which, I think, are new.

The following volume will show how the Revolution with its specific features came out of what is said in the volume I am about to publish. Unless I am mistaken, it will review the general movement both in France and beyond it; and when the Revolution has achieved its work, it will show what in truth this work was, what it had swept away and what it had preserved of the old regime against which it was directed.[3]

[Meanwhile, it was decided in Paris that Tocqueville's book should be entitled *L'Ancien régime et la Révolution*, considering that the existing manuscript dealt only with conditions before the Revolution and that one or more further volumes were to be expected. Reeve wrote that the London bookseller-publisher John Murray had agreed to publish the translation but was uncertain about the title.]

Reeve to Tocqueville   *16 Chester Square, April 18, 1856*

. . . Murray (the bookseller) thinks that the expression *Ancien régime* positively cannot be used in the title of a translated work. I propose therefore "On the State of Society before the Revolution of 1789," which is the equivalent of *Ancien régime*.[4]

[At Tocqueville's suggestion, Reeve added to his proposed title "and on the causes which led to that event." Reeve's title continued to designate the English translation of Tocqueville's book for many years. John Bonner's American translation of 1856 was already called *The Old Regime and the French Revolution*, by which it has been generally known. The book was published by Michel Lévy in Paris in June 1856. By the time of Tocqueville's death in 1859 a fourth printing had appeared in France, with nine thousand copies then in print, a figure thought very high for a book of this kind. In 1873 a second edition of the Reeve translation was published in England (followed by a third in 1888); it included Gustave de Beaumont's re-

[3] OC VI, 1, *Correspondance anglaise*, pp. 160–161.
[4] Ibid., pp. 167–168.

construction after Tocqueville's death of the seven unfinished chapters, of which André Jardin's quite different arrangement is translated in the present volume.

The immediate success of the *Old Regime* encouraged Tocqueville to go to work without delay on its sequel. He was blocked, however, by a problem that he never solved to his own satisfaction: how to avoid a mere recounting of "facts" while portraying the changing "ideas and feelings" of the Revolution. The analytical powers that had served him so well in *Democracy in America* and *The Old Regime and the Revolution* seemed less suited to the understanding of rapid change over a short period of time. He was more interested in continuity than in innovation, more in long-run trends than in the passage from one crisis to another.]

To J. J. Ampère   *Tocqueville, August 3, 1856*

. . . What you tell me of the sale of my book is such good news and so surprising that I cannot help but believe that you have made an error in saying 1,800 copies have been sold. . . . I would not be telling the truth if I didn't say that this whole affair has been a great joy to me and still more to my wife. The fact is, that if the book had fallen flat, with my tendency to *despondency*, it would have had a great effect on all the rest of my life. I had made an immense effort, and if it had been in vain, it would have been hard for me to begin again.

Now, on the contrary, I am eager to get back to work, though I see from a distance that the task presents infinitely more difficulties of all kinds than the one I have just completed. In any case, I have many ideas for this part of my work, which, as you know, was the part that I first had in mind. . . .[5]

To J. J. Ampère   *Tocqueville, August 26, 1856*

. . . I am having a lot of trouble in getting a hold on my great subject. I don't know which end to take it up by, and I want very much for us to talk about it together, in the hope that, as so often in the

[5] OC XI, *Correspondance avec P. P. Royer-Collard et avec J. J. Ampère*, p. 334.

past, the horizon will clear in talking with you, and I can at last see the way that will lead me to my goal. . . .[6]

To Pierre Freslon   *September 20, 1856*

. . . The difficulty in my present enterprise is greater than any I have had before. If I stand off too far from the details of fact while tracing the movements of ideas and feelings during the revolutionary period (which is, strictly speaking, my subject), I become vague and elusive. If I come too close to the details, I fall into an immense ocean that is already well traversed from all directions and is well known. The mere sight of it makes me dizzy. . . . I have not yet reached even the half-light that would let me see enough of the country for me to ask the inhabitants the way. . . .[7]

To George Cornewall Lewis   *October 6, 1856*

. . . Since my object is more to trace the movement of ideas and feelings that produced the events of the Revolution than to narrate these events themselves, it is not so much historical documents that I need as it is writings in which public opinion expressed itself at each period—journals, pamphlets, private letters, administrative correspondence.[8]

[As is evident in the preceding letters, Tocqueville's intention was not to produce another narrative of the Revolution but to write something more in the nature of reflections on its meaning, such as Montesquieu had written on the Romans. Pursuing also his idea of a general European revolution of which the French was the most acute and momentous phase, he read a number of books on Germany and became curious about strange sects and secret societies as omens of imminent change.]

---

[6] Ibid., pp. 341–342.

[7] André Jardin, *Alexis de Tocqueville, 1805–1859*, Paris, 1984, p. 486. This excerpt is from the biography by Jardin, the correspondence with Freslon being not yet published.

[8] Ibid., pp. 486–487.

To J. J. Ampère   *Sunday, January 11, 1857*

Here I am again, dear friend, and still to ask a favor. I think it useful in my work (which I am beginning to take up again in your absence, since the charm of our intimacy when you were here consoled me in my sterility), I think it useful, to repeat, to form an idea of what that sort of feverish dreaming before the Revolution was like—what is called Illuminism, Rosicrucians, Freemasonry . . . which revealed the human mind turning upon itself before aiming at a definite point. . . . Don't bother to send me anything. Simply have with you or at your house the books I am to get. I will send for them. . . .[9]

J. J. Ampère   *Marseille, Wednesday the 21st,*
to Alexis de Tocqueville   *at 7 o'clock in the morning* [1857]

Dear friend, you will find in Grégoire a summary of all the "illuminated" sects that will give you indications on what you are working on at the moment. . . .[10]

[On the very day after writing to Ampère, Tocqueville wrote to another friend, Adolphe de Circourt, putting to him the same question. As early as 1852, he and Circourt had corresponded on the well-known book of Abbé Barruel, who had claimed that the Revolution was caused by a conspiracy of Illuminati and Freemasons. "Nothing seems to me more erroneous," Tocqueville had said in 1852, and he went on to explain to Circourt that he saw in these societies only "symptoms of the malady, not the malady itself, effects and not causes."[11] It is hard to understand why Tocqueville took such a persistent interest in this esoteric subject in 1857.]

[9] OC XI, pp. 361–362.

[10] Ibid., p. 362. The reference is to Abbé Henri Grégoire's book of 1810, republished in six volumes in 1828 and 1845, entitled (if it had been translated) "A history of religious sects which, since the beginning of the last century, have arisen, been modified, or become extinct in the four quarters of the globe."

[11] OC XVIII, *Correspondance avec Adolphe de Circourt et avec Madame de Circourt*, pp. 69–76. On Barruel and his conspiratorial theory, see R. R. Palmer, *The Age of the Democratic Revolution*, Princeton, 1964, vol. II, pp. 251–255.

To A. de Circourt   *Tocqueville, January 12, 1857*

. . . Here is my question now: I am curious to know what that sort of feverish agitation of the human mind consisted in that immediately preceded the French Revolution in all Europe and which manifested itself as Illuminism, the Rosicrucians, Freemasonry, Mesmerism. . . . I know from various works, among others the bad book by Mirabeau on the Prussian monarchy, that in Germany in 1788, the date of the book, all these doctrines had a great many adepts, and vaguely and deeply agitated men's minds. If there were a book or several books giving an exact idea of this singular state of mind, especially in Germany and northern Europe, and that could show what it consisted in, I would try to procure such works. I cannot give the subject much time or prolonged study. But I would hope to see it in general outline and correct perspective, and take account of its character and extent. I should be very glad if you can help me in that. . . .[12]

A. de Circourt   *La Celle, January 15, 1857*
to Alexis de Tocqueville

. . . On that important prologue to the drama of the Revolution that you write about at the beginning of your letter, the only special work that I know of is the *Mémoires sur le jacobinisme* of the Abbé Barruel. But there is a whole literature in German on the subject. The Illuminati controlled Sweden, ruined Prussia, and caused disturbances in Hesse and Bavaria. The Swedenborgians had laid the way for them in Scandinavia. In Germany and France, the Martinists chastened the bizarre tendencies of the Illuminati by trying to have angels do what others attributed to demons. Barruel, in his undigested and inflated compilation, cites a good many German writers in his notes. To enlighten myself I am going to write to the best authority I know in this field; it is [Leopold von] Ranke. I hope that he will reply without too much delay.[13]

[12] OC XVIII, p. 362.
[13] Ibid., pp. 366–367.

A. de Circourt   *Paris, February 12, 1857*
to Alexis de Tocqueville

Ranke has answered me on the subject of the ramifications of the
opinions and revolutionary intrigues of our country in Germany toward the end of the last century. I enclose a transcript of his letter.
Ranke also tells me that he has sent to a common friend a few books
on this matter that he wishes to be sent on to you. . . .

From M. Leopold von Ranke   *Berlin, February 10, 1857*
We have nothing in German of what would be called *standard
works* in England on the subject of the Illuminati and other ramifications that the French philosophic and revolutionary sects had in
Germany in the last years of the past century. The Illuminati sym-
pathized with the French Revolution and, more surprisingly, with
the advent of Napoleon. But none of all that struck any deep roots
in German soil. It was an ephemeral effort to combine the spirit peculiar to the eighteenth century with the hierarchic and hieratic
forms of the sixteenth. . . .[14]

To A. de Circourt   *February 22, 1857*

I should like, dear Monsieur de Circourt, to join a few words to
the letter I have just written to Madame de Circourt to thank you
for your communication on the *Illuminati of Germany*. You tell me
that Ranke is sending a few books. If they come to you, please keep
them until my return, which will be in about three weeks. Does M.
Ranke know that it was for me that you asked him the questions he
answers? That is not evident from the fragment of his letter that you
sent me. If so, and if it were for me that the books he mentions were
to be sent, I should feel obliged to write to him, though I have not
the honor of knowing him personally. It would be a pleasure to enter into direct correspondence with so eminent a man. In that case,
please give me his address. I see, however, that he has completely
mistaken the meaning of the questions I put to him. I have never
thought that the sects of Illuminati had any appreciable influence on
the coming of the French Revolution. I consider them only as one

[14] Ibid., pp. 375–377.

of the numerous symptoms characterizing the state of mind at the time, or the state of mind out of which the Revolution came. . . . I may say confidentially that I understand nothing of an ephemeral effort to *conciliate the spirit peculiar to the eighteenth century with the hierarchic and hieratic forms of the sixteenth*. This must mean that they wanted to animate the body of the old European society with the new spirit. The most distinguished Germans always take pains to cover the clearest ideas with a bit of high-flying nonsense. . . .[15]

To A. de Circourt   *Tocqueville, March 11, 1857*

I take the liberty, dear Monsieur de Circourt, to enclose with this letter one that I have written to M. Ranke, which I would ask you to send on to him after filling in the address. I thought it well to thank M. Ranke directly for the trouble he took in replying to the question you put to him for the purposes of my work. I have now learned on this point what I needed to know, and would not wish to inconvenience M. de Savigny unnecessarily. You know, of course, that my desire to understand the movement of various Masonic and Illuminist sects in Germany did not come from any idea on my part that one of the causes of the French Revolution was to be found in the birth and development of these sects. I was looking in them only for a curious sign of the general spirit of the time. Though interesting, this is not of primary importance and requires no very long or very detailed studies. . . .[16]

[Tocqueville goes on to tell Circourt that he had been reading, besides Mirabeau on the Prussian monarchy, some writings by Ernst Brandes and Johann Georg Forster. The results became apparent later in the first chapter of his unfinished book. See pp. 153–158 above.

Meanwhile, Tocqueville had written in February to his old friend Gustave de Beaumont, who had been his companion in America in 1831–1832, telling him about the progress of his new book. He was working intensively, making notes and digests of his sources. Fortunately for Tocqueville, the Bibliothèque Nationale (called Impériale during these years of the Second Empire) had published in

[15] Ibid., pp. 379–380.
[16] Ibid., pp. 385–386.

1855 the volume of its printed catalogue which related to the French Revolution. Such was Tocqueville's political and literary standing that the famous national library was willing to break its usual rule and send books to him at his home in Normandy.]

To Gustave de Beaumont — *Tocqueville, February 1, 1857*

. . . I am back at work fairly seriously now that we are entirely alone. I am beginning to go forward with some pleasure, but I see a whole world opening before me. The sight of it alarms me. I have not progressed far enough to be sure that I can continue on my course. I am sustained more by the pleasure of the work than by any proud illusion of the importance of such labors. There are times when books are political acts. It has been so in France for a hundred and fifty years with few exceptions. But today books are pure amusements of the mind. You can see this in the praise freely given to a book that goes against your own ideas. It can do so little damage that you like to read it even when disapproving of it.

I have found, especially at the Bibliothèque Impériale, a great deal of good will that is most useful for the work I can do here in the country. They have sent me a copy of the printed catalogue in which works relating to the Revolution are listed. I mark in this book all those that I need, and they send them to me. Many are pamphlets or detached pieces. They have sent me as many as a hundred and fifty at a time. That's what I call being helpful. . . .[17]

[In June 1857 Tocqueville went to England and remained there about a month. His purpose was to consult materials in the British Museum, but he was such a distinguished visitor and had so many friends and admirers in England that much of his time was consumed in social obligations. For reasons that he explains, the trip was not very rewarding so far as his researches were concerned.]

To Gustave de Beaumont — *Tocqueville, July 25, 1857*

. . . The most serious purpose of the trip was to see what is in the British Museum on the Revolution, but this was fulfilled very incompletely because the special library on the Revolution is not cat-

[17] OC VIII, 3, *Correspondance avec Gustave de Beaumont*, p. 456.

alogued.[18] I estimate at no less than 12,000 the number of pamphlets written in France on or during the Revolution that are now brought together in a room at the British Museum. I think it is the greatest collection in existence. But its very extent makes it useless until some easy means of consulting it is provided. I spent hours there, but they were badly employed and I hardly collected anything but dust. I had a more interesting time at the State Paper Office, which, as you know, houses the political archives of the country. All the diplomatic materials are to be found there either in the original or in copies, in big, carefully bound volumes. The rule is not to let anything later than '89 be seen. But Lord Clarendon kindly made an exception in my favor, so that all the diplomatic correspondence from 1787 to 1793, until the rupture of diplomatic relations, was made available to me. I found nothing of great value, except for almost certain proof that the English, at the beginning of our troubles, did not play the Machiavellian role attributed to them. Of course they were not sorry to see our embarrassments, but nothing shows that they tried to increase them, as so many people have said. Incidentally, it is amusing to see how the English, despite their own experiences in revolutions, had no idea how ours would come out. . . .[19]

[After his return from England, he and Mme de Tocqueville entertained house guests for much of the rest of the summer, during which his work was delayed. He felt the need to begin to write, but he lacked the drive of his younger days.]

To Gustave de Beaumont   *Tocqueville, September 25, 1857*

. . . I figure that I shall not be left to myself until October 15. I hope then to have several months of peace for effective work. As you guessed in your last letter, I have done little since my return. I have only brought my preparatory work to the point where I *must* begin composition of the first part of my new book. I count on this labor of composition to restore the impulse that has been lacking for almost a year. For some time I have felt such impatience at my ste-

[18] What Tocqueville saw was the Croker Collection on the French Revolution, for which a guide was published by G. K. Fortescue of the British Museum in 1899.
[19] OC VIII, 3, p. 490.

rility, such a sometimes painful uneasiness, that I hope at last to regain some of my old zest once I am caught up in the effort of writing. But on the other hand, I am alarmed to see how I am more amused or interested than I used to be by little things, insignificant and yet pleasant, that occupy and fill up my life and make it both agreeable and sterile. That is so different from the old man that you have known that I sometimes fear I have lost, along with the faults that often made me insufferable to others and to myself, the very qualities that from time to time made me act with vigor and produce.[20]

[Engaged in the actual writing from October into December, he was still uncertain what his book on the Revolution should contain.]

To J. J. Ampère   *Tocqueville, November 21, 1857*

I think I am back on the right path for my work. But where will this path lead me? That is what I still don't know. But it's something accomplished to have set foot again on my new subject.[21]

[In the following letter Tocqueville explains that, owing to the "panic of 1857" in the United States, he is concerned about his considerable investment in bonds of the Central Michigan Railway and the Galena-Chicago. He was less worried about the capital than about whether the interest would be paid.]

To Gustave de Beaumont   *Tocqueville, December 6, 1857*

. . . All this crisis in America has put me in an unfavorable mood for work. . . . I think that the extreme difficulty I feel comes not only from my own troubled state of mind but from the obstacles presented by the subject. To treat it in a new way would be an almost chimerical attempt, but simply to repeat commonplaces that we have heard since we were born is impossible for me. I would die of boredom myself before boring my reader. In this connection,

[20] Ibid., p. 502.
[21] OC XI, p. 396.

moreover, it is necessary to weave together the ideas and the facts, to say enough of the latter to make the former understandable, to get the reader to sense the interest and importance of the ideas and yet not write a history properly speaking. I sometimes ask myself whether what I am trying to do can be realized. I often doubt it, and yet I see, it seems to me, the object that I want to depict. But the light that illuminates it is vacillating and doesn't yet allow me to seize the image well enough to be able to reproduce it. . . .

. . . To think of the French Revolution requires an effort; to plunge into all the little arrangements for building a stable or a sheepfold, I would only have to let myself go. Nevertheless, from my knowledge of myself, the incurable uneasiness of my mind, the restlessness of my character, I am led to think that I could never reduce my life absolutely to the care of my fields, or at least I could never in that way be contented. . . .[22]

[In his depressed moments Tocqueville wondered whether his work was worth doing.]

To Gustave de Beaumont   *Tocqueville, January 2, 1858*

. . . I have no child that might someday enjoy the little fame that my name may have; I do not believe that the slightest influence is to be gained by writings like mine, in such times as ours, or by any writings except perhaps bad novels that may have the undesirable effect of making us more demoralized and disordered than we are. And yet I get up at five o'clock in the morning, I spend six hours facing a sheet of paper that often remains blank, I lose hope of finding what I am looking for, I then find it halfway and with difficulty, I leave my desk often defeated by my task, dissatisfied with myself and hence with everything else. . . .[23]

[Having drafted his seven chapters on developments up to May 5, 1789, and set them aside for future revision, Tocqueville at last confronted again the problem of the Revolution itself. He was at first more cheerful and optimistic.]

[22] OC VIII, 3, pp. 521–523.
[23] Ibid., p. 529.

To J. J. Ampère   *Tocqueville, February 18, 1858*

. . . I have finished all the work I can do at Tocqueville. It is not much, and I would be ashamed and discouraged to see myself so little advanced, except for my conviction that I shall soon go more rapidly forward. I have come out of the shadowy region in which I have groped for so long. I now see my road; I now perceive the objective I want to reach, and I am ready to go. As soon as I get to Paris, I shall throw myself into the libraries and archives, and I hope to gather enough materials to push the writing pretty far on my return. . . .[24]

[Unfortunately, Tocqueville told neither Ampère nor anyone else what this "road" was. In the following letter to Louis de Kergolay he shows himself again uncertain of his own procedure, still seeing a malady or virus in the Revolution, and still making no distinction between the transitory but widespread radicalism of 1793–1794, at the height of real revolution and war, and the minority of professional and lifelong revolutionaries of his own time, who planned and worked for revolution before it happened. Kergolay, the most aristocratic of his friends, offers an explanation of the "virus," which he located in the faults of the aristocracy.]

To Louis de Kergolay   *Tocqueville, May 16, 1858*

. . . Among the things that I would have liked to talk about with you, my work would have had first place. I am beginning to be a little concerned about it. I am certain that it should not be a long book, but given my way of studying the facts and writing the final draft, I am afraid it will never end. Unfortunately, I don't know what rule to adopt to limit my researches. Between reading everything and saying nothing, I see no middle way. The *literature* of the Revolution, as the Germans call it, is so enormous that a lifetime might pass in trying to know its contents even superficially. You know that what I am looking for in these readings is less the facts than signs of the movement of ideas and feelings. That is what I want to depict: the successive changes in the social state, the insti-

[24] OC XI, pp. 401–402.

tutions, the mindset and general outlook and behavior of the French as the Revolution proceeds. That is my subject. To see it clearly, I have so far found only one method and that is to live, as it were, each moment of the Revolution with its contemporaries, reading not what is said about them or what they said about themselves later, but what they themselves said at the time and, so far as possible, what they really thought. The lesser writings of the time, the private correspondence . . . [dots in original] have more usefulness for this purpose than the debates in assemblies. I am reaching in this way the goal that I set for myself, which is to place myself in the midst of that time. But the process is so slow that I often despair of it. Is there another way?

There is moreover in this malady of the French Revolution something peculiar that I sense without being able to describe it well or analyze its causes. It is a *virus* of a new and unknown kind. There have been violent revolutions in the world, but the character of these Revolutionaries is so immoderate, violent, radical, desperate, audacious, almost insane yet powerful and effective as to have no precedents, it seems to me, in the great social agitations of ages past. Where does this new race come from? Who produced it? Who made it so effective? Who perpetuates it? For we are still facing men like this, although circumstances are different, and they have left their descendants throughout the civilized world. My mind wears itself out in trying to conceive a clear notion of this object and looking for ways to describe it. Beyond everything that can be explained in the French Revolution there remains something unexplained in its spirit and its acts. I sense where this unknown object is, but try as I may, I cannot lift the veil that covers it. I grope as if across a foreign body that prevents me from quite touching it or seeing it.[25]

Louis de Kergolay   *Paris, May 21, 1858*
to Alexis de Tocqueville

. . . I hasten, as is the old habit of our correspondence, to take up the ideas that you throw out for discussion in your letter. The important point in this letter is this question: Why is what you call the

[25] OC XIII, 2, pp. 337–338.

virus of the French Revolution being constantly reborn? Why does this contagion, unlike other physical and moral contagions, have no end? On this question I have a fairly clear idea, and hence I feel no hesitation in presenting it to you. I don't claim that my explanation is complete or adequate to explain everything, but I do think that among many causes it is the dominant one. If, among all the resentments that went into the revolutionary spirit, you try to find the one that is still very much alive, you will see that it is animosity against anything that, rightly or wrongly, can be denounced as aristocratic. All the other revolutionary passions are almost dead. How has that happened? The anti-religious and anti-monarchical passions have not been appeased by the suppression of religion and monarchy, but on the contrary by the fact that religious and monarchical authority has come into the hands of men who were by no means unpopular and who have demonstrated to the crowd something that is popular in all countries of the world—I mean, ability and practical knowledge. . . .

Now, as for the aristocratic fragments still scattered through France and Europe, have they ever for a single day, or on a single issue, risen to the level of the aristocratic calling? Taking them as a whole and disregarding exceptions, they have made the stupid blunder, from one end of Europe to the other, of hiding between the legs of autocracy and so losing all influence and reputation. . . .

There you have, I think, the main cause of this ever-recurring fury. It is like the grotesque fury of 1830 against that poor Charles X, whose only fault was in not being equal to his task. Let there reappear in France or elsewhere in Europe a certain kind of men of a certain worth and importance, to exercise a reasonable, prominent, and advantageous influence in the affairs of nations, then the anti-aristocratic resentment will definitely disappear. It will cease when the aristocratic element, whatever new form it takes, shall have washed its flag. . . .[26]

[Kergolay concludes his letter by urging Tocqueville to go on with his reading of materials contemporary with the Revolution itself.

[26] Ibid., pp. 339–340.

During 1858 Tocqueville's physical condition became increasingly difficult and painful. There were periods of intermission, but on the whole he could do very little. In October he and Mme de Tocqueville, who was also ill, settled in Cannes in the hope of relieving their troubles.]

To Gustave de Beaumont   *Tocqueville, July 4, 1858*

. . . I still find it difficult to work, and any continued concentration makes me ill. I am alarmed at how easily I get used to doing nothing. In my idleness I feel a kind of deep and secret discomfort, but nothing like that almost unbearable moral pain that I felt, not long ago, when for a while I was unable to do anything effective of any kind. I think that if I went on ailing as I am now I could reach a point of doing nothing at all, or what I call nothing; and this condition, while not making me content, would not make me very unhappy. I shall not feel again that enthusiasm which even in sickness and misfortune pushed me on with a desperate ardor to my work. . . .[27]

To J. J. Ampère   *Cannes, December 30, 1858*

. . . I am regaining my strength. I can find something to do outdoors, or in the house. But I cannot do any serious work. . . .[28]

[He died at Cannes on April 16, 1859.]

[27] OC VIII, 3, p. 583.
[28] OC XI, p. 418.

Glossary

à bas les aristocrates!   Down with the aristocrats!

bailliages   In the present context, the principal electoral districts set up for the election of deputies to the Estates General in 1789; they followed the boundaries of existing *bailliages*, which were secondary courts in the judicial system.

cahiers   The *cahiers des doléances*, or "grievance lists," were statements drawn up in electoral districts by assemblies electing deputies to the Estates General in 1789. In each principal district (*bailliage*) the clergy, nobility, and Third Estate each compiled its *cahier*, which in effect constituted its instructions to its deputies.

capitation   A head tax, or tax on individuals, in principle varying according to the taxpayer's presumed level of income, but modified as time passed by various abatements and exemptions.

cens   A payment, usually in money and hence of slight value in the eighteenth century (because of the decline in money values since the Middle Ages), payable by a tenant or owner of land to a *seigneur* or feudal superior; more significant as a sign of social status than as a financial burden.

chambre des comptes   A government office, in dignity just below the Parlement, with a great many functions but chiefly the verification of the king's revenues from the royal domain, taxes, and other sources. There were lesser *chambres des comptes* throughout the country.

chambre des enquêtes   A subdivision of the Parlement of Paris, subordinate to the *grand' chambre*, hearing appeals from lower courts in certain civil and criminal cases, and usually composed of younger members of the Parlement.

compte-rendu   A report or accounting, specifically in the present context the report of Necker to Louis XVI in 1781 on the state of the government finances. The unusual fact of its publication caused much public discussion and dispute.

corvée   Unpaid labor; specifically, the days of work required by the royal government of the rural population living within a few miles of the principal roads. Virtually everyone was exempt except peasants.

cours des aides   Law courts having jurisdiction in matters of taxation. The one of Paris, with jurisdiction over a large part of France, stood just below the Parlement of Paris in ceremonial rank.

curé   A priest in charge of a parish and its parishioners, often on a small salary with the income of the parish going to others.

ducs et pairs   The "dukes-and-peers" were the highest order of the French nobility, numbering forty-three in 1789, by which time they had mainly ceremonial functions, but on rare special occasions they could sit in the Parlement of Paris.

franc fief   A payment to the royal government by a non-noble purchasing noble land, generally complained of in the eighteenth century by both nobles and non-nobles as interfering with the real estate market.

gabelle   The salt tax and government monopoly on the sale of salt, requiring the purchase of a certain amount.

Garde française   A regiment permanently stationed in Paris, composed of men who, though professional soldiers, were in many cases married and in close daily touch with the ordinary people of the city.

généralité   One of the thirty-four areas into which France was divided, each under an intendant who exercised virtually all powers of the royal government except military.

grand' chambre   The highest of the chambers into which the Parlement of Paris was divided, acting as a court of first instance for certain privileged cases and exercising leadership in all actions of the Parlement.

grands bailliages   Law courts just below the parlements as proposed (but never implemented) in the government's reform plan of May 1788.

Hôtel de Ville   The town hall.

lettres de cachet   "Sealed" letters (*cachet*, the royal seal) ordering the arrest and confinement of a person without further procedure or publicity.

lit de justice   A solemn occasion on which the king, as the ultimate source of all judicial authority, appeared in the Parlement and formally commanded it to obey his will.

mainmorte   A payment to the royal government by colleges, guilds, religious houses, and other "undying" corporations on the acquisition of real property, in compensation for the loss of future taxes to the government.

maréchal de camp   A military rank, the lowest grade of general officer.

parlement   The Parlement of Paris and twelve provincial parlements, each within its area of jurisdiction, were primarily the highest courts of the realm, rendering justice in particular cases; but they had administrative functions also and claimed the right to "verify" royal edicts to ascertain their conformity to existing law, hence to "remonstrate" against proposed edicts that they found contrary to this law. Their remonstrances could be overruled in a *lit de justice*. The Parlement of Paris had jurisdiction in about half the country.

pays d'états   Those provinces (and *généralités*) in which meetings of the three estates (*états*)—clergy, nobility, and Third—continued to take place in the eighteenth century. Brittany and Languedoc were the most important *pays d'états*. In most of France they had fallen into disuse.

rentes   Income regularly received from land, annuities, or other proprietary rights. *Rentes* included "rent" in the modern sense of rental under terminable leases; perpetual income from feudal or seigneurial rights; and income from

246

loans made to the royal government, the clergy, other public bodies, or individuals, that is, what would later be called interest.

seigneur   A person, usually a noble, but in some cases a non-noble or an institution, entitled to receive the income and enjoy the honors arising from the manorial or feudal system of land tenure.

taille   The basic tax of the French monarchy, dating from the fifteenth century, with exemption for nobles and clergy and, by the eighteenth century, for most townspeople, officeholders, and others, so that the *taille personelle* was paid in general only by the peasantry and was a sign of inferior status. In some parts of France, where the land itself was defined as noble or non-noble, a noble owning non-noble land would be liable for the *taille réelle*.

vingtième   A more modern tax, the "twentieth," introduced in 1749 (after earlier experiments with the *dixième*, or tenth), consisting in principle of a twentieth of all income, and in practice falling only on the imputed income from lands. In principle payable by persons of all social classes, but subject to many special arrangements.

Vive le roi!, vive la reine!, vive la Nation!   Cheers for the king, the queen, the Nation!

A few words are so common to French and English as to justify special comment:

bureau   The Assembly of Notables of 1787 and 1788 divided itself into seven *bureaux* of about twenty persons each to facilitate discussion. They were not committees, though sometimes translated as such; each considered all matters before the Notables, and they are called "bureaus" in the present translations.

bourgeois, bourgeoisie   These words were not regarded as English until the later years of the nineteenth century, and since then there has sometimes been a hesitation to use them lest they suggest a Marxist interpretation. A *bourgeois* was someone who was not a noble and not of the laboring class, and who generally possessed some education and assured income. The *bourgeoisie* was a category somewhat indefinite at the edges. Where the Tocquevilles say *bourgeois*, we translate as "bourgeois," and where they say *classes moyennes*, we say "middle classes."

gentilhomme   This word never developed in France the broader range of meaning that "gentleman" took on in English. Newly made nobles were not *gentilhommes*, since *gentilhomme* referred to purity or antiquity of lineage and good breeding, not to legal status. Where the Tocquevilles say *gentilhomme*, we translate as "gentleman," using an old-fashioned sense of the word.

Monsieur, Messieurs   These French terms of address are retained, since to say "Sir" or "Gentlemen" would strike a false note. When the king addressed an assembly as *Messieurs*, he politely included those who were not "gentlemen."

Index

NOTE: Readers wishing to compare the two Tocquevilles should note that references to pages 41–143 relate to passages written by Hervé, those to pages after 144 refer to passages written by Alexis.

Library of Congress Cataloging-in-Publication Data

The Two Tocquevilles, father and son.
Includes index.
1. France—History—Revolution, 1789-1799—Collected works.
2. France—History—Revolution, 1789-1799—Historiography.
3. Tocqueville, Hervé de, d. 1856—Views on French Revolution.
4. Tocqueville, Alexis de, 1805-1859—Views on French Revolution.
I. Tocqueville, Hervé de, d. 1856. Coup d'oeil sur le règne
de Louis XVI. English. Selections, 1987.
II. Tocqueville, Alexis de, 1805-1859. Selections. English. 1987.
III. Palmer, R. R. (Robert Roswell), 1909-

DC142.T86 1987 944.04 86-30244
ISBN 0-691-05495-9